Grade 1

PRACTICE - ASSESS - DIAGNOSE

180 Days of MATH for First Grade

Developed by
Jodene Smith

Publishing Credits

Dona Herweck Rice, *Editor-in-Chief*; Lee Aucoin, *Creative Director;*
Don Tran, *Print Production Manager;* Timothy J. Bradley, *Illustration Manager*;
Chris McIntyre, M.A.Ed., *Editorial Director*; Sara Johnson, M.S.Ed., *Senior Editor*;
Aubrie Nielsen, M.S.Ed., *Associate Education Editor*; Juan Chavolla, *Cover/Interior Layout Designer;*
Grace Alba, *Production Artist;* Ana Clark, *Illustrator;* Corinne Burton, M.A.Ed., *Publisher*

Shell Education
5301 Oceanus Drive
Huntington Beach, CA 92649-1030
http://www.shelleducation.com

ISBN 978-1-4258-0804-4

Reprinted 2013

TABLE OF CONTENTS

Introduction and Research 3
How to Use This Book 4
Daily Practice Pages 11
Answer Key 191
References Cited 207
Contents of the Teacher Resource CD 208

INTRODUCTION AND RESEARCH

The Need for Practice

In order to be successful in today's mathematics classroom, students must deeply understand both concepts and procedures so that they can discuss and demonstrate their understanding. Demonstrating understanding is a process that must be continually practiced in order for students to be successful. According to Marzano (2010, 83), "practice has always been, and will always be, a necessary ingredient to learning procedural knowledge at a level at which students execute it independently." Practice is especially important to help students apply their concrete, conceptual understanding to a particular procedural skill.

Understanding Assessment

In addition to providing opportunities for frequent practice, teachers must be able to assess students' understanding of mathematical procedures, terms, concepts, and reasoning (Kilpatrick, Swafford, and Findell 2001). This is important so that teachers can adequately address students' misconceptions, build on their current understanding, and challenge them appropriately.

Assessment is a long-term process that often involves careful analysis of student responses from a lesson discussion, project, practice sheet, or test. When analyzing the data, it is important for teachers to reflect on how their teaching practices may have influenced students' responses and to identify those areas where additional instruction may be required. In short, the data gathered from assessments should be used to inform instruction: slow down, speed up, or reteach. This type of assessment is called *formative assessment* and is used to provide a seamless connection between instruction and assessment (McIntosh 1997).

HOW TO USE THIS BOOK

180 Days of Math for First Grade offers teachers and parents a full page of daily mathematics practice activities for each day of the school year.

Easy to Use and Standards-Based

These activities reinforce grade-level skills across a variety of mathematical concepts. The questions are provided as a full practice page, making them easy to prepare and implement as part of a classroom morning routine, at the beginning of each mathematics lesson, or as homework.

Every first-grade practice page provides 8 questions, each tied to a specific mathematical concept. Students are given the opportunity for regular practice in each mathematical concept, allowing them to build confidence through these quick standards-based activities.

Question	Mathematics Concept	NCTM Standards
1	**Number Sense**	Understands numbers, ways of representing numbers, relationships among numbers, and number systems
2	**Addition**	Understands meanings of operations and how they relate to one another; Computes fluently and makes reasonable estimates; Develops and uses strategies for whole-number computations, with a focus on addition and subtraction
3	**Subtraction**	
4	**Algebraic Thinking**	Understands patterns, relations, and functions; Models situations that involve the addition and subtraction of whole numbers, using objects, pictures, and symbols
5	**Geometry**	Analyzes characteristics and properties of two-dimensional and three-dimensional geometric shapes and develops mathematical arguments about geometric relationships; Describes attributes and parts of two- and three-dimensional shapes
6	**Measurement**	Understands measurable attributes of objects and the units, systems, and processes of measurement; Recognizes the attributes of length, volume, weight, area, and time
7	**Data Analysis**	Formulates questions that can be addressed with data and collects, organizes, and displays relevant data to answer them
8	**Word Problem/Logic Problem or Mathematical Reasoning**	Builds new mathematical knowledge through problem solving; Solves problems that arise in mathematics and in other contexts

Standards are listed with the permission of the National Council of Teachers of Mathematics (NCTM). NCTM does not endorse the content or validity of these alignments.

HOW TO USE THIS BOOK *(cont.)*

Using the Practice Pages

As outlined on page 4, every question is aligned to a mathematics concept and standard.

Practice pages provide instruction and assessment opportunities for each day of the school year.

Each question ties student practice to a specific mathematics concept.

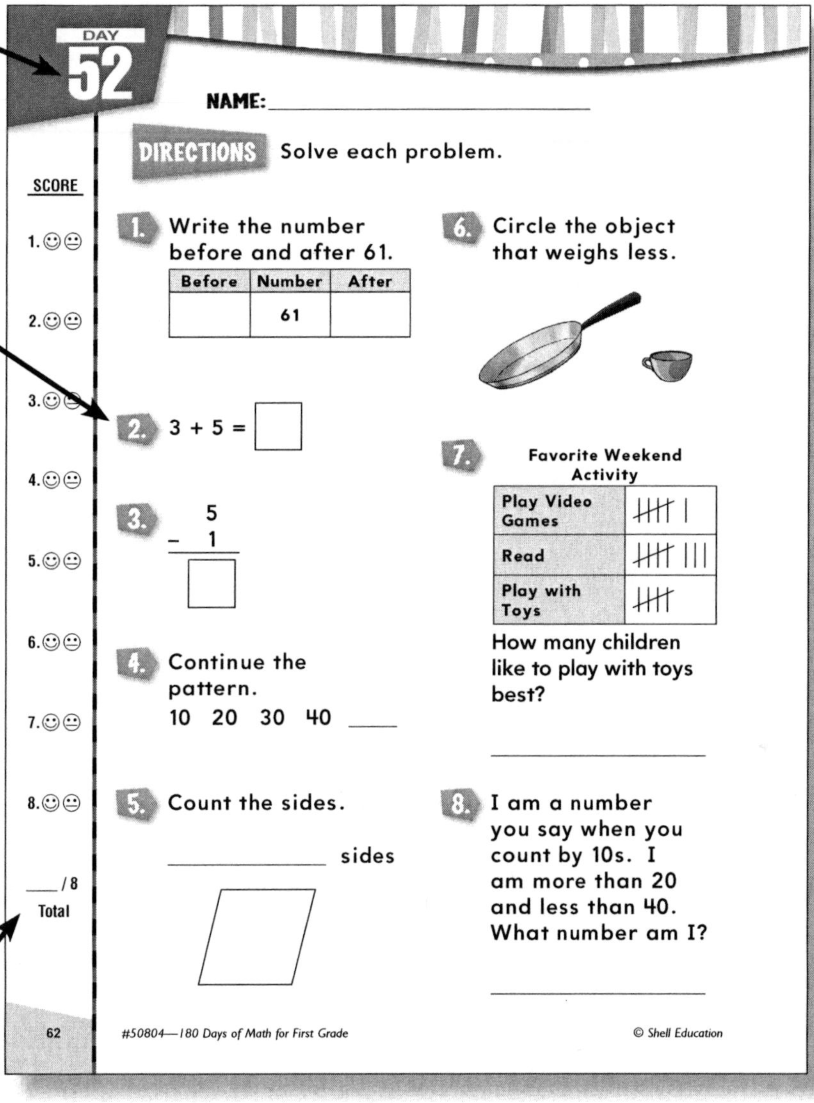

DAY 52

NAME:________________

DIRECTIONS Solve each problem.

SCORE

1.☺☹ 2.☺☹ 3.☺☹ 4.☺☹ 5.☺☹ 6.☺☹ 7.☺☹ 8.☺☹

____ /8 Total

1. Write the number before and after 61.

Before	Number	After
	61	

2. 3 + 5 = ☐

3. 5 − 1 = ☐

4. Continue the pattern.
10 20 30 40 ____

5. Count the sides.
________ sides

6. Circle the object that weighs less.

7. Favorite Weekend Activity

Play Video Games	卌 I
Read	卌 III
Play with Toys	卌

How many children like to play with toys best?
____

8. I am a number you say when you count by 10s. I am more than 20 and less than 40. What number am I?
____

62 #50804—180 Days of Math for First Grade © Shell Education

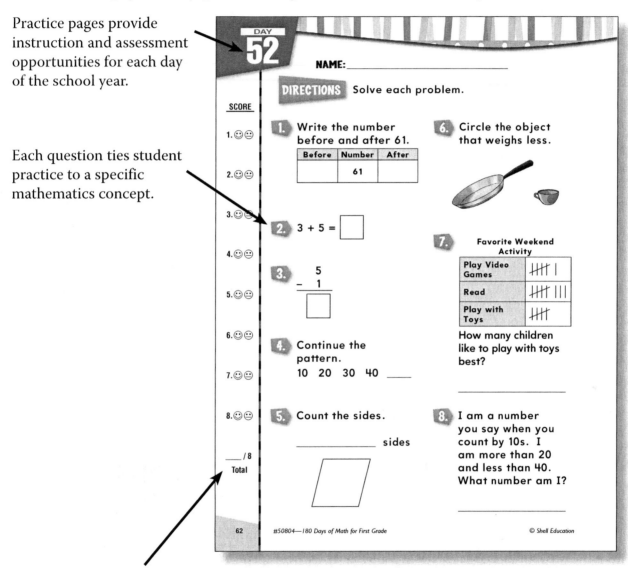

Using the Scoring Guide

Use the scoring guide along the side of each practice page to check answers and see at a glance which skills may need more reinforcement.

Fill in the appropriate circle for each problem to indicate correct (☺) or incorrect (☹) responses. You might wish to indicate only incorrect responses to focus on those skills. (For example, if students consistently miss numbers 2 and 6, they may need additional help with those concepts as outlined in the table on page 4.) Use the answer key at the back of the book to score the problems, or you may call out answers to have students self-score or peer-score their work.

HOW TO USE THIS BOOK *(cont.)*

Diagnostic Assessment

Teachers can use the practice pages as diagnostic assessments. The data-analysis tools included with the book enable teachers or parents to quickly score students' work and monitor their progress. Teachers and parents can see at a glance which mathematics concepts or skills students may need to target in order to develop proficiency.

After students complete a practice page, grade each page using the answer key (pages 191–206). Then, complete the *Practice Page Item Analysis* (page 7, or pageitem.pdf) for the whole class, or the *Student Item Analysis* (page 8, or studentitem.pdf) for individual students. These charts are also provided as both *Microsoft Word*® files (pageitem.doc and studentitem.doc) and as *Microsoft Excel*® files (pageitem.xls and studentitem.xls). Teachers can input data into the electronic files directly on the computer, or they can print the pages and analyze students' work using paper and pencil.

To complete the Practice Page Item Analysis:

- Write or type students' names in the far-left column. Depending on the number of students, more than one copy of the form may be needed or you may need to add rows.
- The question numbers are included across the top of the chart. Each item correlates with the matching question number from the practice page.
- For each student, record an *X* in the column if the student has the item incorrect. If the item is correct, leave the item blank.
- If you are using the *Excel* file, totals will be automatically generated. If you are using the *Word* file or if you have printed the PDF, you will need to compute the totals. Count the *X*s in each row and column and fill in the correct boxes.

To complete the Student Item Analysis:

- Write or type the student's name on the top row. This form tracks the on-going progress of each student, so one copy per student is necessary.
- The question numbers are included across the top of the chart. Each item correlates with the matching question number from the practice page.
- For each day, record an *X* in the column if the student has the item incorrect. If the item is correct, leave the item blank.
- If you are using the *Excel* file, totals will be automatically generated. If you are using the *Word* file or if you have printed the PDF, you will need to compute the totals. Count the *X*s in each row and column and fill in the correct boxes.

Practice Page Item Analysis

Directions: Record an *X* in cells to indicate where students have missed questions. Add up the totals. You can view: (1) which questions/concepts were missed per student; (2) the total correct score for each student; and (3) the total number of students who missed each question.

Day: ______ Question #	1	2	3	4	5	6	7	8	# Correct
Student Name									
Sample Student		X			X	X			5/8
# of Students Missing Each Question									

HOW TO USE THIS BOOK *(cont.)*

Student Item Analysis

Directions: Record an *X* in cells to indicate where the student has missed questions. Add up the totals. You can view: (1) which questions/concepts the student missed; (2) the total correct score per day; and (3) the total number of times each question/concept was missed.

Student Name: Sample Student									
Question	**1**	**2**	**3**	**4**	**5**	**6**	**7**	**8**	**# Correct**
Day									
1		X			X	X			5/8
Total									

HOW TO USE THIS BOOK *(cont.)*

Using the Results to Differentiate Instruction

Once data is gathered and analyzed, teachers can use the results to inform the way they differentiate instruction. The data can help determine which concepts are the most difficult for students and which need additional instructional support and continued practice. Depending on how often the practice pages are scored, results can be considered for instructional support on a daily or weekly basis.

Whole-Class Support

The results of the diagnostic analysis may show that the entire class is struggling with a particular concept or group of concepts. If these concepts have been taught in the past, this indicates that further instruction or reteaching is necessary. If these concepts have not been taught in the past, this data is a great pre-assessment and demonstrates that students do not have a working knowledge of the concepts. Thus, careful planning for the length of the unit(s) or lesson(s) must be considered, and extra frontloading may be required.

Small-Group or Individual Support

The results of the diagnostic analysis may show that an individual or small group of students is struggling with a particular concept or group of concepts. If these concepts have been taught in the past, this indicates that further instruction or reteaching is necessary. Consider pulling aside these students while others are working independently to instruct further on the concept(s). Teachers can also use the results to help identify individuals or groups of proficient students who are ready for enrichment or above-grade level instruction. These students may benefit from independent learning contracts or more challenging activities. Students may also benefit from extra practice using games or computer-based resources.

Teacher Resource CD

The Teacher Resource CD provides the following resources:

- NCTM Correlations Chart
- Reproducible PDFs of each practice page
- Directions for completing the diagnostic Item Analysis forms
- Practice Page Item Analysis PDF, *Word* document, and *Excel* spreadsheet
- Student Item Analysis PDF, *Word* document, and *Excel* spreadsheet

HOW TO USE THIS BOOK *(cont.)*

NCTM Standards

The lessons in this book are aligned to the National Council of Teachers of Mathematics (NCTM) standards. The standards listed on page 4 support the concepts and skills that are consistently presented on each of the practice pages.

Standards Correlations

Shell Education is committed to producing educational materials that are research and standards based. In this effort, we have correlated all of our products to the academic standards of all 50 states, the District of Columbia, and the Department of Defense Dependent Schools, as well as to the Common Core Standards.

How to Find Standards Correlations

To print a customized correlation report of this product for your state, visit our website at **http://www.shelleducation.com** and follow the on-screen directions. If you require assistance in printing correlation reports, please contact Customer Service at 1-877-777-3450.

Purpose and Intent of Standards

The No Child Left Behind legislation mandates that all states adopt academic standards that identify the skills students will learn in kindergarten through grade twelve. While many states had already adopted academic standards prior to NCLB, the legislation set requirements to ensure the standards were detailed and comprehensive.

Standards are designed to focus instruction and guide adoption of curricula. Standards are statements that describe the criteria necessary for students to meet specific academic goals. They define the knowledge, skills, and content students should acquire at each level. Standards are also used to develop standardized tests to evaluate students' academic progress.

Teachers are required to demonstrate how their lessons meet state standards. State standards are used in development of all of our products, so educators can be assured they meet the academic requirements of each state.

NAME: ____________________________

DIRECTIONS Solve each problem.

1. Count how many.

★ ★ ★ ★ ★ ★ ★ ★
★ ★ ★ ★ ★ ★ ★ ★

____

2. How many in all?

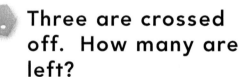

 and 

____

3. Three are crossed off. How many are left?

____

4. 1 + ☐ = 2

5. Color the circle.

6. Circle the longer snake.

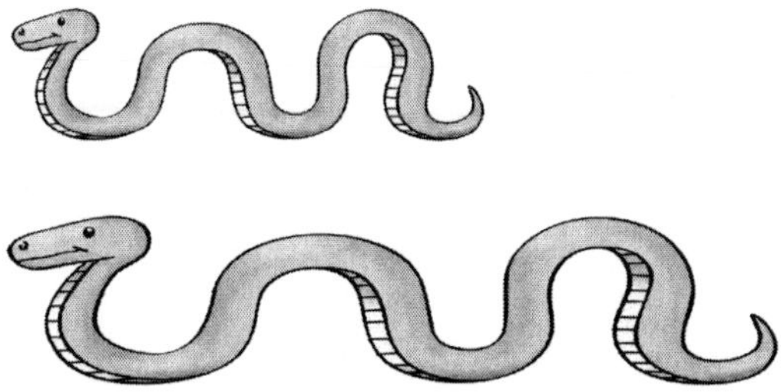

7. Count how many. Record with tally marks.

Item	Tally

8. Draw a circle around the group that has less.

SCORE

1.
2.
3.
4.
5.
6.
7.
8.

___ / 8
Total

NAME: ____________________

DIRECTIONS Solve each problem.

SCORE

1. ☺ ☹
2. ☺ ☹
3. ☺ ☹
4. ☺ ☹
5. ☺ ☹
6. ☺ ☹
7. ☺ ☹
8. ☺ ☹

___ / 8
Total

1. Write the number before and after 6.

Before	Number	After
	6	

2. How many in all?

and

____

3. Two are crossed off. How many are left?

____

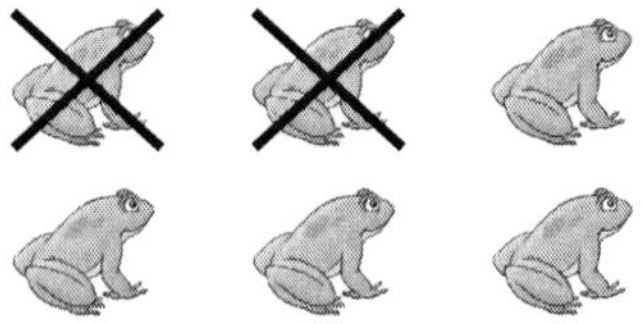

4. Continue the pattern.

A B A B A ___ ___

5. Count the sides.

__________ sides

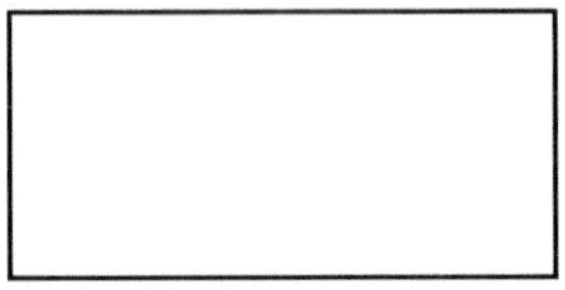

6. Circle the heavier object.

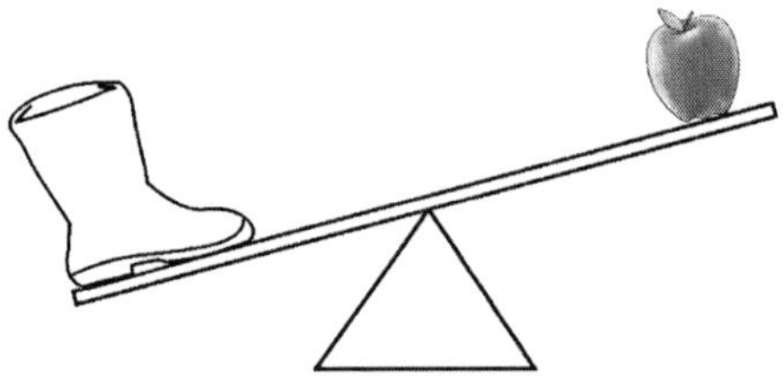

7. Number of Home Runs

Marc	Ramon	Jamal
7	4	15

How many home runs did Ramon hit?

____

8. I am the number that comes after 3. What number am I?

____

NAME: ____________________

DIRECTIONS Solve each problem.

1. Write the numeral for six.

____

2. How many in all?

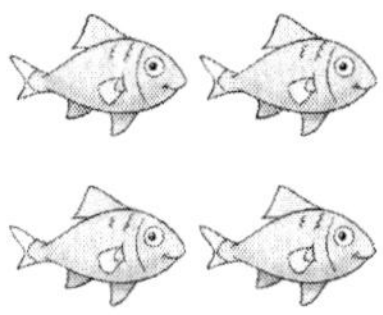
and
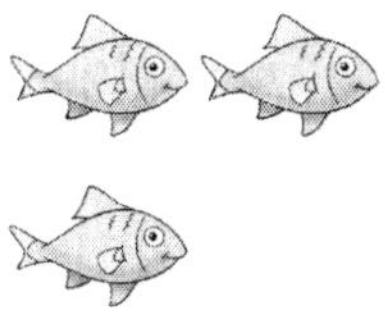

____

3. One is crossed off. How many are left?

____

4. 4 – ☐ = 2

5. Will the object stack?

Circle: yes no

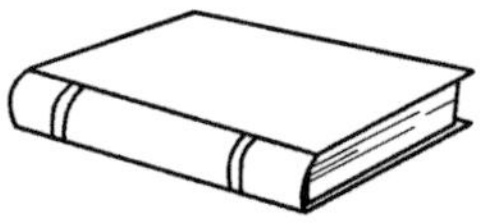

6. What time is it?

__________ o'clock

7. **Pencil Colors**

Red	𝍸
Green	𝍸 III
Blue	III

How many pencils are blue?

____

8. Mom has 3 flowers. I give her 1 more. How many flowers does she have in all?

____

SCORE

1. ☺ 😐
2. ☺ 😐
3. ☺ 😐
4. ☺ 😐
5. ☺ 😐
6. ☺ 😐
7. ☺ 😐
8. ☺ 😐

___ / 8
Total

NAME: ______________________________

DIRECTIONS Solve each problem.

SCORE

1. ☺ 😐
2. ☺ 😐
3. ☺ 😐
4. ☺ 😐
5. ☺ 😐
6. ☺ 😐
7. ☺ 😐
8. ☺ 😐

____ / 8
Total

1. Circle the larger number.

3 8

2. How many in all?

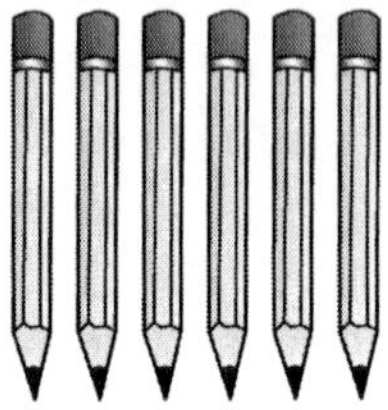

and

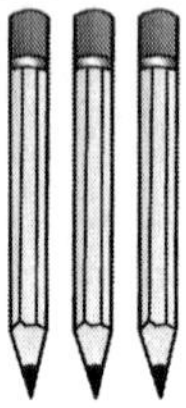

____

3. Two are crossed off. How many are left?

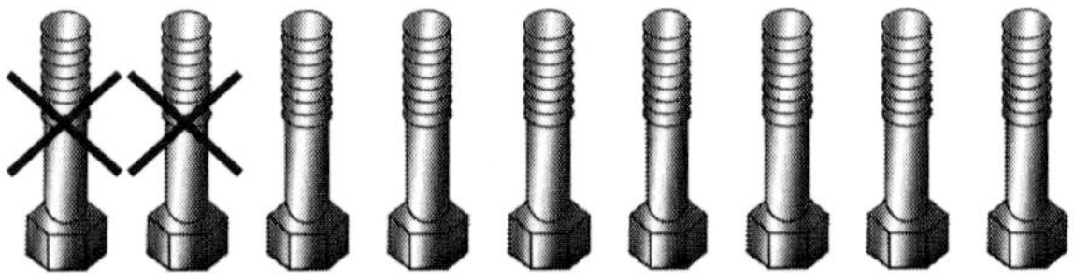

____

4. Write the missing sign.

2 ☐ 1 = 3

5. Draw a line of symmetry.

6. Circle the container that holds more.

7. Favorite Ice Cream

Chocolate Ice Cream	
Strawberry Ice Cream	

How many children like strawberry ice cream?

____

8. Willis has 2 cats. His mom brings home 1 more. How many cats does Willis have now?

____

NAME: ____________________

DIRECTIONS Solve each problem.

1. Write the numeral for the ordinal number second.

____

2. How many in all?

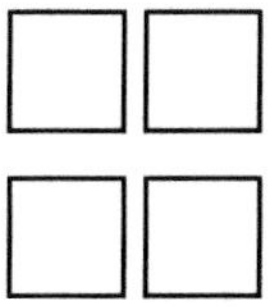
and
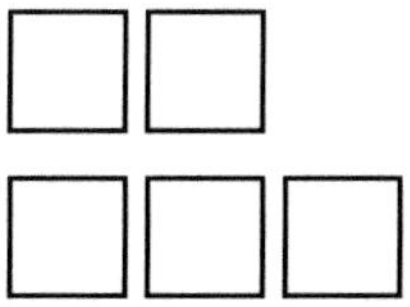

____

3. Four are crossed off. How many are left?

____

4. Circle the number sentences that equal four.

1 + 3   2 + 4

2 + 2   4 + 0

5. Circle the object that looks like the solid.

6. Is the object shorter than your arm?

Circle: yes no

7.

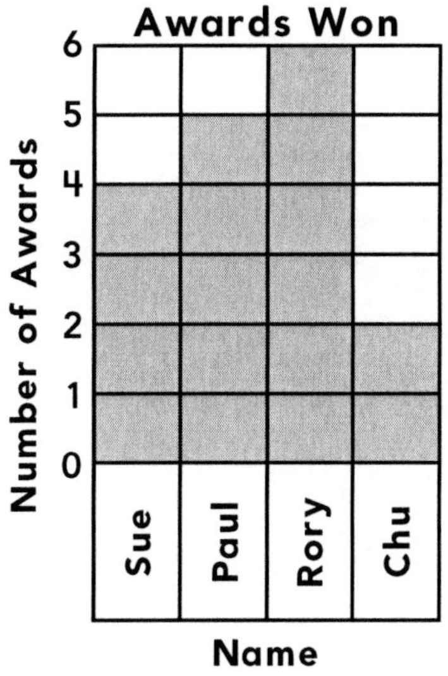

How many awards does Paul have?

____

8. How many wheels are on 2 tricycles?

____

SCORE

1.

2.

3.

4.

5.

6.

7.

8.

____ / 8

Total

DAY 6

NAME: ______________________________

DIRECTIONS Solve each problem.

SCORE

1. ☺ 😐
2. ☺ 😐
3. ☺ 😐
4. ☺ 😐
5. ☺ 😐
6. ☺ 😐
7. ☺ 😐
8. ☺ 😐

____ / 8
Total

1. Write the numeral.

●	●	●	●	●	●	●	●	●	●
●	●								

____

2. Add. How many in all?

[4] + [3] = [ ]

3. Subtract. Cross off two. How many are left?

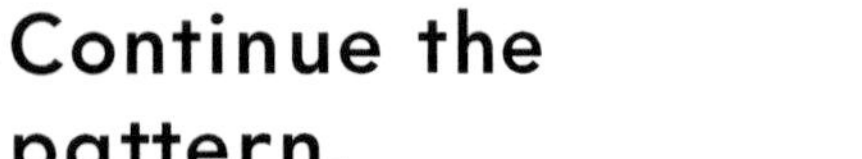

[5] – [2] = [ ]

4. Continue the pattern.

1 2 1 2 1 ____ ____

5. Draw a fish inside the box.

[ ]

6. Circle the shorter pants.

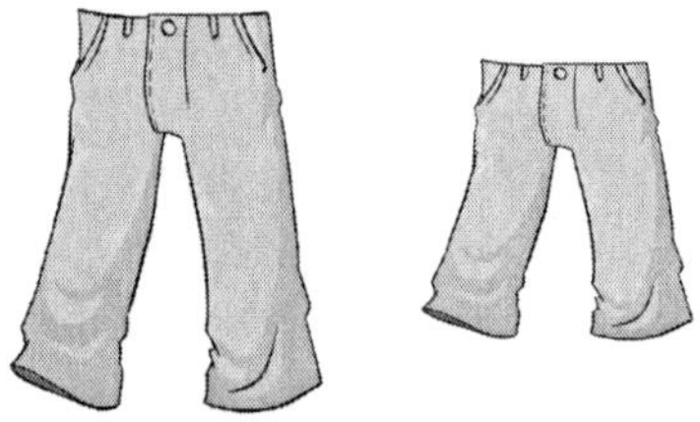

7. Count the tally marks. Write the numeral.

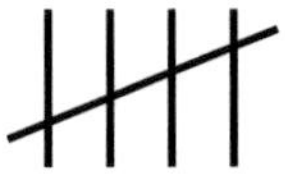

____

8. Irene gets an ice cream with 3 scoops on it. She eats 1 scoop. How many scoops does she have left?

____

NAME: ______________________

DIRECTIONS Solve each problem.

1. How many sticks?

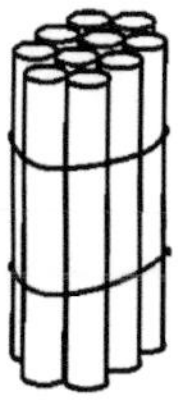

______

2. Add. How many in all?

3 + 5 = ☐

3. Subtract. Cross off two. How many are left?

6 – 2 = ☐

4. 2 – ☐ = 2

5. Does the ball have any flat surfaces?

Circle: yes no

6. Circle the object that is heavier.

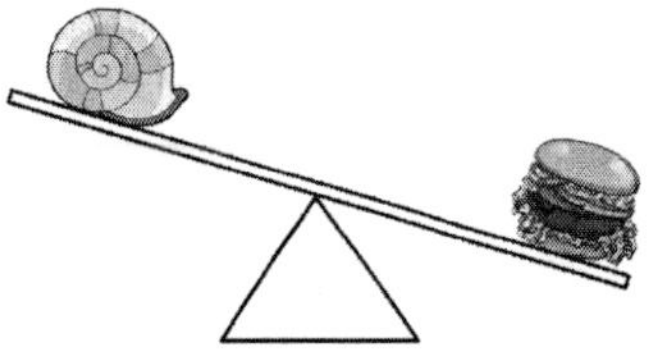

7. Favorite Subject

Math	☺ ☺ ☺ ☺ ☺ ☺
Reading	☺ ☺ ☺ ☺
Science	☺ ☺ ☺ ☺ ☺ ☺ ☺

How many children say science is their favorite subject?

____

8. Write an addition number sentence using the numbers 1, 3, and 4.

____

SCORE

1. ☺ 😐
2. ☺ 😐
3. ☺ 😐
4. ☺ 😐
5. ☺ 😐
6. ☺ 😐
7. ☺ 😐
8. ☺ 😐

____ / 8 Total

DAY 8

NAME: ____________________

DIRECTIONS Solve each problem.

SCORE

1.
2.
3.
4.
5.
6.
7.
8.

___ / 8 Total

1. Write the number before and after 13.

Before	Number	After
	13	

2. Add. How many in all?

[5] + [3] = [ ]

3. Subtract. Cross off two. How many are left?

[4] − [2] = [ ]

4.

  3
+ [ ]
―――
  3

5. Draw a square. Put a dot outside the square.

6. What time is it?

__________ o'clock

7. Favorite Activity

Swings	Slide	Monkey Bars	Balance Beam
8	5	7	2

How many children like the swings?

____

8. Jenny is last. Monique is first. Sara is in the middle. Write 1, 2, or 3 to show the order.

Sara	Jenny	Monique
______	______	______

NAME: ____________________

DIRECTIONS Solve each problem.

1. Write the numeral.

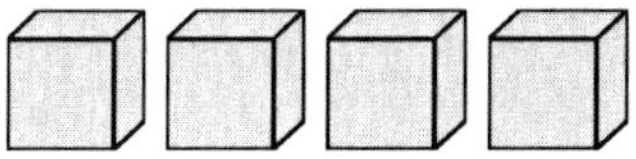

____

2. Add. How many in all?

[3] + [3] = [ ]

3. Subtract. Cross off three. How many are left?

[7] – [3] = [ ]

4. 2 [ ] 2 = 4

5. Draw a circle.

6. Is the object shorter than your arm?

Circle: yes no

7. Favorite Recess Game

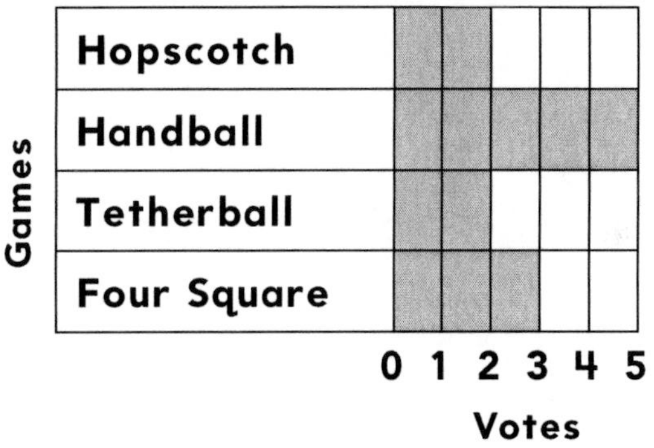

How many children like hopscotch?

____

8. Which has more legs: a bird or a dog?

____

SCORE

1.

2.

3.

4.

5.

6.

7.

8.

___ / 8

Total

DAY 10

NAME: ______________________

DIRECTIONS Solve each problem.

1. Count the squares. Draw 1 more. Write how many squares there are now.

____

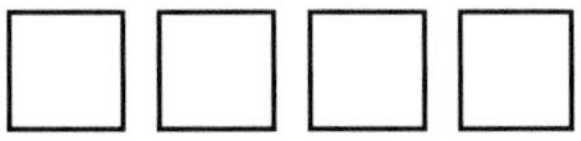

2. Add. How many in all?

[2] + [7] = [ ]

3. Subtract. Cross off two. How many are left?

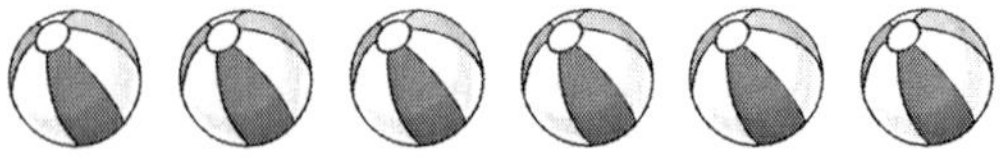

[6] – [2] = [ ]

4. Write the missing number.

0 + [ ] = 4

5. Is the pencil on the right or on the left?

____

6. Circle the container that holds more.

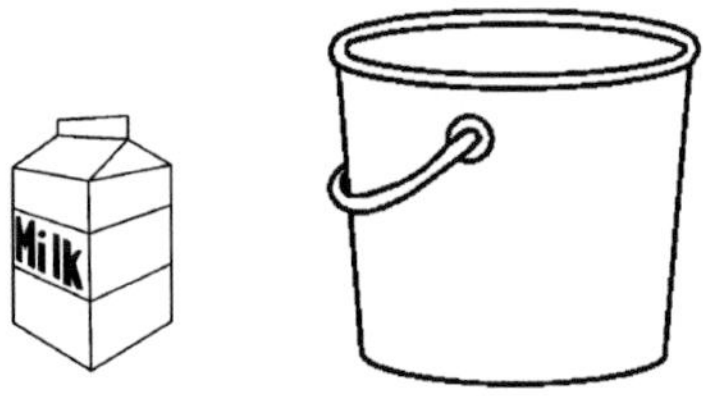

7. Favorite Type of Movie

Funny	Cartoon	Scary	3-D
|||	𝍸 |||	|	𝍸

How many children like funny movies?

____

8. What day comes after Tuesday?

____

SCORE

1. ☺ 😐
2. ☺ 😐
3. ☺ 😐
4. ☺ 😐
5. ☺ 😐
6. ☺ 😐
7. ☺ 😐
8. ☺ 😐

____ / 8 Total

NAME: ______________________________

DIRECTIONS Solve each problem.

1. Count how many.

★★★★★★★★

★★★★★★★

____

2. Add.

☐ + ☐ = ☐

3. Subtract.

☐ – ☐ = ☐

4. Continue the pattern.

○□○□○ ___ ___

5. Color the square.

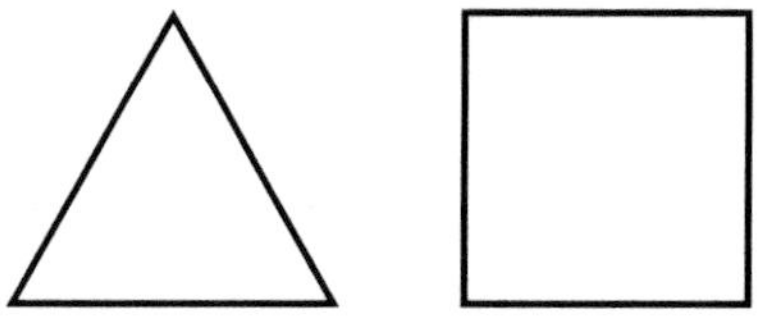

6. Circle the taller camel.

7. Count how many. Write the number for each.

Boys	Girls

______ Boys ______ Girls

8. Circle the group that has more.

★★★
★★★

★★★★★
★★★★★

SCORE

1. ☺ 😐
2. ☺ 😐
3. ☺ 😐
4. ☺ 😐
5. ☺ 😐
6. ☺ 😐
7. ☺ 😐
8. ☺ 😐

___ / 8 Total

NAME: ____________________

DIRECTIONS Solve each problem.

SCORE

1. ☺ 😐
2. ☺ 😐
3. ☺ 😐
4. ☺ 😐
5. ☺ 😐
6. ☺ 😐
7. ☺ 😐
8. ☺ 😐

____ / 8
Total

1. Write the numeral for zero.

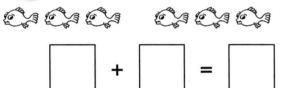

____

2. Add.

☐ + ☐ = ☐

3. Subtract.

☐ − ☐ = ☐

4.

$$\begin{array}{r} 1 \\ -\ \square \\ \hline 0 \end{array}$$

5. Count the sides.

__________ sides

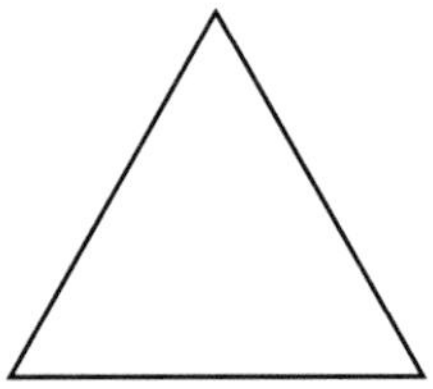

6. Mark the circle that takes up the most space.

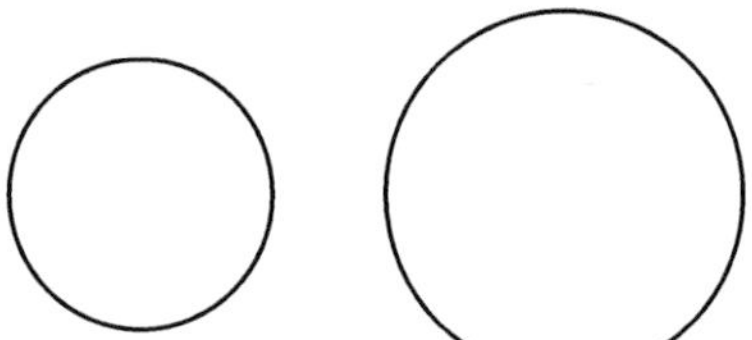

7. Number of Home Runs

Marc	Ramon	Jamal
7	4	15

How many home runs did Jamal hit?

____

8. I am the number that is less than 10 and more than 8. What number am I?

____

NAME: ____________________

DIRECTIONS Solve each problem.

1. Write the number that comes between.

8 ____ 10

2. Add.

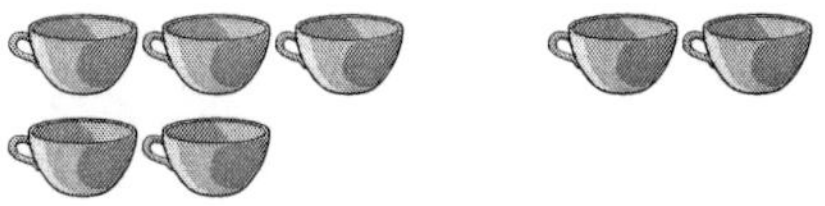

☐ + ☐ = ☐

3. Subtract.

☐ – ☐ = ☐

4. Circle the ways to make 5.

1 + 3

2 + 3

3 + 2

4 + 1

5. Will the object roll?
Circle: yes no

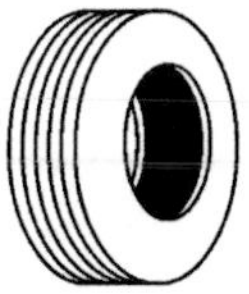

6. Circle the object that weighs more.

7.

Pencil Colors

Red	𝍸
Green	𝍸 |||
Blue	|||

How many pencils are red?

____

8. Anita has 7 stickers. She gives 3 away. How many stickers does Anita have left?

____

SCORE

1. ☺ 😐
2. ☺ 😐
3. ☺ 😐
4. ☺ 😐
5. ☺ 😐
6. ☺ 😐
7. ☺ 😐
8. ☺ 😐

____ / 8
Total

DAY
14

NAME: ____________________

DIRECTIONS Solve each problem.

SCORE

1. ☺ 😐
2. ☺ 😐
3. ☺ 😐
4. ☺ 😐
5. ☺ 😐
6. ☺ 😐
7. ☺ 😐
8. ☺ 😐

____ / 8
Total

1. Write the number before and after 20.

Before	Number	After
	20	

2. Add.

☐ + ☐ = ☐

3. Subtract.

☐ – ☐ = ☐

4. Write the missing sign.

3 ☐ 1 = 2

5. Draw a line of symmetry.

☐

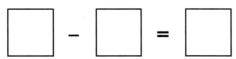

6. What time is it?

__________ o'clock

7. Favorite Weekend Activity

Play Video Games	
Read	
Play with Toys	

How many chose reading as their favorite weekend activity?

____

8. DeShawn had 4 crackers. He ate 2. How many crackers does he have left?

____

NAME: ______________________________

DIRECTIONS Solve each problem.

1. Write the numeral for the ordinal number seventh.

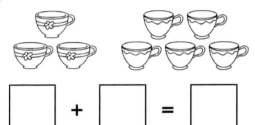

____

2. Add.

☐ + ☐ = ☐

3. Subtract.

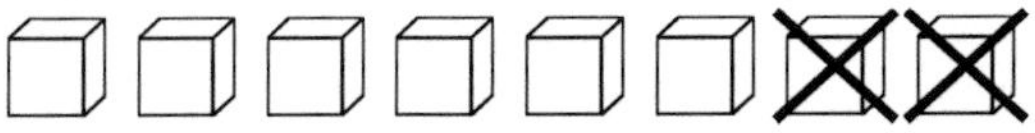

☐ − ☐ = ☐

4.

$$\begin{array}{r} \square \\ +\ 2 \\ \hline 4 \end{array}$$

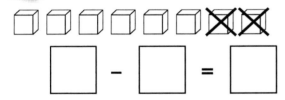

5. Circle the object that looks like the solid.

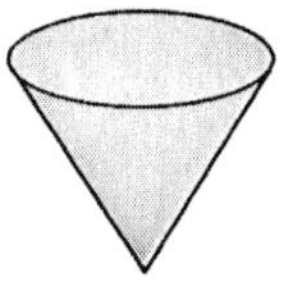

6. Is the object shorter than your arm?

____

7.

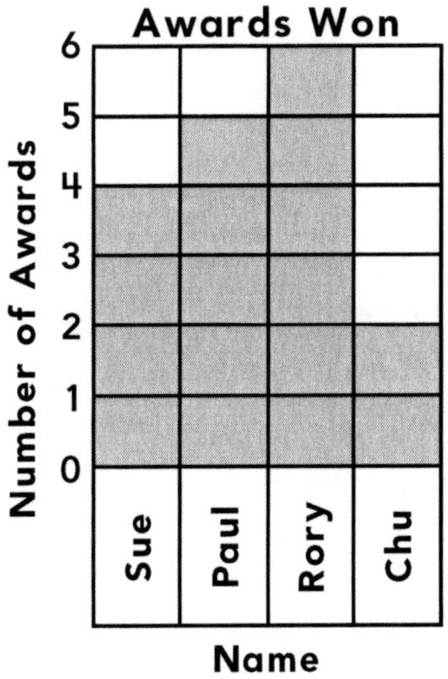

How many awards does Chu have?

____

8. Mary is 2 years older than Trent. Trent is 4. How old is Mary?

____

SCORE

1. ☺ 😐
2. ☺ 😐
3. ☺ 😐
4. ☺ 😐
5. ☺ 😐
6. ☺ 😐
7. ☺ 😐
8. ☺ 😐

____ / 8
Total

NAME: ____________________

DIRECTIONS Solve each problem.

SCORE

1. ☺ 😐
2. ☺ 😐
3. ☺ 😐
4. ☺ 😐
5. ☺ 😐
6. ☺ 😐
7. ☺ 😐
8. ☺ 😐

____ / 8

Total

1. Count all the sticks. Write the numeral.

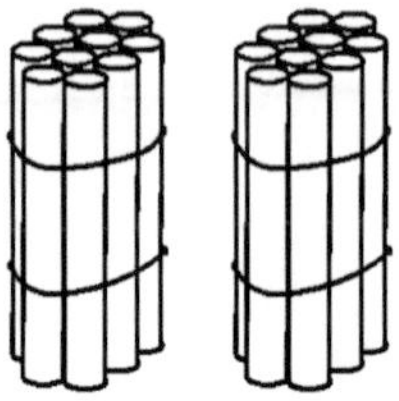

____

2. Add.

☐ + ☐ = ☐

3. Subtract.

☐ – ☐ = ☐

4. 5 – ☐ = 2

5. Is the book in front of the pitcher?

Circle: yes no

6. Circle the bigger frog.

7. Count the tally marks. Write the numeral.

____

8. Tom has 4 toy cars. Jim gives him 2 more. How many toy cars does Tom have in all?

____

NAME: ______________________________

DIRECTIONS Solve each problem.

1. Write the numeral.

●	●	●	●	●	●	●	●	●	●
●	●	●	●						

____

2. Add.

☐ + ☐ = ☐

3. Subtract.

☐ – ☐ = ☐

4. Write the missing number.

3 + ☐ = 3

5. Draw a tree. Draw a sun above the tree.

6. Record the line length.

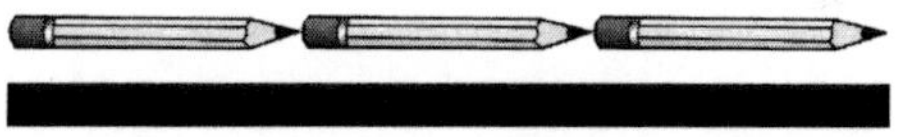

____________ pencils

7. Create a tally chart from the data:

- There are 7 cats.
- There are 9 dogs.

Cats	Dogs

8. Circle each number that has only straight lines.

0 1 2 3 4

5 6 7 8 9

SCORE

1. ☺ 😐
2. ☺ 😐
3. ☺ 😐
4. ☺ 😐
5. ☺ 😐
6. ☺ 😐
7. ☺ 😐
8. ☺ 😐

___ / 8
Total

DAY 18

NAME: ____________________

DIRECTIONS Solve each problem.

SCORE

1. ☺ ☹
2. ☺ ☹
3. ☺ ☹
4. ☺ ☹
5. ☺ ☹
6. ☺ ☹
7. ☺ ☹
8. ☺ ☹

___ / 8
Total

1. Write the numeral.

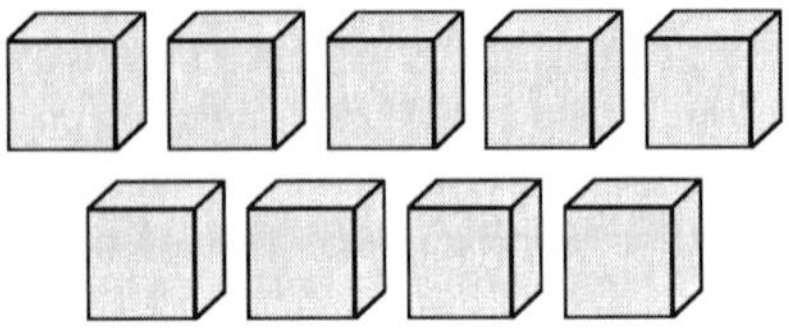

____

2. Add.

☐ + ☐ = ☐

3. Subtract.

☐ - ☐ = ☐

4. Continue the pattern.

A B B A B ___ ___

5. Does the cube have flat surfaces?

Circle: yes no

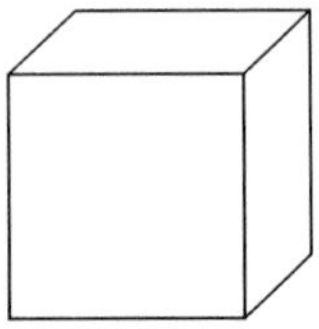

6. Circle the container that holds more.

7. Record the data in the chart. Use tally marks.

- Three people like water parks.
- Five people like amusement parks.

Water Parks	
Amusement Parks	

8. Bikes come in yellow and red. There are three bikes for sale. Only one is red. How many are yellow?

____

NAME: ______________________

DIRECTIONS Solve each problem.

1. Write the number before and after 35.

Before	Number	After
	35	

2. Add.

☐ + ☐ = ☐

3. Subtract.

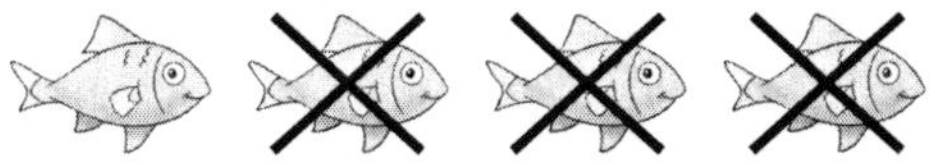

☐ – ☐ = ☐

4. 4 + ☐ = 5

5. Draw a square.

6. Circle the longest line.

7. Favorite Activity

Swings	Slide	Monkey Bars	Balance Beam
8	5	7	2

How many children like the slide?

____

8. There is a bowl of fruit with 3 apples and 2 oranges. Should Winnie add or subtract to find out how many pieces of fruit are in the bowl?

____

SCORE

1. ☺ 😐
2. ☺ 😐
3. ☺ 😐
4. ☺ 😐
5. ☺ 😐
6. ☺ 😐
7. ☺ 😐
8. ☺ 😐

___ / 8 Total

NAME: ____________________

DIRECTIONS Solve each problem.

SCORE

1. ☺ 😐
2. ☺ 😐
3. ☺ 😐
4. ☺ 😐
5. ☺ 😐
6. ☺ 😐
7. ☺ 😐
8. ☺ 😐

____ / 8
Total

1. Count the circles. Draw 2 more. Write how many circles there are now.

____

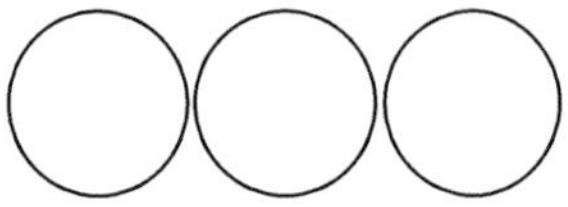

2. Add.

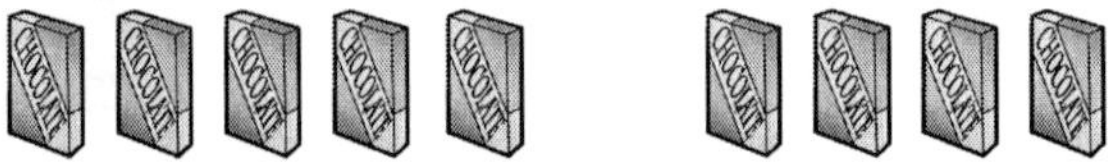

☐ + ☐ = ☐

3. Subtract.

☐ − ☐ = ☐

4. Write the missing sign.

4 ☐ 1 = 5

5. Draw a circle above the square.

6. Is the mass equal?

Circle: yes no

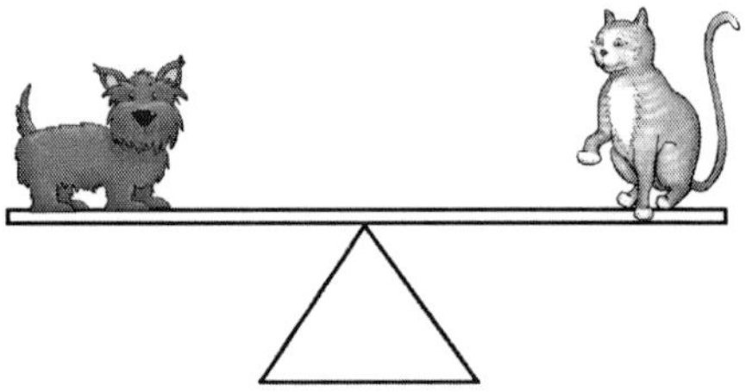

7. What question would you ask to find out about your friends' favorite animals?

____

____

8. What month comes after December?

____

NAME: ______________________________

DIRECTIONS Solve each problem.

1. Circle the smaller number.

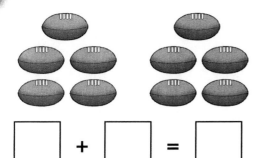

18 12

2. Add.

☐ + ☐ = ☐

3. Subtract.

☐ – ☐ = ☐

4.

☐
– 3
1

5. Color the triangle.

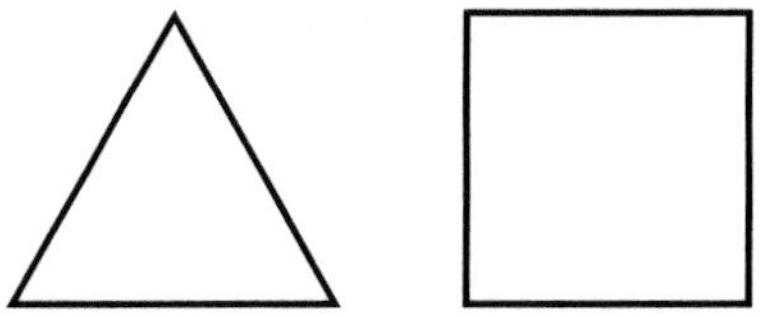

6. Is the object shorter than your arm?

Circle: yes no

7. Count how many. Record with tally marks.

Type of Fish	Tally

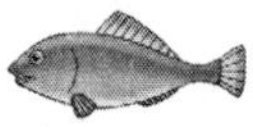	

8. Circle the groups that have the same amount.

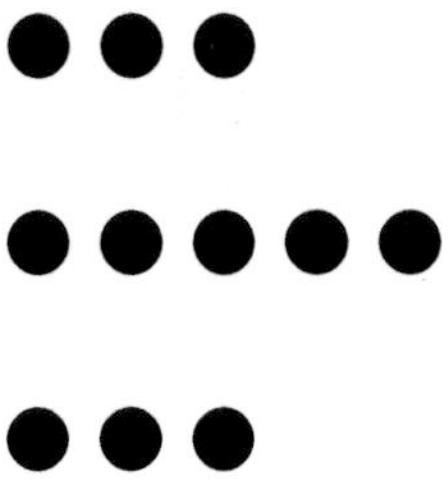

SCORE

1. ☺ 😐
2. ☺ 😐
3. ☺ 😐
4. ☺ 😐
5. ☺ 😐
6. ☺ 😐
7. ☺ 😐
8. ☺ 😐

___ / 8 Total

DAY 22

NAME: ____________________

DIRECTIONS Solve each problem.

SCORE

1. ☺ 😐
2. ☺ 😐
3. ☺ 😐
4. ☺ 😐
5. ☺ 😐
6. ☺ 😐
7. ☺ 😐
8. ☺ 😐

___ / 8
Total

1. Count how many.

★ ★ ★ ★ ★ ★
★ ★ ★ ★ ★ ★
★ ★ ★ ★ ★ ★

____

2. Add.

☐ + ☐ = ☐

3. Subtract.

☐ − ☐ = ☐

4. Write the missing number.

3 + ☐ = 5

5. Count the corners.

__________ corners

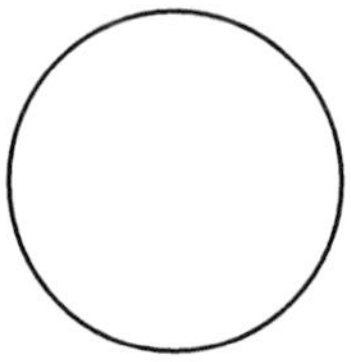

6. What time is it?

_____ : _____

7.

Number of Home Runs

Marc	Ramon	Jamal
7	4	15

How many home runs did Marc hit?

____

8. I am the number that is right before 9. What number am I?

____

NAME: ______________________________

DIRECTIONS Solve each problem.

1. Write the number before and after 30.

Before	Number	After
	30	

2. Add.

☐ + ☐ = ☐

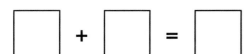

3. Subtract.

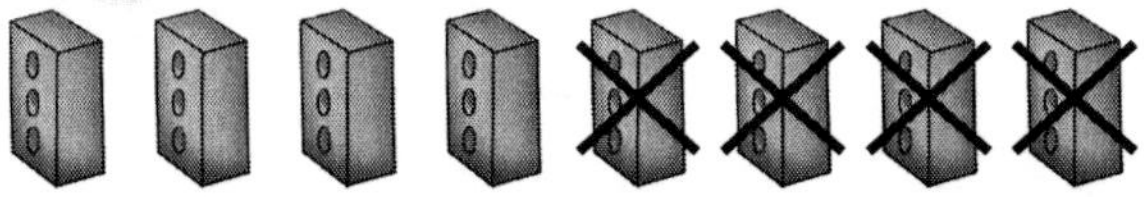

☐ – ☐ = ☐

4. Continue the pattern.

 ____ ____

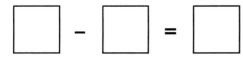

5. Will the object stack?

Circle: yes no

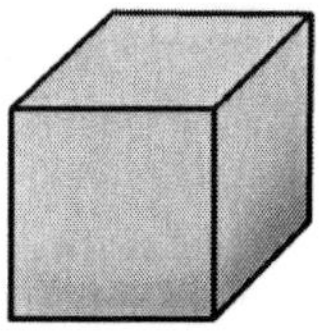

6. Circle the square with the larger area.

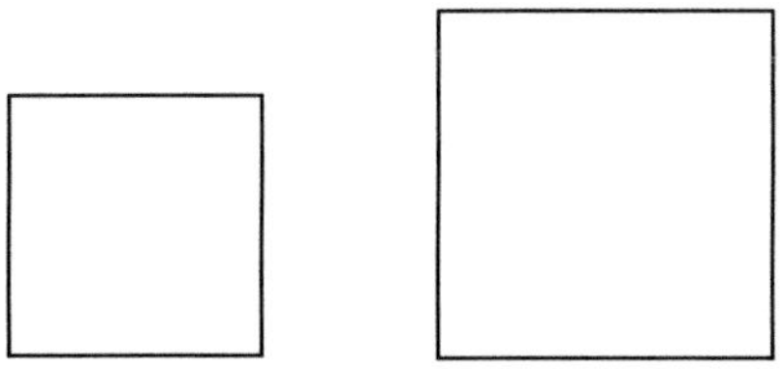

7.

Pencil Colors

Red	卌
Green	卌 |||
Blue	|||

How many pencils are green?

____

8. Abdul has 5 stickers. He earns 4 more. How many stickers does Abdul have now?

____

SCORE

1.
2.
3.
4.
5.
6.
7.
8.

____ / 8 Total

DAY
24

NAME: ____________________

DIRECTIONS Solve each problem.

SCORE

1. ☺ 😐
2. ☺ 😐
3. ☺ 😐
4. ☺ 😐
5. ☺ 😐
6. ☺ 😐
7. ☺ 😐
8. ☺ 😐

____ / 8
Total

1. Write the numeral for one.

____

2. Add.

☐ + ☐ = ☐

3. Subtract.

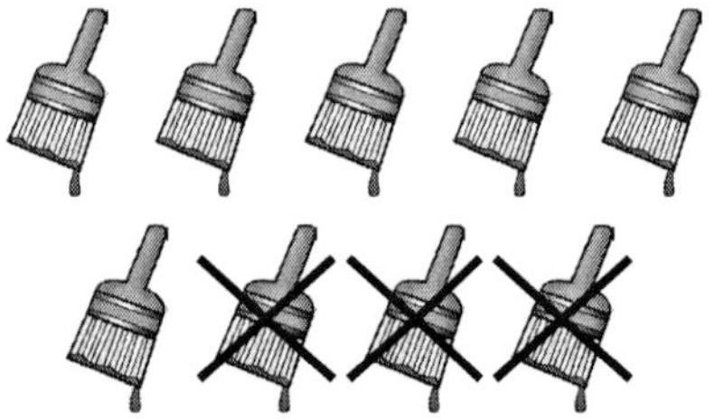

☐ − ☐ = ☐

4.

$$\begin{array}{r} \square \\ +\ 4 \\ \hline 4 \end{array}$$

5. Draw a line of symmetry.

6. Circle the container that holds more.

7. Count the tally marks. Write the numeral.

____

8. Sherry has 5 carrots. Her rabbit eats 2 carrots. How many carrots does Sherry have left?

____

NAME: ____________________

DIRECTIONS Solve each problem.

1. Count. Write the numeral.

____

2. Add.

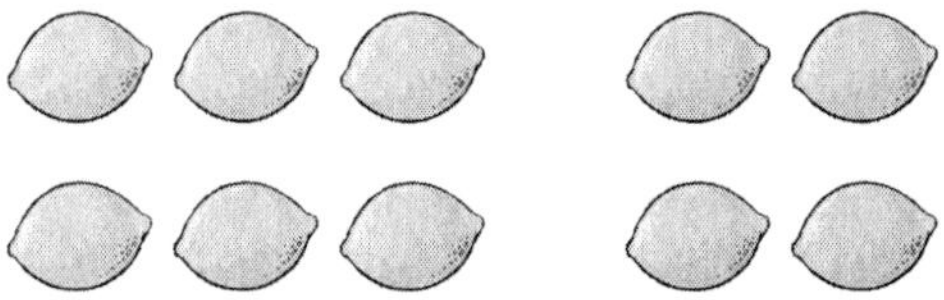

☐ + ☐ = ☐

3. Subtract.

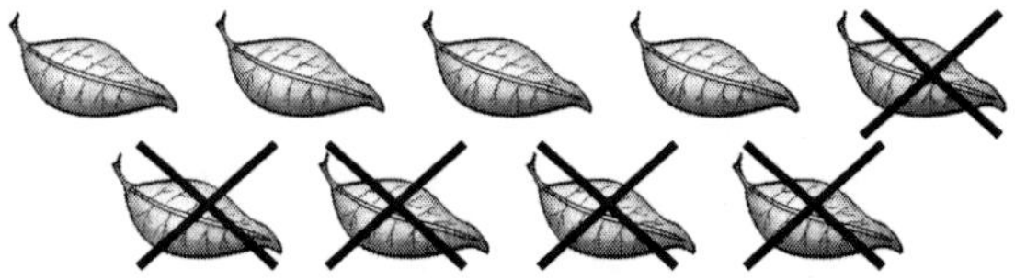

☐ – ☐ = ☐

4. Circle the number sentences that equal 2.

1 + 1

2 + 1

2 + 2

0 + 2

5. Circle the object that looks like the solid.

6. Record the line length.

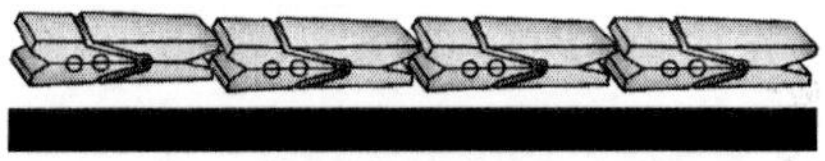

______ clothes pins

7.

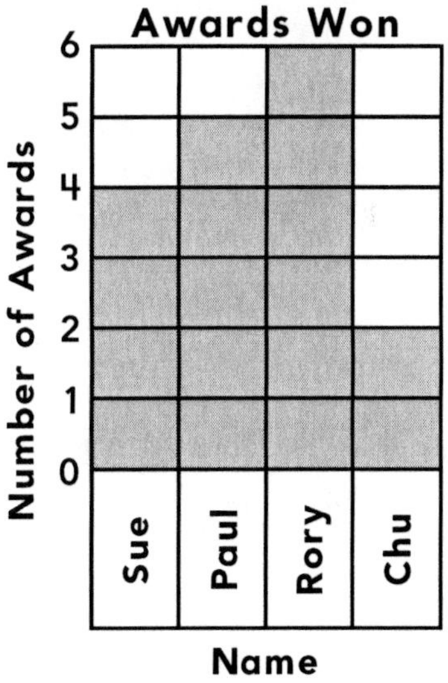

How many awards does Sue have?

____

8. How many sides are on 3 triangles?

____

SCORE

1. ☺ 😐

2. ☺ 😐

3. ☺ 😐

4. ☺ 😐

5. ☺ 😐

6. ☺ 😐

7. ☺ 😐

8. ☺ 😐

____ / 8

Total

NAME: ____________________

DIRECTIONS Solve each problem.

SCORE

1. ☺ 😐
2. ☺ 😐
3. ☺ 😐
4. ☺ 😐
5. ☺ 😐
6. ☺ 😐
7. ☺ 😐
8. ☺ 😐

____ / 8 Total

1. Write the numeral.

●	●	●	●	●	●	●	●	●	●
●	●	●							

____

2. 2 + 0 = ☐

3. Subtract.

☐ – ☐ = ☐

4. Write the missing number.

5 + ☐ = 7

5. Draw a frog on the lily pad.

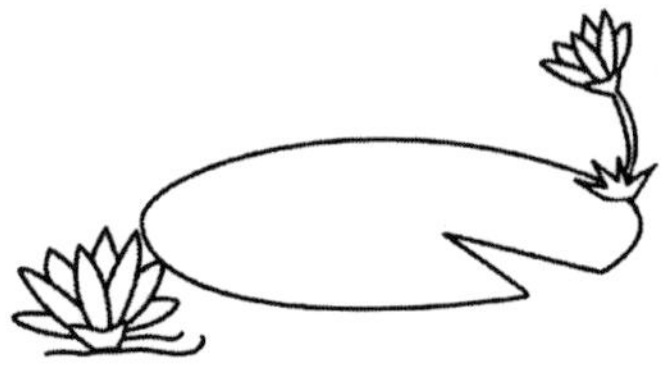

6. Is the object shorter than your arm?

Circle: yes no

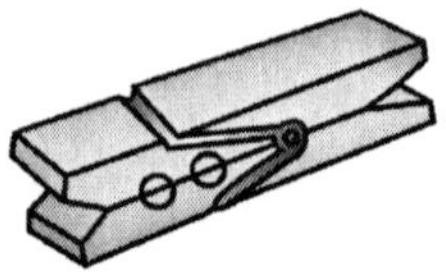

7. Favorite Ice Cream

How many children like chocolate ice cream?

____

8. Rex, the dog, had 5 bones buried in the yard. He eats 1 of them. How many bones are still buried?

____

NAME: ______________________

DIRECTIONS Solve each problem.

1. Write the numeral.

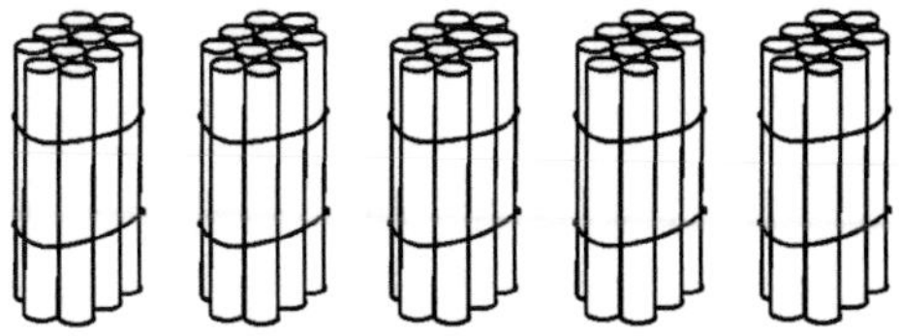

____

2. 3 + 1 = ☐

3. Subtract.

☐ – ☐ = ☐

4.

$$\begin{array}{r} \square \\ +\ 2 \\ \hline 3 \end{array}$$

5. Will the solid roll?

Circle: yes no

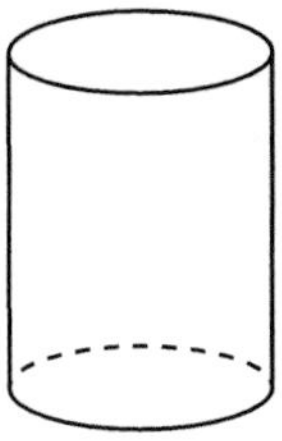

6. Circle the heavier object.

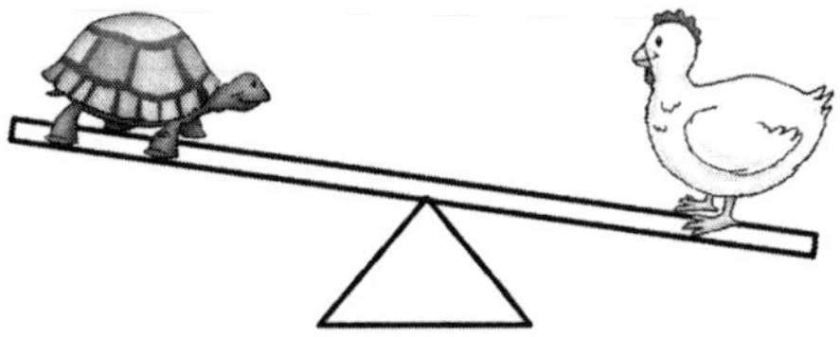

7.

Favorite Subject

Math	☺ ☺ ☺ ☺ ☺ ☺
Reading	☺ ☺ ☺ ☺
Science	☺ ☺ ☺ ☺ ☺ ☺ ☺

How many children like math?

____

8. Write an addition number sentence using the numbers 2, 3, and 5.

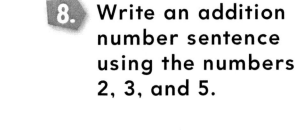

____

SCORE

1. ☺ 😐
2. ☺ 😐
3. ☺ 😐
4. ☺ 😐
5. ☺ 😐
6. ☺ 😐
7. ☺ 😐
8. ☺ 😐

___ / 8 Total

DAY
28

NAME: ____________________

DIRECTIONS Solve each problem.

SCORE

1. ☺ 😐
2. ☺ 😐
3. ☺ 😐
4. ☺ 😐
5. ☺ 😐
6. ☺ 😐
7. ☺ 😐
8. ☺ 😐

____ / 8
Total

1. Count the happy faces. Draw 3 more. Write how many happy faces there are now.

____

2. 1 + 0 = ☐

3. Subtract.

☐ – ☐ = ☐

4. Continue the pattern.

↑ ↑ ↓ ↑ ↑ ____

5. Does the solid have any curved surfaces?

Circle: yes no

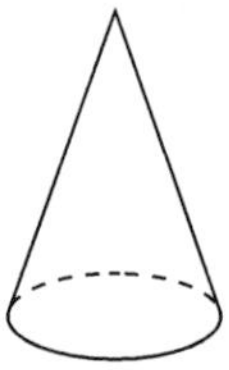

6. Circle the container that holds more.

7. 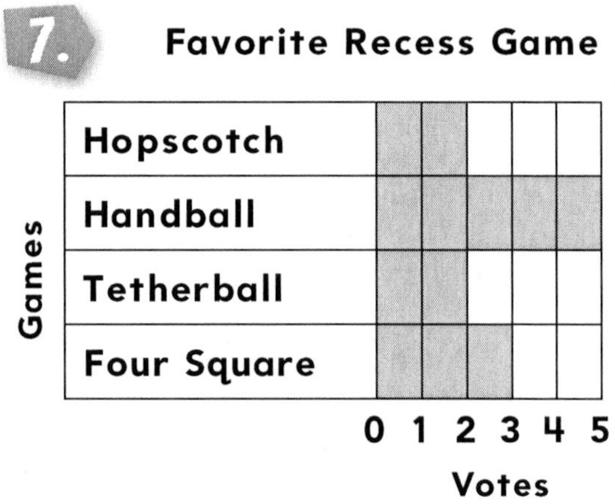

How many children like to play handball?

____

8. Jack and Elly each have a bike. One is blue and one is red. Jack's bike is not red. Which color bike does each child have?

__________ __________
Jack Elly

NAME: ______________________________

DIRECTIONS Solve each problem.

1. Write the numeral for the ordinal number tenth.

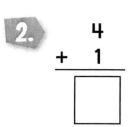

____

2.

$$\begin{array}{r} 4 \\ +\ 1 \\ \hline \square \end{array}$$

3. Subtract.

☐ – ☐ = ☐

4.

$$\begin{array}{r} 5 \\ -\ \square \\ \hline 5 \end{array}$$

5. Draw a triangle.

6. Write the time.

______________ o'clock

7. **Favorite Type of Movie**

Funny	Cartoon	Scary	3-D
III	~~IIII~~ III	I	~~IIII~~

How many children chose 3-D as their favorite type of movie?

____

8. Which has fewer legs: a horse or a man?

____

SCORE

1. ☺ 😐
2. ☺ 😐
3. ☺ 😐
4. ☺ 😐
5. ☺ 😐
6. ☺ 😐
7. ☺ 😐
8. ☺ 😐

____ / 8 Total

DAY 30

NAME: ____________________

DIRECTIONS Solve each problem.

SCORE

1. ☺ 😐
2. ☺ 😐
3. ☺ 😐
4. ☺ 😐
5. ☺ 😐
6. ☺ 😐
7. ☺ 😐
8. ☺ 😐

____ / 8

Total

1. Write the number before and after 42.

Before	Number	After
	42	

2. 3 + 2 = ☐

3. Subtract.

☐ – ☐ = ☐

4. Write the missing sign.

4 ☐ 2 = 6

5. Is the door on the right or left?

____

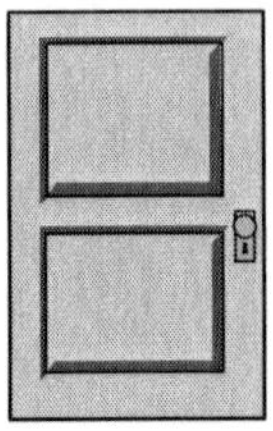

6. Circle the smaller object.

7.

Children in Class

Boys	Girls
7	10

Are there more boys or more girls in the class?

____

8. I start playing tennis at 2:00. I play for 1 hour. At what time do I stop?

____

NAME: ____________________

DIRECTIONS Solve each problem.

1. Write the numeral.

____

2.

$$\begin{array}{r} 2 \\ +\ 1 \\ \hline \square \end{array}$$

3. Subtract.

☐ – ☐ = ☐

4.

$$\begin{array}{r} 1 \\ +\ \square \\ \hline 2 \end{array}$$

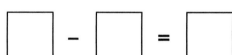

5. Color the rectangle.

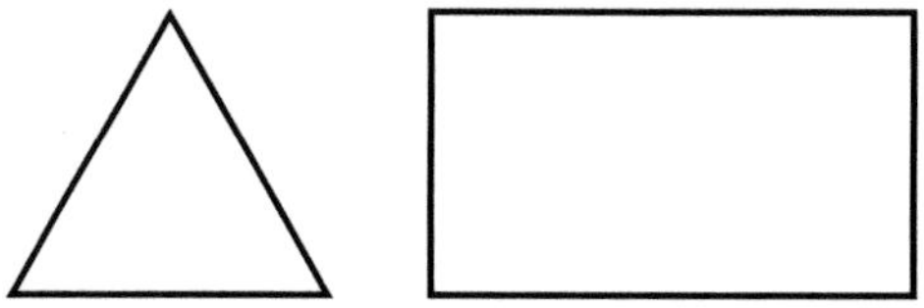

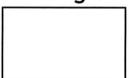

6. Write the time.

____________ o'clock

7. Count how many. Record with numbers.

Cats	Dogs	Birds

8. Start at 10. Write the next five numbers.

____

SCORE

1. ☺ 😐
2. ☺ 😐
3. ☺ 😐
4. ☺ 😐
5. ☺ 😐
6. ☺ 😐
7. ☺ 😐
8. ☺ 😐

___ / 8
Total

DAY 32

NAME: ____________________

DIRECTIONS Solve each problem.

SCORE

1. ☺ 😐
2. ☺ 😐
3. ☺ 😐
4. ☺ 😐
5. ☺ 😐
6. ☺ 😐
7. ☺ 😐
8. ☺ 😐

____ / 8 Total

1. Write the missing number.

23, ______, 25

2. 1 + 1 = ☐

3. Subtract.

☐ – ☐ = ☐

4. Continue the pattern.

● ○ ● ○ ● ____

5. Count the sides.

____________ sides

6. Is the mass equal?

Circle: yes no

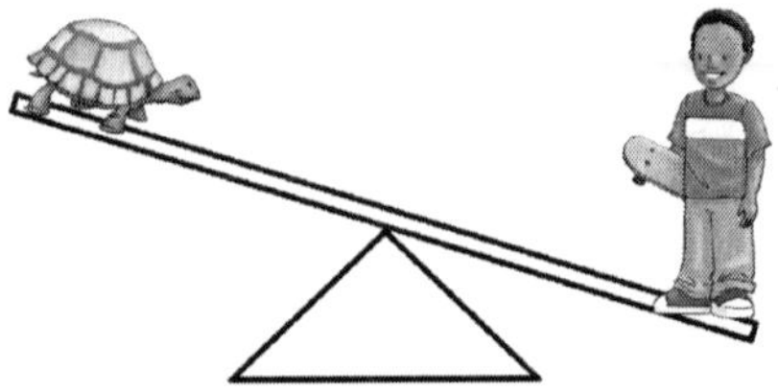

7. Number of Home Runs

Marc	Ramon	Jamal
7	4	15

Who hit the most home runs?

____

8. I am the number that is less than 15 and more than 13. What number am I?

____

NAME: ______________________________

DIRECTIONS Solve each problem.

1. Count how many.

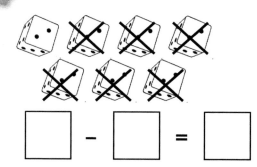

★ ★ ★ ★ ★ ★ ★
★ ★ ★ ★ ★ ★ ★
★ ★ ★ ★ ★

____

2.

$$\begin{array}{r} 3 \\ +\ 0 \\ \hline \square \end{array}$$

3. Subtract.

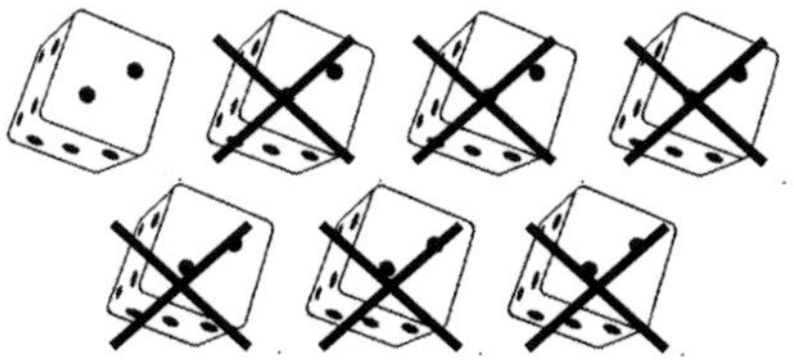

☐ – ☐ = ☐

4. 3 – ☐ = 2

5. Will the object roll?

Circle: yes no

6. Is the object shorter than your leg?

Circle: yes no

7. Pencil Colors

Red	𝍸
Green	𝍸 𝍷𝍷𝍷
Blue	𝍷𝍷𝍷

Are there more red pencils than blue pencils?

____

8. Nine birds are sitting on a fence. Three fly away. How many birds are left?

____

SCORE

1. ☺ 😐
2. ☺ 😐
3. ☺ 😐
4. ☺ 😐
5. ☺ 😐
6. ☺ 😐
7. ☺ 😐
8. ☺ 😐

____ / 8
Total

NAME: ______________________

DIRECTIONS Solve each problem.

SCORE

1. ☺ 😐
2. ☺ 😐
3. ☺ 😐
4. ☺ 😐
5. ☺ 😐
6. ☺ 😐
7. ☺ 😐
8. ☺ 😐

____ / 8 Total

1. Write the numeral for ten.

____

2. 2 + 2 = ☐

3. Subtract.

☐ – ☐ = ☐

4. Circle the ways to make 5.

5 + 0   1 + 4

2 + 2   3 + 2

5. Draw a line of symmetry.

6. Circle the coin that takes up more space.

7. Count the tally marks. Write the numeral.

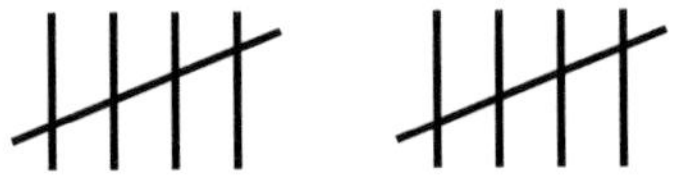

____

8. There is a baseball game every Saturday. The team practices the day before the game. On what day does the team practice?

____

NAME: ______________________

DIRECTIONS Solve each problem.

1. Write the number before and after 23.

Before	Number	After
	23	

2.

$$\begin{array}{r} 5 \\ +\ 0 \\ \hline \square \end{array}$$

3. Subtract.

☐ – ☐ = ☐

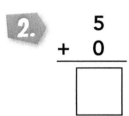

4. Write the missing number.

☐ + 3 = 7

5. Circle the object that looks like the solid.

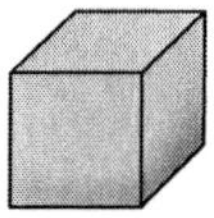

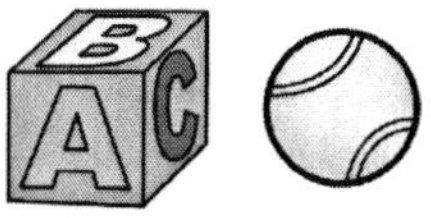

6. Circle the object that weighs less.

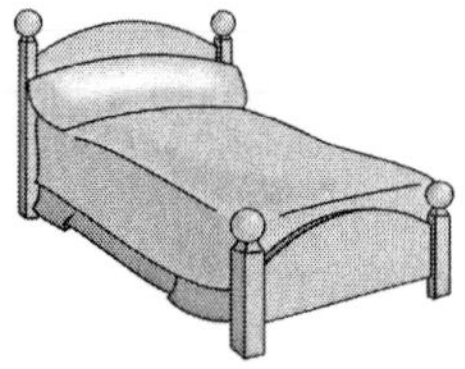

7.

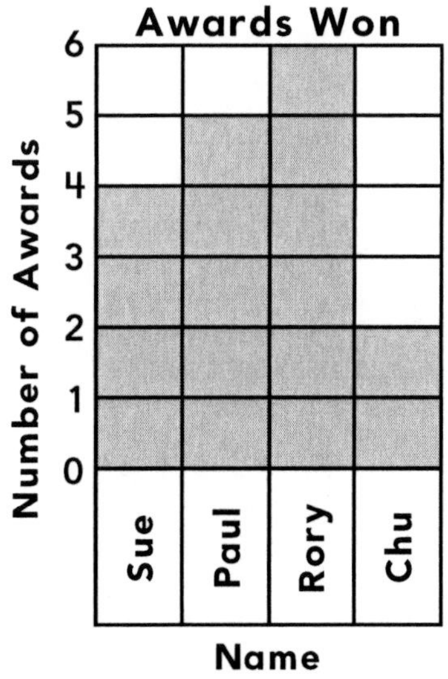

How many awards does Rory have?

____

8. The children took off their shoes. There are 4 shoes on the floor. How many children are there?

____

SCORE

1.

2.

3.

4.

5.

6.

7.

8.

___ / 8
Total

DAY
36

NAME: ____________________

DIRECTIONS Solve each problem.

SCORE

1. ☺ 😐
2. ☺ 😐
3. ☺ 😐
4. ☺ 😐
5. ☺ 😐
6. ☺ 😐
7. ☺ 😐
8. ☺ 😐

____ / 8

Total

1. Write the numeral for the ordinal number first.

____

2. 4 + 0 = ☐

3.

$$\begin{array}{r} 1 \\ -\ 0 \\ \hline \square \end{array}$$

4. 4 − ☐ = 3

5. Is the fork next to the knife?

Circle: yes no

6. What month comes after January?

____

7. Favorite Activity

Swings	Slide	Monkey Bars	Balance Beam
8	5	7	2

How many children like the monkey bars?

____

8. Janai has 3 stickers. Her mom buys her 2 more. How many stickers does Janai have now?

____

DAY
37

NAME: ______________________________

DIRECTIONS Solve each problem.

1. Write the numeral.

● ● ● ● ● ● ● ● ● ●
● ● ● ● ● ●

____

2.

$$\begin{array}{r} 1 \\ +\ 2 \\ \hline \square \end{array}$$

3. $2 - 2 = \square$

4. Continue the pattern.

1 2 3 4 5 _____

5. What shape is a basketball?

____

6. Write the time.

____________ o'clock

7. **Favorite Weekend Activity**

Play Video Games	𝍸 |
Read	𝍸 |||
Play with Toys	𝍸

How many children like video games best?

____

8. Circle the numbers that have only curved lines.

0 1 2 3 4

5 6 7 8 9

SCORE

1. ☺ 😐
2. ☺ 😐
3. ☺ 😐
4. ☺ 😐
5. ☺ 😐
6. ☺ 😐
7. ☺ 😐
8. ☺ 😐

____ / 8

Total

DAY
38

NAME: ______________________________

DIRECTIONS Solve each problem.

SCORE

1. ☺ ☹
2. ☺ ☹
3. ☺ ☹
4. ☺ ☹
5. ☺ ☹
6. ☺ ☹
7. ☺ ☹
8. ☺ ☹

____ / 8

Total

1. Write the numeral.

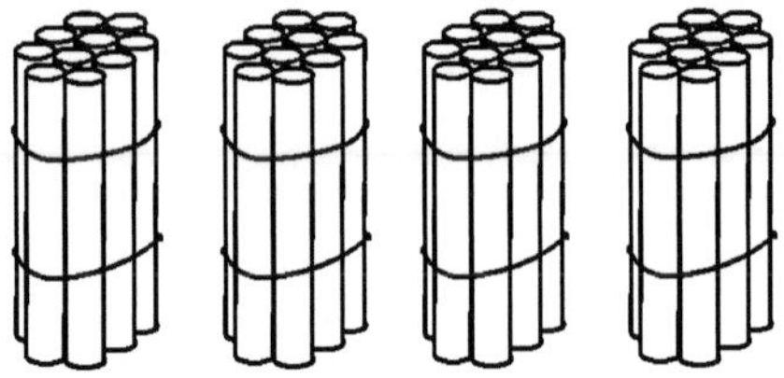

____

2. 2 + 3 = ☐

3.

$$\begin{array}{r} 3 \\ -\ 1 \\ \hline \square \end{array}$$

4. ☐ + 3 = 5

5. Will the solid roll?

Circle: yes no

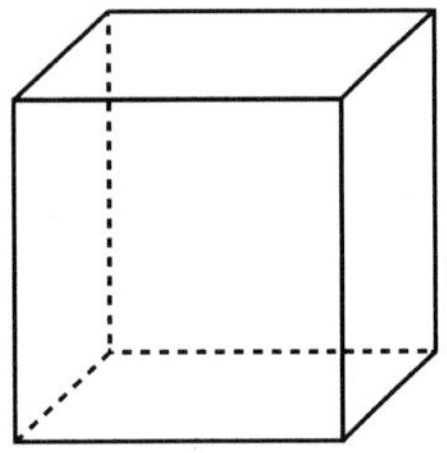

6. Circle the heavier object.

7. Write a good title for this chart.

____

Cats	Dogs
7	9

8. There are 4 wheels on the street. How many cars are there?

____

NAME: ______________________________

DIRECTIONS Solve each problem.

1. Write the number before and after 49.

Before	Number	After
	49	

2.

$$\begin{array}{r} 0 \\ +\ 2 \\ \hline \square \end{array}$$

3. $4 - 3 = \square$

4. Write the missing sign.

$$\begin{array}{r} 5 \\ \square\ 3 \\ \hline 2 \end{array}$$

5. Draw a rectangle.

6. Record the line length.

_______ spiders

7. Record the data in the pictograph. Use happy faces.

- Four people like tacos.
- Six people like pizza.

Favorite Food

Tacos	
Pizza	

8. Which is greater: the number of legs on a spider or the number of legs on a cat?

____

SCORE

1. ☺ ☹
2. ☺ ☹
3. ☺ ☹
4. ☺ ☹
5. ☺ ☹
6. ☺ ☹
7. ☺ ☹
8. ☺ ☹

___ / 8 Total

DAY
40

NAME: ______________________________

DIRECTIONS Solve each problem.

SCORE

1.
2.
3.
4.
5.
6.
7.
8.

___ / 8
Total

1. Count the triangles. Draw 2 more. Write how many now.

____

2. 1 + 3 = ☐

3.

$$\begin{array}{r} 5 \\ -\ 4 \\ \hline \square \end{array}$$

4. Write the missing number.

6 + ☐ = 7

5. Draw a square below the triangle.

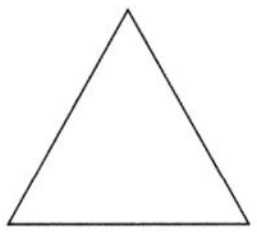

6. Circle the smaller object.

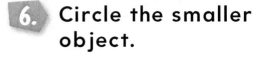

7. What question would you ask to find out about your friend's favorite color?

____

____

____

8. Tasha's birthday is in the first month of the year. In what month is Tasha's birthday?

____

NAME: ____________________

DIRECTIONS Solve each problem.

1. Write the numeral.

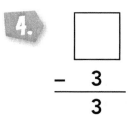

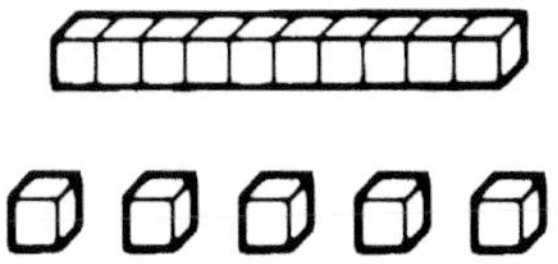

____

2.

$$\begin{array}{r} 2 \\ +\ 2 \\ \hline \square \end{array}$$

3. 3 – 0 = $\square$

4.

$$\begin{array}{r} \square \\ -\ 3 \\ \hline 3 \end{array}$$

5. Name the shape.

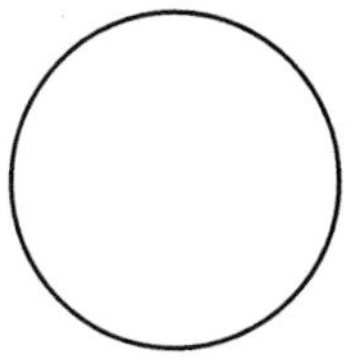

____

6. Is the object shorter than your arm?

Circle: yes no

7. Count how many. Record with tallies.

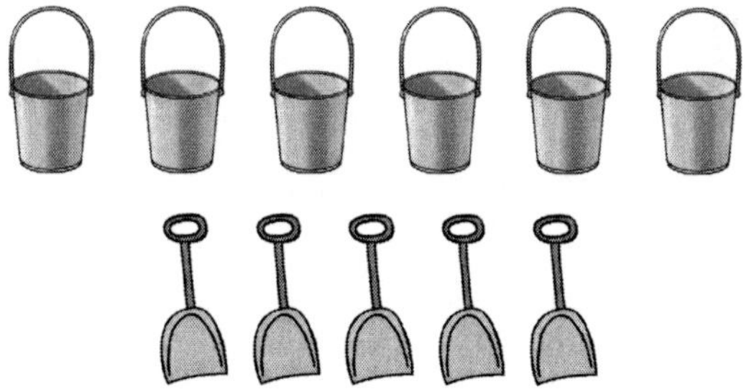

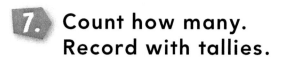

Buckets	
Shovels	

8. There are 5 apples in a basket. I eat 1 of them. How many apples are left in the basket?

____

SCORE

1. ☺ 😐
2. ☺ 😐
3. ☺ 😐
4. ☺ 😐
5. ☺ 😐
6. ☺ 😐
7. ☺ 😐
8. ☺ 😐

___ / 8 Total

DAY
42

NAME: ____________________

DIRECTIONS Solve each problem.

SCORE

1. ☺ 😐
2. ☺ 😐
3. ☺ 😐
4. ☺ 😐
5. ☺ 😐
6. ☺ 😐
7. ☺ 😐
8. ☺ 😐

____ / 8

Total

1. Write the numeral.

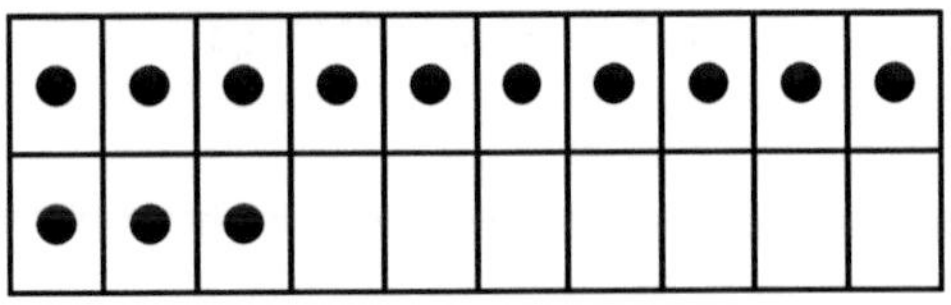

____

2. 0 + 1 = ☐

3.

$$\begin{array}{r} 5 \\ -\ 2 \\ \hline \square \end{array}$$

4. ☐ + 4 = 5

5. Count the corners.

__________ corners

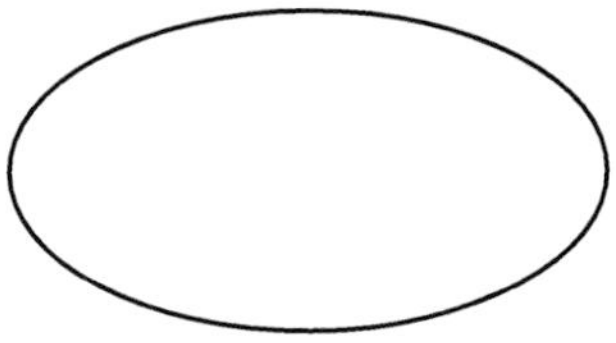

6. Write the time.

_____ : _____

7.

Number of Home Runs

Marc	Ramon	Jamal
7	4	15

Who hit the fewest home runs?

____

8. I am the number that is 5 more than 10. What number am I?

____

NAME: ______________________________

DIRECTIONS Solve each problem.

1. Write the numeral for thirteen.

____

2.

$$\begin{array}{r} 1 \\ +\ 4 \\ \hline \square \end{array}$$

3. $2 - 1 = \square$

4.

$$\begin{array}{r} 0 \\ +\ \square \\ \hline 2 \end{array}$$

5. Will the object stack?

Circle: yes no

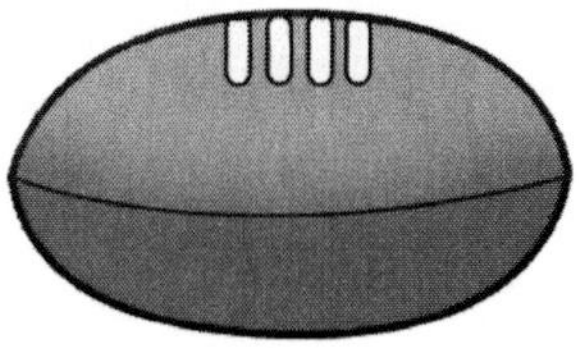

6. Circle the sign that takes up more space.

7. Pencil Colors

Red	𝍸
Green	𝍸 𝍷𝍷𝍷
Blue	𝍷𝍷𝍷

Are there more red pencils than green pencils?

____

8. Guy has 6 marbles. He wins 2 more. How many marbles does Guy have now?

____

SCORE

1. ☺ 😐
2. ☺ 😐
3. ☺ 😐
4. ☺ 😐
5. ☺ 😐
6. ☺ 😐
7. ☺ 😐
8. ☺ 😐

____ / 8

Total

DAY 44

NAME: ____________________________

DIRECTIONS Solve each problem.

SCORE

1. ☺ 😐
2. ☺ 😐
3. ☺ 😐
4. ☺ 😐
5. ☺ 😐
6. ☺ 😐
7. ☺ 😐
8. ☺ 😐

____ / 8
Total

1. Circle the larger number.

12 21

2. 0 + 3 = ☐

3.

$$\begin{array}{r} 4 \\ -\ 2 \\ \hline \square \end{array}$$

4. Continue the pattern.

← → → ← → ____

5. Draw a line of symmetry.

☐

6. Circle the object that weighs less.

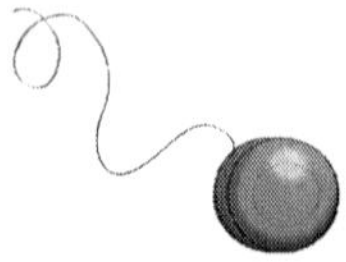

7.

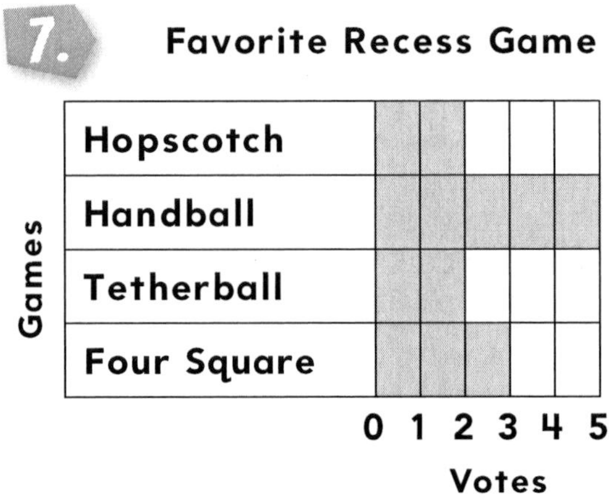

How many children like to play tetherball?

____

8. Write the number sentence:

Five plus two equals seven.

____

NAME: ______________________________

DIRECTIONS Solve each problem.

1. Circle the 5th star.

★ ★ ★ ★ ★ ★ ★

2.

$$\begin{array}{r} 1 \\ +\ 1 \\ \hline \square \end{array}$$

3. 5 – 0 = ☐

4. Circle the ways to make 8.

4 + 4

2 + 3

6 + 2

10 – 2

5. Circle the object that looks like the solid.

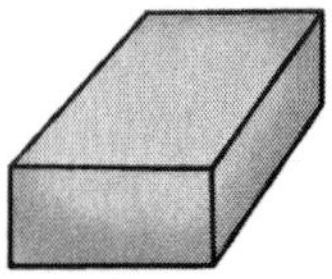

6. Record the line length.

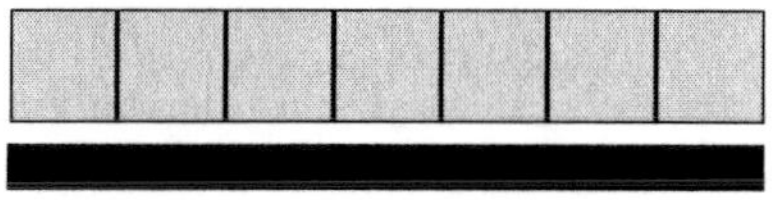

__________ squares

7.

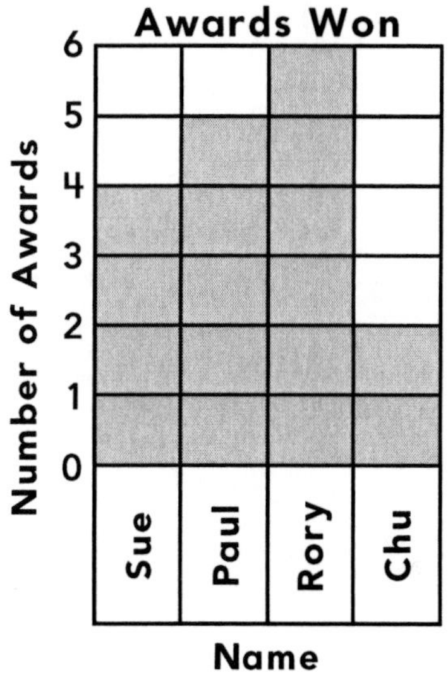

Who has the most awards?

____

8. How many sides are there on 2 squares?

____

SCORE

1. ☺ 😐
2. ☺ 😐
3. ☺ 😐
4. ☺ 😐
5. ☺ 😐
6. ☺ 😐
7. ☺ 😐
8. ☺ 😐

____ / 8 Total

NAME: ____________________

DIRECTIONS Solve each problem.

SCORE

1. ☺ ☹
2. ☺ ☹
3. ☺ ☹
4. ☺ ☹
5. ☺ ☹
6. ☺ ☹
7. ☺ ☹
8. ☺ ☹

____ / 8
Total

1. Write the number before and after 27.

Before	Number	After
	27	

2. 5 + 0 = ☐

3.
$$\begin{array}{r} 3 \\ -\ 3 \\ \hline \square \end{array}$$

4. Write the missing sign.

4 ☐ 1 = 5

5. Draw a boy beside the pig.

6. Is the mass equal?
Circle: yes no

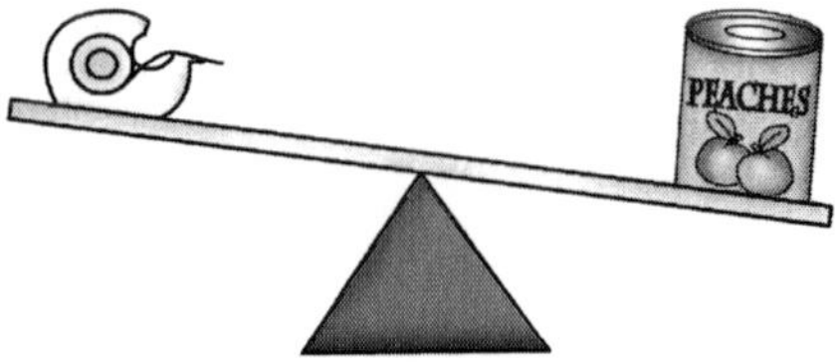

7. Count the tally marks. Write the numeral.

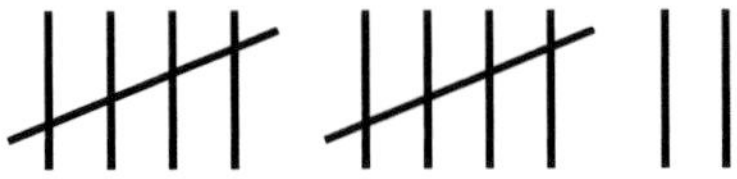

____

8. Pauline has 8 marshmallows in her hot chocolate. She eats 4 of them. How many marshmallows are left in her hot chocolate?

____

NAME: ____________________

DIRECTIONS Solve each problem.

1. Write the numeral.

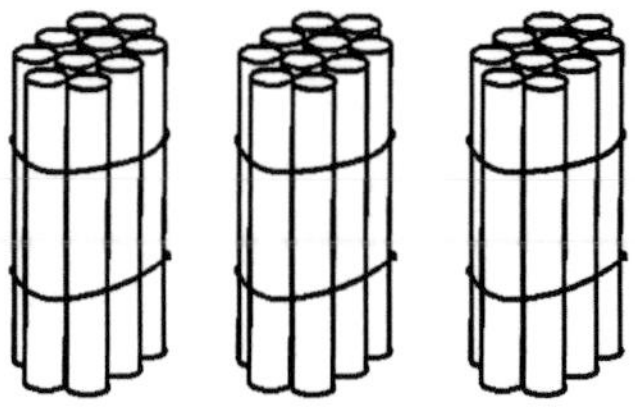

____

2. 2 + 5 = ☐

3. 4 − 1 = ☐

4. 7 − ☐ = 5

5. How many flat surfaces does the solid have?

____

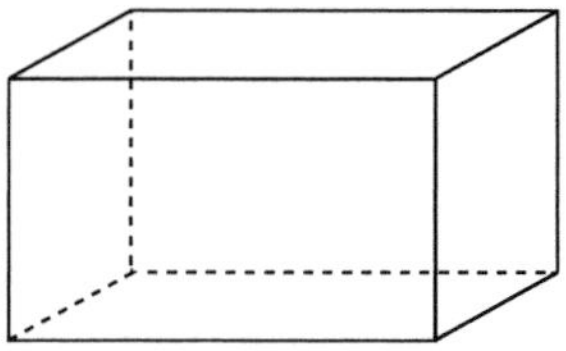

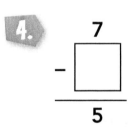

6. Circle the smaller object.

7. Favorite Subject

Math	☺☺☺☺☺☺
Reading	☺☺☺☺
Science	☺☺☺☺☺☺☺

How many children like reading best?

____

8. Write an addition number sentence using the numbers 3, 3, and 6.

____

SCORE

1. ☺ 😐

2. ☺ 😐

3. ☺ 😐

4. ☺ 😐

5. ☺ 😐

6. ☺ 😐

7. ☺ 😐

8. ☺ 😐

___ / 8 Total

NAME: ____________________

DIRECTIONS Solve each problem.

SCORE

1. ☺ 😐
2. ☺ 😐
3. ☺ 😐
4. ☺ 😐
5. ☺ 😐
6. ☺ 😐
7. ☺ 😐
8. ☺ 😐

____ / 8 Total

1. Count how many.

★ ★ ★ ★ ★ ★ ★ ★ ★ ★

★ ★ ★ ★ ★ ★ ★ ★ ★ ★

____

2. $1 + 7 = \square$

3.

$$\begin{array}{r} 2 \\ -\ 0 \\ \hline \square \end{array}$$

4. Continue the pattern.

□ □ ○ □ □ ____

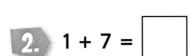

5. What shape is a sheet of paper?

____

6. Count the blocks.

____

7. Favorite Type of Movie

Funny	Cartoon	Scary	3-D
|||	~~||||~~ |||	|	~~||||~~

How many children like scary movies best?

____

8. Draw a line from each person's name to their favorite fruit.

- Brandon's favorite fruit is apples.
- Allison's favorite is not bananas.
- Brandon and Craig do not like oranges as their favorite.

Allison 

Craig 

Brandon 

NAME: ______________________

DIRECTIONS Solve each problem.

SCORE

1. Count the shells. Draw 5 more. Write how many shells there are now.

____

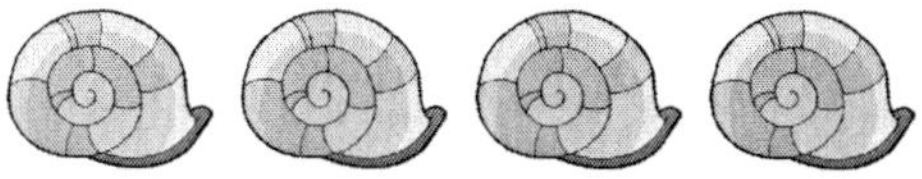

2.

$$\begin{array}{r} 3 \\ +\ 3 \\ \hline \square \end{array}$$

3. $0 - 0 = \square$

4. Circle the ways to make 6.

3 + 3   2 + 4

6 – 0   8 – 2

5. Draw an oval.

6. Is the object shorter than your arm?

Circle: yes no

7. Children in Class

Boys	Girls
7	10

How many children are in the class?

____

8. There are 3 pairs of shoes. How many shoes are there in all?

____

1. ☺ 😐
2. ☺ 😐
3. ☺ 😐
4. ☺ 😐
5. ☺ 😐
6. ☺ 😐
7. ☺ 😐
8. ☺ 😐

____ / 8
Total

DAY 50

NAME: ____________________

DIRECTIONS Solve each problem.

SCORE

1. ☺ ☹
2. ☺ ☹
3. ☺ ☹
4. ☺ ☹
5. ☺ ☹
6. ☺ ☹
7. ☺ ☹
8. ☺ ☹

____ / 8 Total

1. Write the numeral for the ordinal number twentieth.

____

2. $8 + 0 = \square$

3.

$$\begin{array}{r} 5 \\ -\ 5 \\ \hline \square \end{array}$$

4. Write the missing number.

$9 - 5 = \square$

5. Is the flashlight on the right or left?

____

6. Write the time.

__________ o'clock

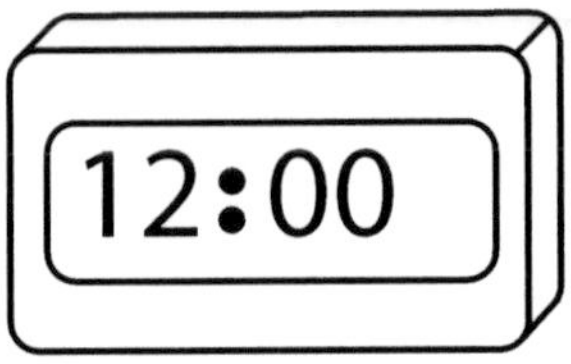

7.

Favorite Animal

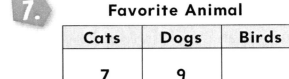

Cats	Dogs	Birds
7	9	

There are more birds than cats. There are more dogs than birds. Write the number of birds in the table.

8. Which would hold more water: a bathtub or a swimming pool?

____

NAME: ______________________

DIRECTIONS Solve each problem.

1. Put these numbers in order from smallest to largest.

9 5 7

_____ _____ _____

2.

$$\begin{array}{r} 1 \\ +\ 6 \\ \hline \square \end{array}$$

3. $3 - 2 = \square$

4.

$$\begin{array}{r} 3 \\ +\ \square \\ \hline 4 \end{array}$$

5. Name the shape.

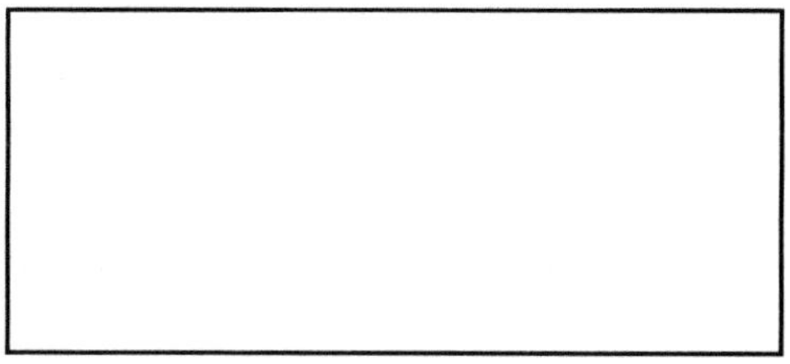

____

6. Record the line length.

_____ dinosaurs

7. Write the number of objects in the chart.

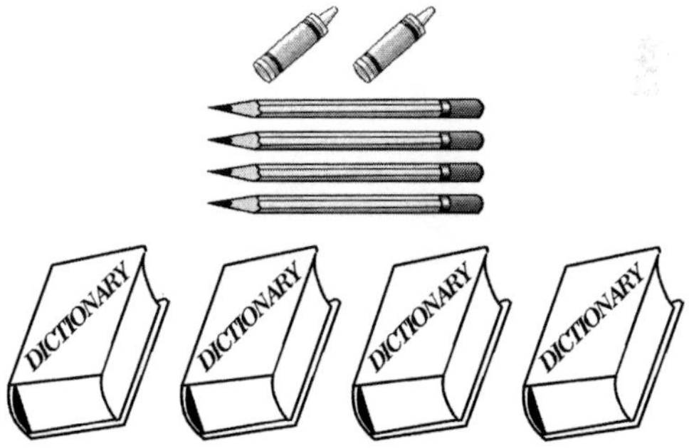

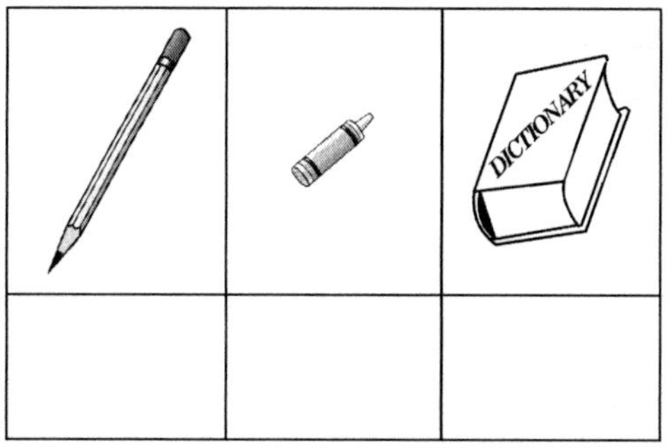

8. Show how you can add numbers in any order. Write the matching addition number sentence.

$2 + 3 = 5$

____

SCORE

1. ☺ ☹

2. ☺ ☹

3. ☺ ☹

4. ☺ ☹

5. ☺ ☹

6. ☺ ☹

7. ☺ ☹

8. ☺ ☹

___ / 8 Total

DAY 52

NAME: ______________________

DIRECTIONS Solve each problem.

SCORE

1. ☺ 😐
2. ☺ 😐
3. ☺ 😐
4. ☺ 😐
5. ☺ 😐
6. ☺ 😐
7. ☺ 😐
8. ☺ 😐

____ / 8
Total

1. Write the number before and after 61.

Before	Number	After
	61	

2. 3 + 5 = ☐

3.

$$\begin{array}{r} 5 \\ -\ 1 \\ \hline \square \end{array}$$

4. Continue the pattern.

10   20   30   40   ____

5. Count the sides.

______________ sides

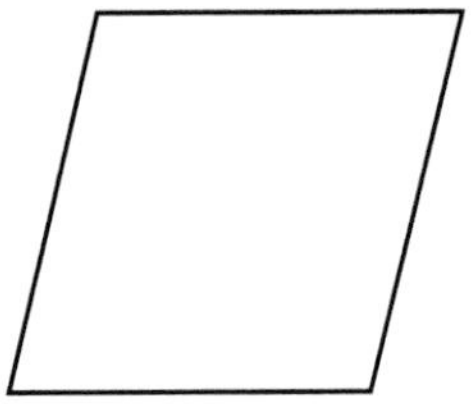

6. Circle the object that weighs less.

7.

Favorite Weekend Activity

Play Video Games	卌 |
Read	卌 |||
Play with Toys	卌

How many children like to play with toys best?

____

8. I am a number you say when you count by 10s. I am more than 20 and less than 40. What number am I?

____

DAY 53

NAME: ____________________

DIRECTIONS Solve each problem.

1. Write the numeral.

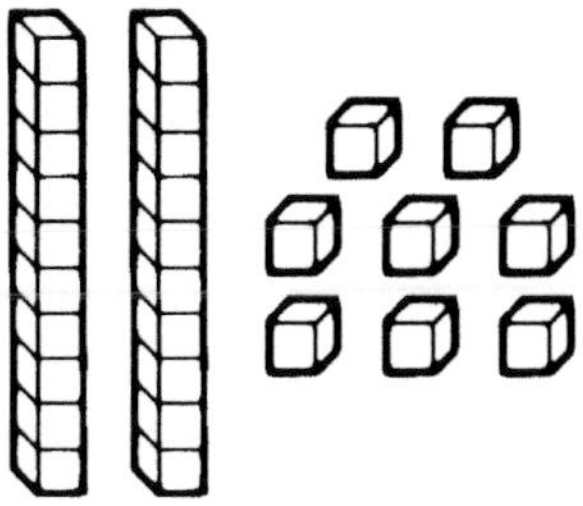

____

2.

$$\begin{array}{r} 2 \\ +\ 7 \\ \hline \square \end{array}$$

3. 1 – 1 = ☐

4. Write the missing number.

☐ + 3 = 9

5. Will the object stack?

Circle: yes no

6. Is the object longer than your finger?

Circle: yes no

7.

Pencil Colors

Red	𝍸
Green	𝍸 |||
Blue	|||

Are there more green pencils than blue pencils?

____

8. There are 7 bananas in a bunch. Frannie eats one of the bananas. How many bananas are left?

____

SCORE

1. ☺ 😐
2. ☺ 😐
3. ☺ 😐
4. ☺ 😐
5. ☺ 😐
6. ☺ 😐
7. ☺ 😐
8. ☺ 😐

___ / 8

Total

NAME: ____________________

DIRECTIONS Solve each problem.

SCORE

1.
2.
3.
4.
5.
6.
7.
8.

___ /8 Total

1. Write the numeral.

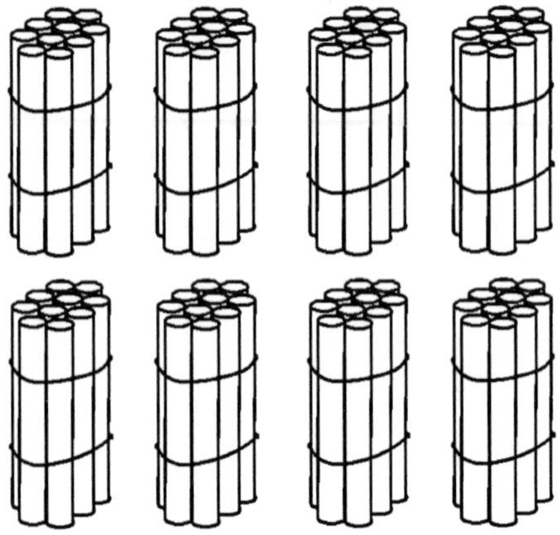

____

2. 1 + 5 = ☐

3.

$$\begin{array}{r} 4 \\ -\ 4 \\ \hline \square \end{array}$$

4. Write the missing sign.

5 ☐ 2 = 7

5. Draw a line of symmetry.

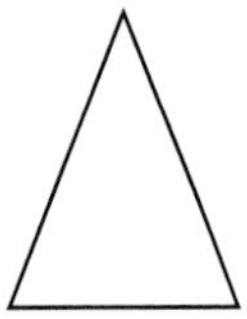

6. Record the line length.

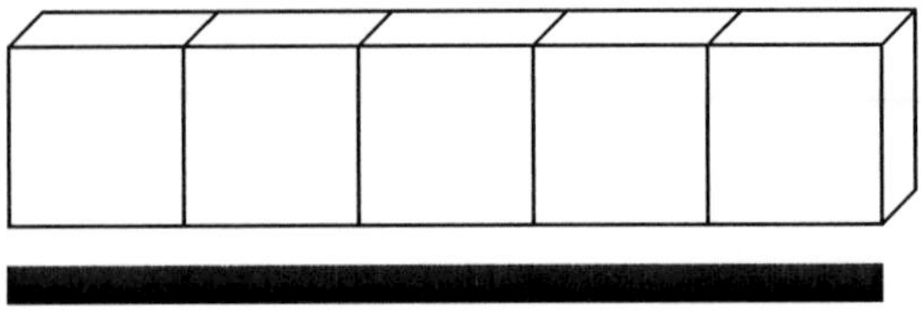

__________ blocks

7. Favorite Ice Cream

Chocolate Ice Cream	
Strawberry Ice Cream	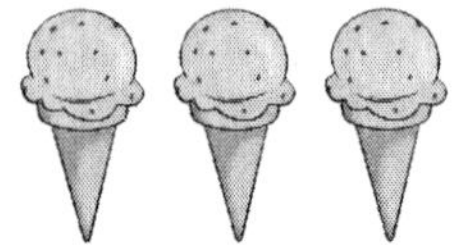

How many children in all were asked about ice cream?

____

8. Harmony drinks 5 cups of water each day. How many cups of water will she drink in 2 days?

____

NAME: ______________________

DIRECTIONS Solve each problem.

1. Write the numeral for twenty-two.

____

2.

$$\begin{array}{r} 0 \\ +\ 7 \\ \hline \square \end{array}$$

3. $4 - 0 = \square$

4.

$$\begin{array}{r} 7 \\ -\ \square \\ \hline 0 \end{array}$$

5. Circle the object that is a cube.

6. How many days are in one week?

____

7.

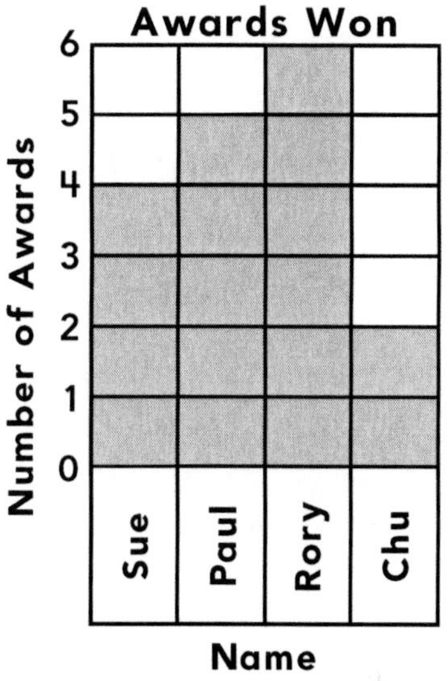

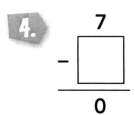

Who has the fewest awards?

____

8. How many fingers are on two hands?

____

SCORE

1. ☺ 😐
2. ☺ 😐
3. ☺ 😐
4. ☺ 😐
5. ☺ 😐
6. ☺ 😐
7. ☺ 😐
8. ☺ 😐

____ / 8
Total

NAME: ____________________

DIRECTIONS Solve each problem.

SCORE

1. 🙂 😐
2. 🙂 😐
3. 🙂 😐
4. 🙂 😐
5. 🙂 😐
6. 🙂 😐
7. 🙂 😐
8. 🙂 😐

____ / 8 Total

1. Write the missing number.

38, ______, 40

2. 4 + 5 = ☐

3.
$$\begin{array}{r} 6 \\ -\ 4 \\ \hline \square \end{array}$$

4. Circle the ways to make 7.

9 – 2   7 – 0

6 – 1   8 – 2

5. Is the shovel near the ball or the pail?

____

6. Record the line length.

____________ forks

7. Count the tally marks. Write the numeral.

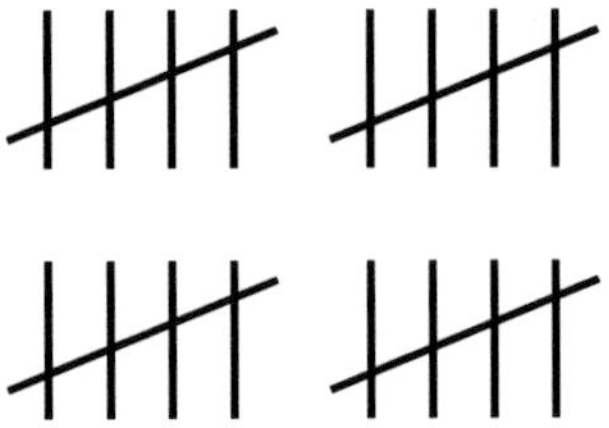

____

8. Yani has 10 pieces of candy. Her mom gives her 3 more. How many pieces of candy does she have now?

____

NAME: ______________________

DIRECTIONS Solve each problem.

1. Draw dots to finish the ten frame. How many more dots were needed to make ten?

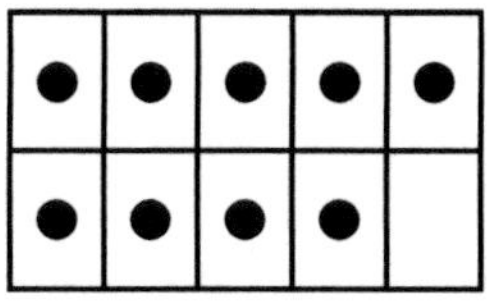

____

2.

$$\begin{array}{r} 6 \\ +\ 2 \\ \hline \square \end{array}$$

3. 8 – 5 = ☐

4. Complete the pattern.

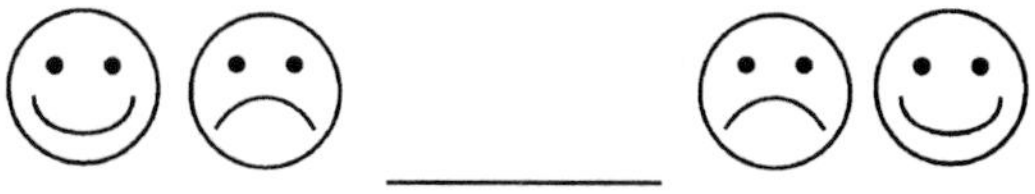

5. Will the solid roll?

Circle: yes no

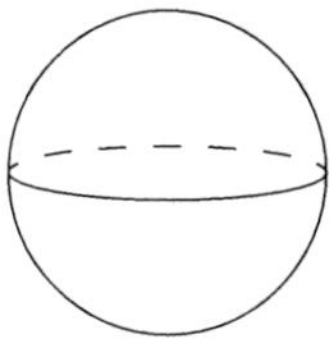

6. Is the mass equal?

Circle: yes no

7. Favorite Activity

Swings	Slide	Monkey Bars	Balance Beam
8	5	7	2

How many children like the balance beam?

____

8. Circle the numbers that have both straight and curved lines.

0 1 2 3 4

5 6 7 8 9

SCORE

1. ☺ 😐
2. ☺ 😐
3. ☺ 😐
4. ☺ 😐
5. ☺ 😐
6. ☺ 😐
7. ☺ 😐
8. ☺ 😐

____ /8

Total

DAY 58

NAME: ______________________

DIRECTIONS Solve each problem.

SCORE

1. ☺ ☹
2. ☺ ☹
3. ☺ ☹
4. ☺ ☹
5. ☺ ☹
6. ☺ ☹
7. ☺ ☹
8. ☺ ☹

____ / 8

Total

1. Count the apples. Draw 4 more. Write how many apples there are now.

____

2. $4 + 3 = \square$

3.

$$\begin{array}{r} 7 \\ -\ 6 \\ \hline \square \end{array}$$

4. $\square + 1 = 3$

5. Trent has 6 blocks. Can he stack them?

Circle: yes no

6. Is the object longer than your finger?

Circle: yes no

7. Number of Home Runs

Marc	Ramon	Jamal
7	4	15

How many more home runs did Marc hit than Ramon?

____

8. Raj checks out 4 books from the library. He returns 1 book early. How many books does he keep?

____

NAME: ______________________

DIRECTIONS Solve each problem.

1. Write the number before and after 79.

Before	Number	After
	79	

2.

$$\begin{array}{r} 7 \\ +\ 2 \\ \hline \square \end{array}$$

3. 8 − 4 = ☐

4. Write the missing number.

☐ + 2 = 8

5. Draw a hexagon.

6. Circle the smaller object.

7. Record the data in the chart. Use numbers.

- Three boys like balls.
- Six boys like action figures.
- Five boys like robots.

Favorite Types of Toys

Action Figures	
Robots	
Balls	

8. It is 8:00 right now. What time will it be in 1 hour?

____

SCORE

1. ☺ 😐
2. ☺ 😐
3. ☺ 😐
4. ☺ 😐
5. ☺ 😐
6. ☺ 😐
7. ☺ 😐
8. ☺ 😐

____ / 8 Total

DAY
60

NAME: ____________________

DIRECTIONS Solve each problem.

SCORE

1. ☺ 😐
2. ☺ 😐
3. ☺ 😐
4. ☺ 😐
5. ☺ 😐
6. ☺ 😐
7. ☺ 😐
8. ☺ 😐

____ / 8
Total

1. Write the numeral for twenty-one.

____

2. $0 + 6 = \square$

3.
$$\begin{array}{r} 7 \\ -\ 3 \\ \hline \square \end{array}$$

4. Write the missing sign.
$$\begin{array}{r} 4 \\ \square\ 4 \\ \hline 8 \end{array}$$

5. Draw a sun above the dog.

6. Write the time.

_____ : _____

7. **Favorite Type of Movie**

<table>
<tr><th>Funny</th><th>Cartoon</th><th>Scary</th><th>3-D</th></tr>
<tr><td>|||</td><td>𝍸 |||</td><td>|</td><td>𝍸</td></tr>
</table>

How many children like cartoons best?

____

8. Write these in order from tallest to shortest.

door cat boy

____

____

____

DAY 61

NAME: ______________________

DIRECTIONS Solve each problem.

1. Put these numbers in order from least to greatest.

13 18 12

_____ _____ _____

2.

$$\begin{array}{r} 8 \\ +\ 1 \\ \hline \square \end{array}$$

3. $9 - 4 = \square$

4.

$$\begin{array}{r} 2 \\ +\ \square \\ \hline 4 \end{array}$$

5. Name the shape.

____

6. Circle the object that weighs less.

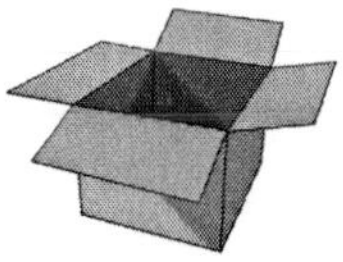

7. Count how many of each item. Record the numbers in the chart.

Fruit

Oranges	
Bananas	
Apples	

8. Show how you can add numbers in any order. Write the matching addition number sentence.

$4 + 1 = 5$

____

SCORE

1. ☺ 😐
2. ☺ 😐
3. ☺ 😐
4. ☺ 😐
5. ☺ 😐
6. ☺ 😐
7. ☺ 😐
8. ☺ 😐

____ / 8 Total

DAY **62**

NAME: ____________________

DIRECTIONS Solve each problem.

SCORE

1. ☺ 😐

2. ☺ 😐

3. ☺ 😐

4. ☺ 😐

5. ☺ 😐

6. ☺ 😐

7. ☺ 😐

8. ☺ 😐

____ / 8
Total

1. Write the numeral for the ordinal number for fifteenth.

____

2. 4 + 2 = ☐

3.

$$\begin{array}{r} 8 \\ -\ 3 \\ \hline \square \end{array}$$

4. Complete the pattern.

25, ____ 27, ____

5. Count the sides.

____________ sides

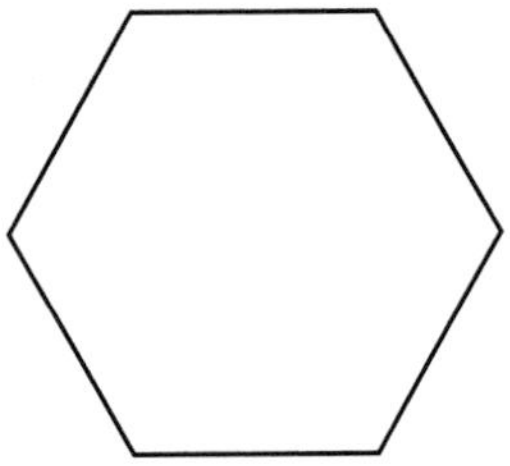

6. Is the mass equal?

Circle: yes no

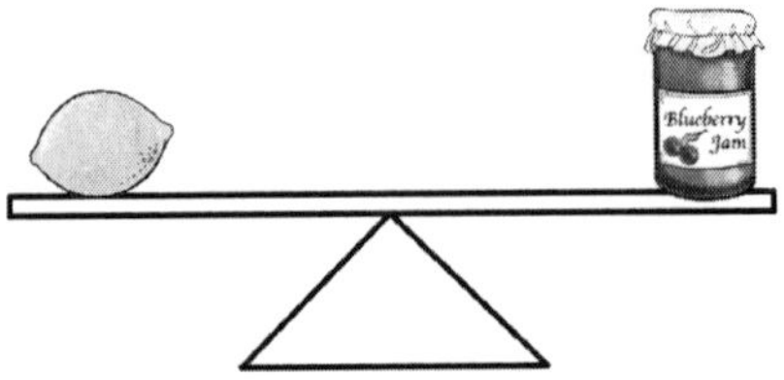

7. What question would you ask to find out about your friends' favorite TV shows?

____

____

____

____

8. I am 10 more than 20. What number am I?

____

DAY 63

NAME: ______________________________

DIRECTIONS Solve each problem.

1. Circle the smaller number.

23 28

2.

$$\begin{array}{r} 3 \\ +\ 6 \\ \hline \square \end{array}$$

3. $10 - 0 = \square$

4. Write the missing number.

$1 + \square = 9$

5. Will the brick stack?

Circle: yes no

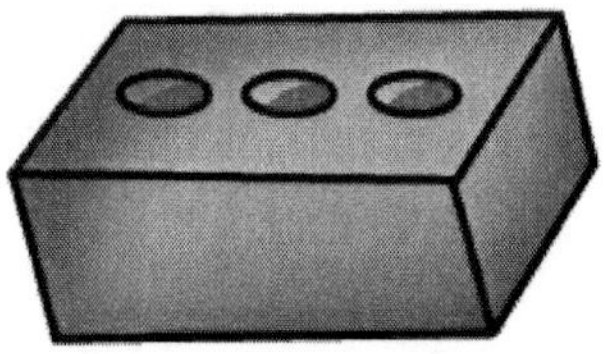

6. Record the line length.

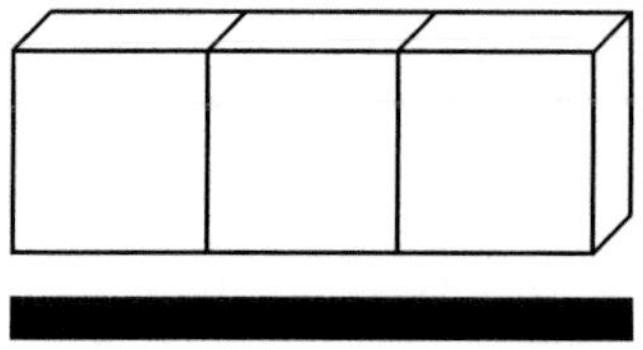

________ blocks

7. Count the tally marks. Write the numeral.

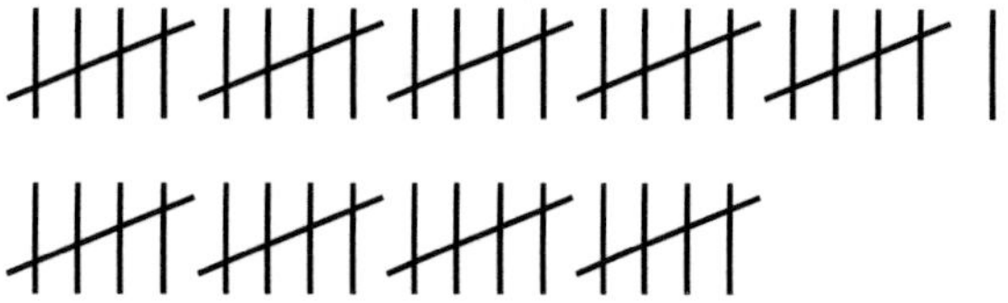

____

8. Daniel received 5 presents for his birthday. His grandma gave him 2 more. How many presents did Daniel receive altogether?

____

SCORE

1.

2.

3.

4.

5.

6.

7.

8.

____ / 8

Total

DAY 64

NAME: ____________________

DIRECTIONS Solve each problem.

SCORE

1. ☺ 😐
2. ☺ 😐
3. ☺ 😐
4. ☺ 😐
5. ☺ 😐
6. ☺ 😐
7. ☺ 😐
8. ☺ 😐

____ / 8 Total

1. Write the numeral.

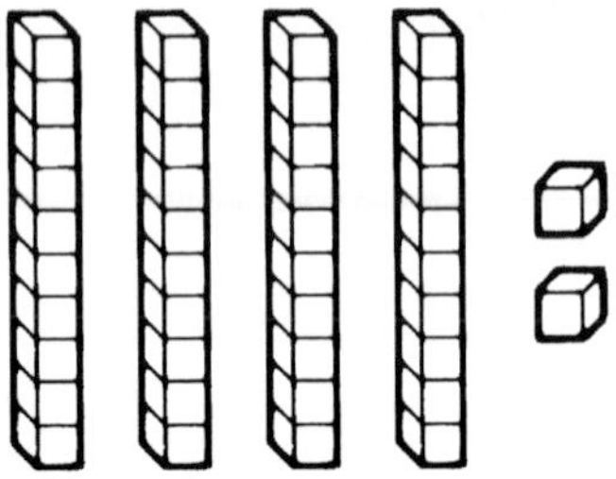

____

2. 4 + 4 = ☐

3.

$$\begin{array}{r} 7 \\ -\ 2 \\ \hline \square \end{array}$$

4. 3 + ☐ = 6

5. Draw a line of symmetry.

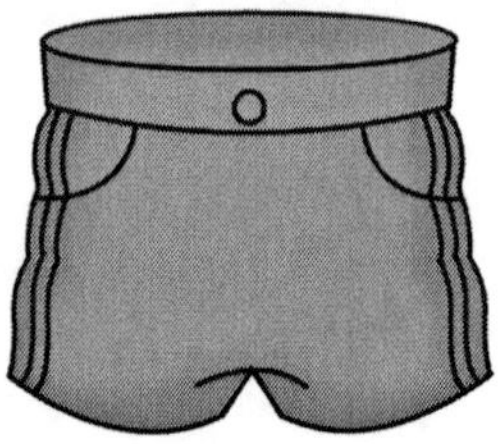

6. What month comes after October?

____

7. Favorite Recess Game

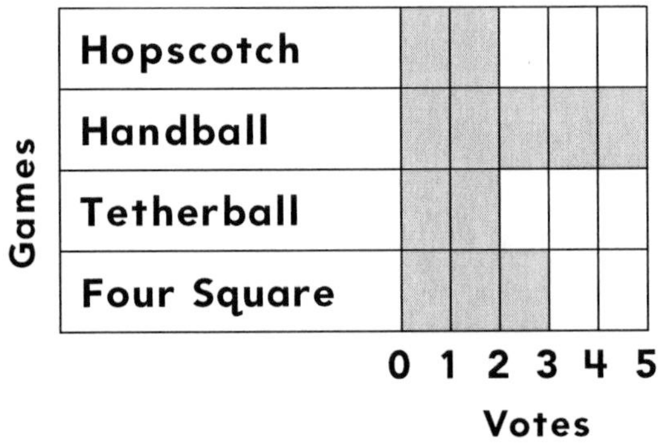

Which game do students like the most?

____

8. Homework is passed out on Monday. It is due on the last day of the school week. On what day is the homework due?

____

NAME: ______________________________

DIRECTIONS Solve each problem.

1. Write the number before and after 85.

Before	Number	After
	85	

2.

$$\begin{array}{r} 5 \\ +\ 1 \\ \hline \square \end{array}$$

3. 6 – 5 = ☐

4. Circle the ways to make 8.

5 + 3

2 + 4

10 – 2

9 – 2

5. Circle the object that is a sphere.

6. Is the object longer than your finger?

Circle: yes no

7.

Favorite Weekend Activity

Play Video Games	卌 |
Read	卌 |||
Play with Toys	卌

Which weekend activity is liked the most?

____

8. How many wheels are on 4 bicycles?

____

SCORE

1. ☺ 😐

2. ☺ 😐

3. ☺ 😐

4. ☺ 😐

5. ☺ 😐

6. ☺ 😐

7. ☺ 😐

8. ☺ 😐

___ / 8 Total

DAY 66

NAME: ______________________

DIRECTIONS Solve each problem.

SCORE

1. ☺ ☹
2. ☺ ☹
3. ☺ ☹
4. ☺ ☹
5. ☺ ☹
6. ☺ ☹
7. ☺ ☹
8. ☺ ☹

____ / 8 Total

1. Write the numeral for forty-three.

____

2. $5 + 2 = \square$

3. $8 - 8 = \square$

4. $4 - \square = 0$

5. Draw a circle around the pencil.

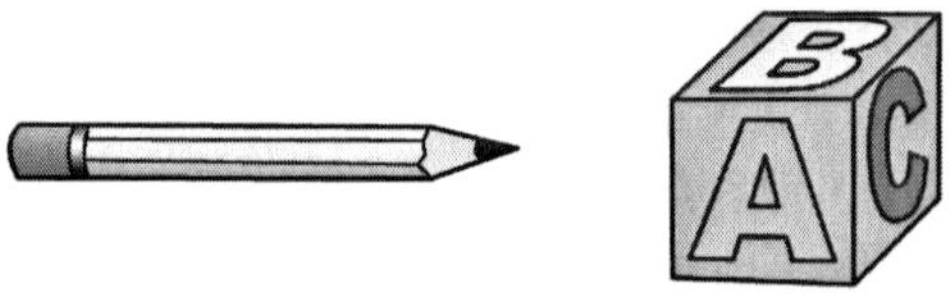

6. What day comes after Friday?

____

7. Children in Class

Boys	Girls
7	10

The class gets a new boy student. Now how many boys are in the class?

____

8. Six robots are in a toy store. Three people come and each buy a robot. How many robots are left in the toy store?

____

NAME: ______________________

DIRECTIONS Solve each problem.

1. Write the numeral.

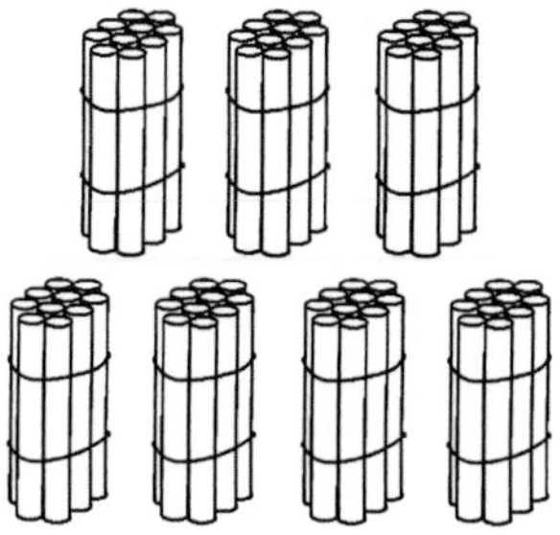

____

2.

$$\begin{array}{r} 6 \\ +\ 0 \\ \hline \square \end{array}$$

3. 9 – 7 = ☐

4. 8 – ☐ = 4

5. How many flat faces does the solid have?

____

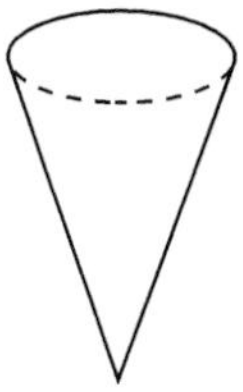

6. Show 1 o'clock.

7. Favorite Subject

Math	☺ ☺ ☺ ☺ ☺ ☺
Reading	☺ ☺ ☺ ☺
Science	☺ ☺ ☺ ☺ ☺ ☺ ☺

Which subject was chosen the most?

____

8. Write a subtraction number sentence using the numbers 2, 4, and 6.

____

SCORE

1. ☺ 😐
2. ☺ 😐
3. ☺ 😐
4. ☺ 😐
5. ☺ 😐
6. ☺ 😐
7. ☺ 😐
8. ☺ 😐

____ / 8
Total

DAY 68

NAME: ____________________

DIRECTIONS Solve each problem.

SCORE

1. ☺ 😐
2. ☺ 😐
3. ☺ 😐
4. ☺ 😐
5. ☺ 😐
6. ☺ 😐
7. ☺ 😐
8. ☺ 😐

____ / 8
Total

1. Circle the third star.

2. 7 + 1 = ☐

3.

$$\begin{array}{r} 6 \\ -\ 2 \\ \hline \square \end{array}$$

4. ☐ + 3 = 7

5. Circle the shape of a can of soup.

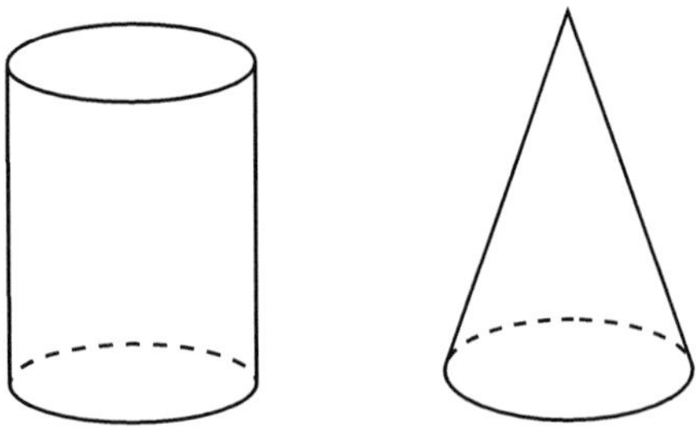

6. Circle the heavier object.

7. Count the tally marks. Write the numeral.

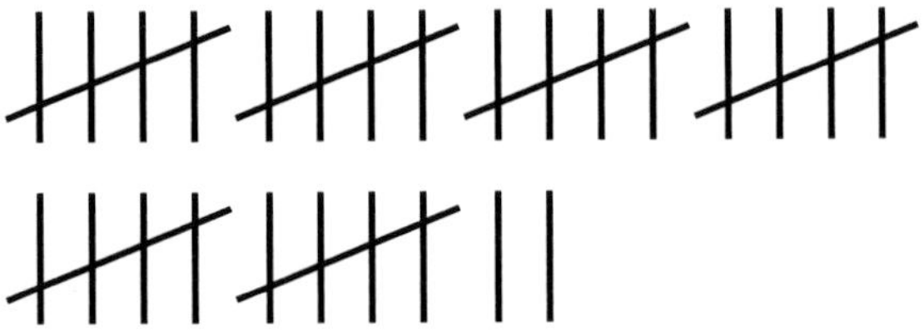

____

8. Pham eats 2 sandwiches each day for 2 days. How many sandwiches does Pham eat?

____

DAY
69

NAME: ______________________________

DIRECTIONS Solve each problem.

1. Draw dots to finish the ten frame. How many more dots are needed to make ten?

●	●	●	●	●
●	●			

____

2.

$$\begin{array}{r} 3 \\ +\ 4 \\ \hline \square \end{array}$$

3. 9 – 3 = ☐

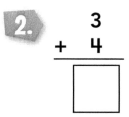

4. Circle the ways to make 2.

10 – 4

8 – 6

7 – 3

5 – 3

5. Draw a pentagon.

6. What month comes after August?

____

7.

Favorite Animal

Cats	Dogs	Birds
7	9	4

Write a question about cats and dogs using the data above.

____

____

____

8. There are 19 birds sitting on a wire. Seven of the birds fly away. Will you add or subtract to find out how many birds are still on the wire?

____

SCORE

1. ☺ 😐
2. ☺ 😐
3. ☺ 😐
4. ☺ 😐
5. ☺ 😐
6. ☺ 😐
7. ☺ 😐
8. ☺ 😐

____ / 8

Total

NAME: ______________________

DIRECTIONS Solve each problem.

SCORE

1. ☺ 😐
2. ☺ 😐
3. ☺ 😐
4. ☺ 😐
5. ☺ 😐
6. ☺ 😐
7. ☺ 😐
8. ☺ 😐

____ / 8
Total

1. Count the circles. Draw 6 more. Write how many circles there are now.

____

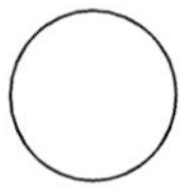

2. 0 + 9 = ☐

3.

$$\begin{array}{r} 7 \\ -\ 1 \\ \hline \square \end{array}$$

4. Continue the pattern.

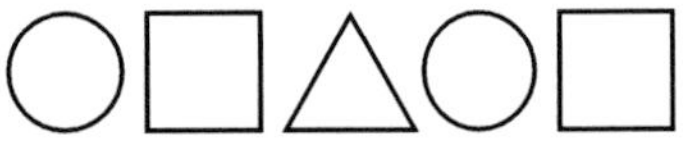 ____

5. Is the toothbrush on the right or on the left?

____

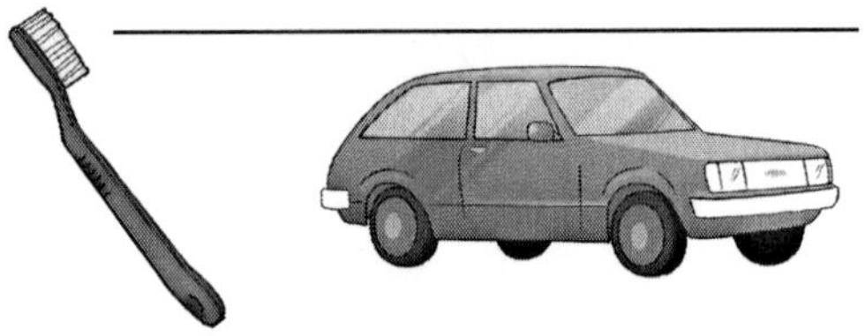

6. Circle the smaller object.

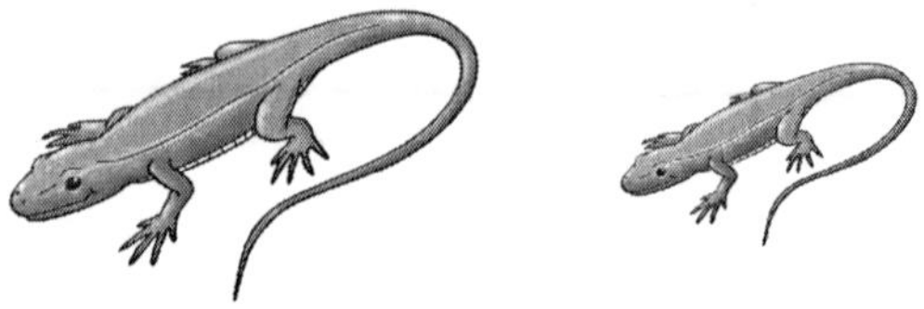

7. Use the data from the chart below. Write a statement about how many children walk to school.

Ways We Get to School

Car	Bike	Bus	Walk
6	2	10	7

____

____

____

____

8. Jerome's birthday is in the last month of the year. In what month is Jerome's birthday?

____

NAME: ______________________

DIRECTIONS Solve each problem.

1. Put these numbers in order from least to greatest.

25 17 21

____ ____ ____

2.

$$\begin{array}{r} 2 \\ +\ 4 \\ \hline \square \end{array}$$

3. 9 – 5 = ☐

4. 10 – ☐ = 7

5. Name the shape.

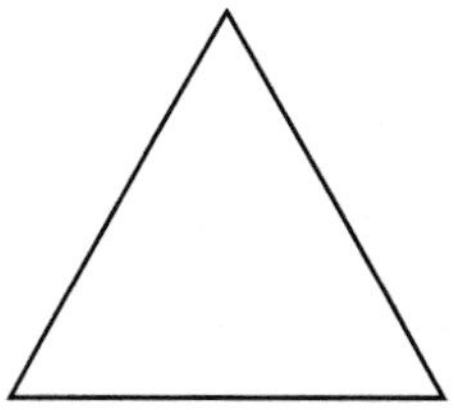

____

6. Is the object longer than your finger?

Circle: yes no

7. Count how many. Record in the chart. Use tally marks.

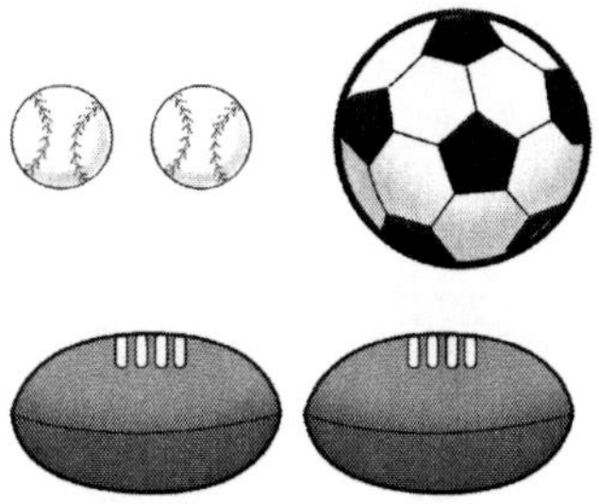

Baseballs	Soccer Balls	Footballs

8. Write the number sentence using numerals.

Ten minus four equals six.

____

SCORE

1. ☺ 😐
2. ☺ 😐
3. ☺ 😐
4. ☺ 😐
5. ☺ 😐
6. ☺ 😐
7. ☺ 😐
8. ☺ 😐

___ / 8

Total

NAME: ______________________

DIRECTIONS Solve each problem.

SCORE
1.
2.
3.
4.
5.
6.
7.
8.
___ / 8 Total

1. Write the number before and after 91.

Before	Number	After
	91	

2. 6 + 2 = ☐

3.
$$\begin{array}{r} 6 \\ -\ 0 \\ \hline \square \end{array}$$

4. ☐ − 1 = 5

5. Count the sides.

______________ sides

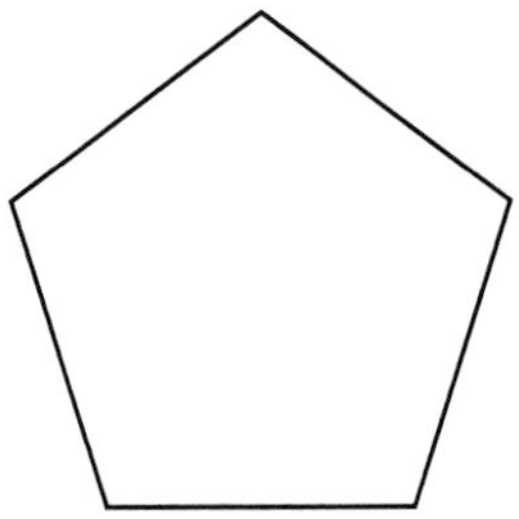

6. Write the time.

______________ o'clock

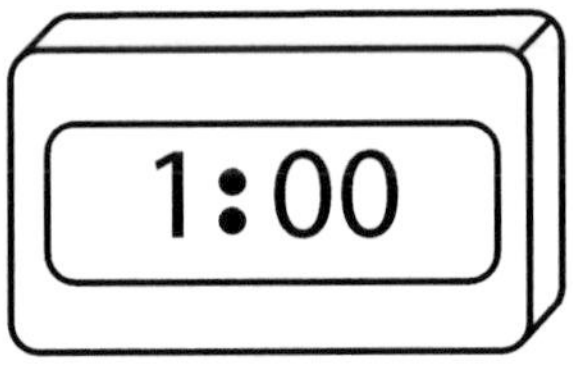

7. Favorite Activity

Swings	Slide	Monkey Bars	Balance Beam
8	5	7	2

Which activity did the most children like?

____

8. I am a number you say when you count by 5s. I am more than 30 and less than 40. What number am I?

____

NAME: ____________________________________

DIRECTIONS Solve each problem.

1. Write the numeral for the ordinal number thirty-first.

____

2.

$$\begin{array}{r} 5 \\ +\ 4 \\ \hline \square \end{array}$$

3. $8 - 2 = \square$

4.

$$\begin{array}{r} 2 \\ +\ \square \\ \hline 6 \end{array}$$

5. Will the object roll?

Circle: yes no

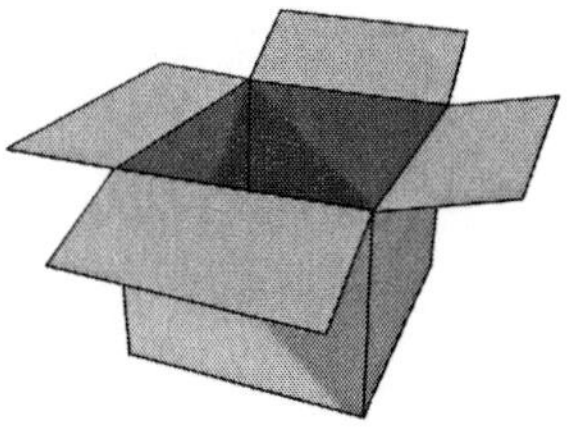

6. Circle the heavier object.

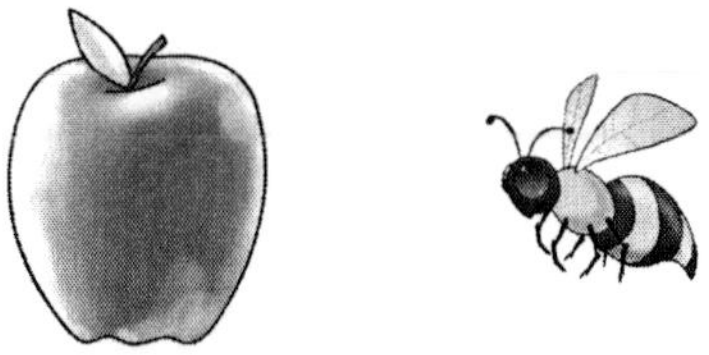

7.

Pencil Colors

Red	卌
Green	卌 |||
Blue	|||

Which pencil color is the most popular?

____

8. Mom cooks 10 ears of corn for dinner. The family eats 7 of them. How many ears of corn are not eaten?

____

SCORE

1. ☺ 😐

2. ☺ 😐

3. ☺ 😐

4. ☺ 😐

5. ☺ 😐

6. ☺ 😐

7. ☺ 😐

8. ☺ 😐

____ / 8

Total

DAY 74

NAME: ______________________

DIRECTIONS Solve each problem.

SCORE

1.

2.

3.

4.

5.

6.

7.

8.

____ / 8

Total

1. Write the missing number.

45, ______, 47

2. 7 + 0 = ☐

3.

$$\begin{array}{r} 9 \\ -\ 8 \\ \hline \square \end{array}$$

4. Continue the pattern.

2 4 6 8 ____

5. Draw a line of symmetry.

6. Record the line length.

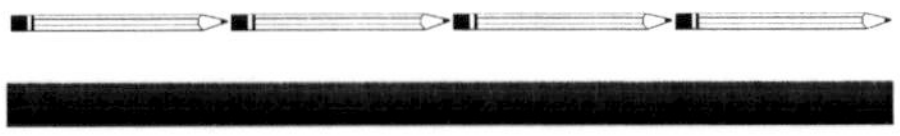

______ pencils

7. Count the tally marks. Write the numeral.

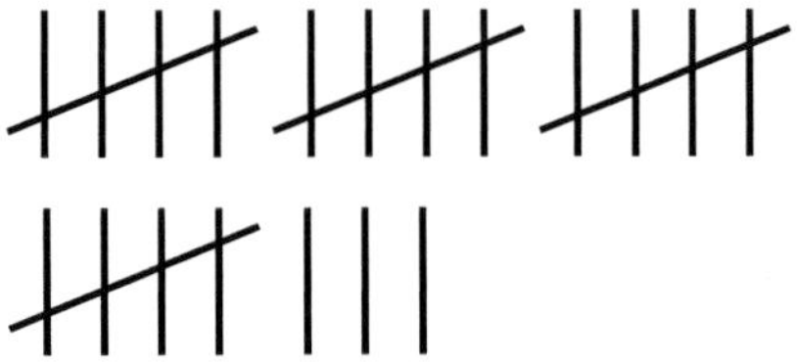

____

8. A horse eats 2 apples every day. How many apples will he eat in 2 days?

____

NAME: ____________________

DIRECTIONS Solve each problem.

1. Write the numeral.

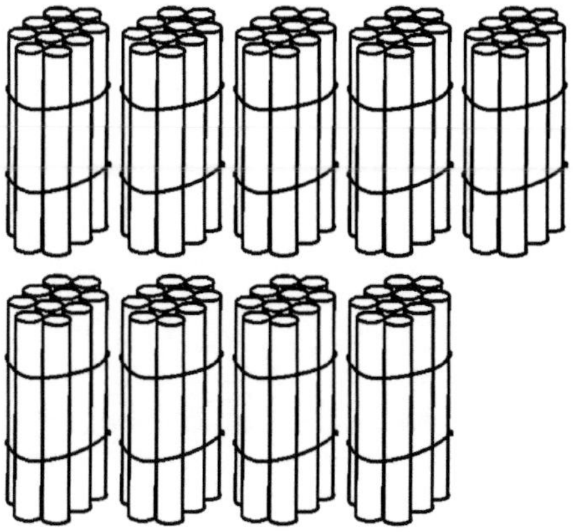

____

2.

$$\begin{array}{r} 5 \\ +\ 3 \\ \hline \square \end{array}$$

3. $7 - 0 = \square$

4. Write the missing sign.

$$\begin{array}{r} 6 \\ \square\ 3 \\ \hline 9 \end{array}$$

5. Circle the cylinder.

6. What is the last month of the year?

____

7. Favorite Type of Movie

<table>
<tr><th>Funny</th><th>Cartoon</th><th>Scary</th><th>3-D</th></tr>
<tr><td>|||</td><td>𝍸 |||</td><td>|</td><td>𝍸</td></tr>
</table>

Which type of movie do most children like best?

____

8. How many corners are on 5 squares?

____

SCORE

1. ☺ 😐
2. ☺ 😐
3. ☺ 😐
4. ☺ 😐
5. ☺ 😐
6. ☺ 😐
7. ☺ 😐
8. ☺ 😐

___ / 8 Total

NAME: ____________________

DIRECTIONS Solve each problem.

SCORE

1. ☺😐
2. ☺😐
3. ☺😐
4. ☺😐
5. ☺😐
6. ☺😐
7. ☺😐
8. ☺😐

____ / 8 Total

1. Write the numeral for sixty-one.

____

2. $6 + 3 = \square$

3.

$$\begin{array}{r} 8 \\ -\ 6 \\ \hline \square \end{array}$$

4. Write the missing number.

$8 - \square = 4$

5. Is the knife beside the plate?

Circle: yes no

6. Write the day that comes after Tuesday.

____

7.

Favorite Ice Cream

Chocolate Ice Cream	
Strawberry Ice Cream	

Which flavor of ice cream do the children like most?

____

8. Emily paints 12 pictures. Then she paints 3 more. How many pictures has Emily painted?

____

NAME: ______________________________

DIRECTIONS Solve each problem.

1. Write the number before and after 66.

Before	Number	After
	66	

2.

$$\begin{array}{r} 9 \\ +\ 0 \\ \hline \square \end{array}$$

3. $6 - 3 = \square$

4.

$$\begin{array}{r} 8 \\ -\ \square \\ \hline 3 \end{array}$$

5. Will the solid roll?

Circle: yes no

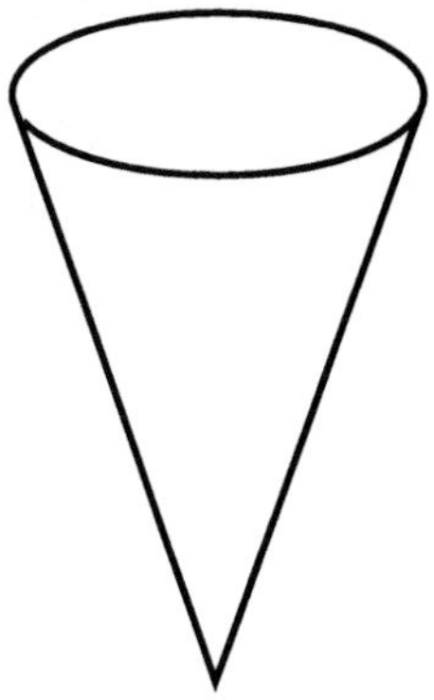

6. Is the object longer than your finger?

Circle: yes no

7.

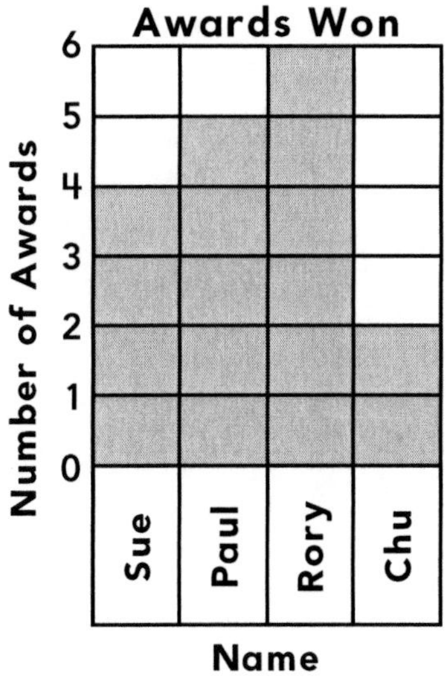

How many more awards does Paul have than Sue?

____

8. Name a shape that has only curved lines.

____

SCORE

1. ☺ 😐
2. ☺ 😐
3. ☺ 😐
4. ☺ 😐
5. ☺ 😐
6. ☺ 😐
7. ☺ 😐
8. ☺ 😐

____ / 8 Total

DAY 78

NAME: ____________________

DIRECTIONS Solve each problem.

SCORE

1. ☺ 😐
2. ☺ 😐
3. ☺ 😐
4. ☺ 😐
5. ☺ 😐
6. ☺ 😐
7. ☺ 😐
8. ☺ 😐

___ / 8
Total

1. Write the numeral.

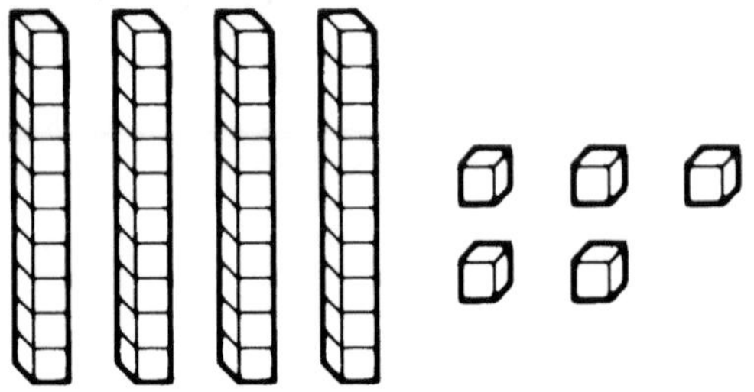

____

2. 6 + 1 = ☐

3.

```
  9
- 2
---
  ☐
```

4. Circle the ways to make 6.

3 + 3

2 + 4

2 + 5

13 – 7

5. What smaller shapes are used to make this rectangle?

____

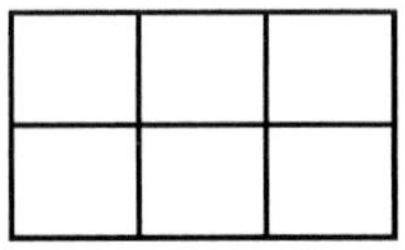

6. Show 3 o'clock.

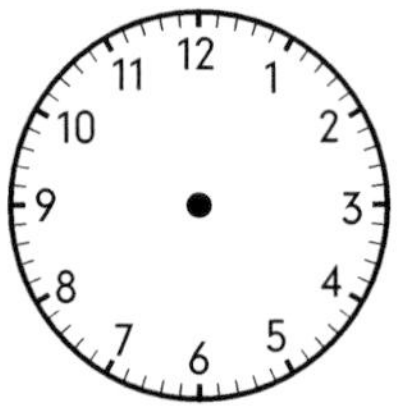

7. Number of Home Runs

Marc	Ramon	Jamal
7	4	15

How many more home runs did Jamal hit than Marc?

____

8. Write a matching addition problem using the same numerals.

6 – 3 = 3

____

NAME: ____________________

DIRECTIONS Solve each problem.

1. Draw dots to finish the ten frame. How many more dots are needed to make ten?

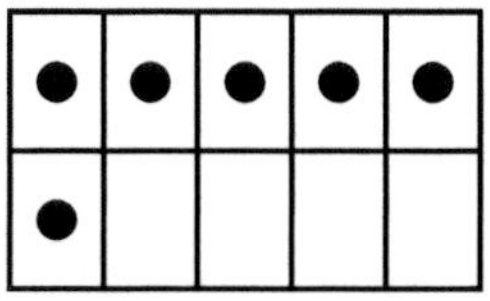

____

2.

$$\begin{array}{r} 0 \\ +\ 8 \\ \hline \square \end{array}$$

3. $7 - 4 = \square$

4. Continue the pattern.

15 14 13 12 11 ____

5. Draw an octagon.

6. How many cubes make this solid?

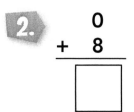

__________ cubes

7. Favorite Recess Game

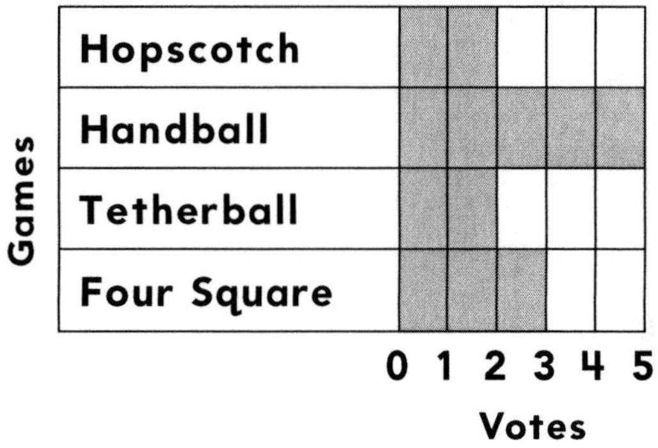

Which games did students like least?

____

____

8. Are there more days in a week or months in a year?

____

SCORE

1. ☺ 😐
2. ☺ 😐
3. ☺ 😐
4. ☺ 😐
5. ☺ 😐
6. ☺ 😐
7. ☺ 😐
8. ☺ 😐

____ / 8 Total

DAY
80

NAME: ______________________________

DIRECTIONS Solve each problem.

SCORE

1. ☺ 😐
2. ☺ 😐
3. ☺ 😐
4. ☺ 😐
5. ☺ 😐
6. ☺ 😐
7. ☺ 😐
8. ☺ 😐

____ / 8
Total

1. Count the squares. Draw 3 more. Write how many squares there are now.

____

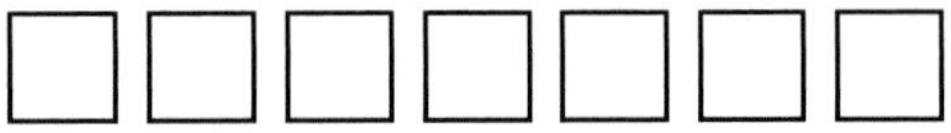

2. 1 + 8 = ☐

3.

$$\begin{array}{r} 9 \\ -\ 6 \\ \hline \square \end{array}$$

4. ☐ + 3 = 8

5. Draw a rock under the turtle.

6. Record the line length.

________ sticks

7.

Favorite Weekend Activity

Play Video Games	𝍸 |
Read	𝍸 |
Play with Toys	𝍸

Which weekend activity is liked the least?

____

8. Which is taller: a dog or a giraffe?

____

NAME: ____________________

DIRECTIONS Solve each problem.

1. Put these numbers in order from least to greatest.

36 14 23

_____ _____ _____

2.

$$\begin{array}{r} 10 \\ +\ 2 \\ \hline \square \end{array}$$

3. $10 - 3 = \square$

4.

$$\begin{array}{r} \square \\ -\ 3 \\ \hline 4 \end{array}$$

5. Name the shape.

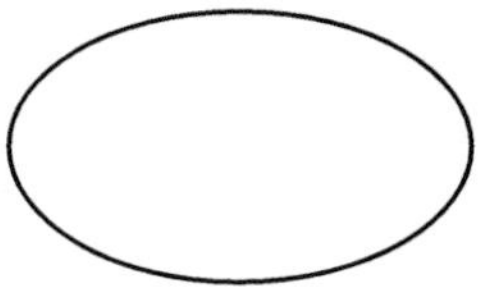

____

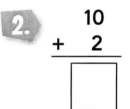

6. What time is it?

_____ : _____

7. Count how many. Record with tallies.

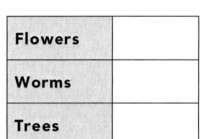

Flowers	
Worms	
Trees	

8. Today is Wednesday. Sally's piano recital is in 3 days. On what day of the week is Sally's recital?

____

SCORE

1. ☺ 😐
2. ☺ 😐
3. ☺ 😐
4. ☺ 😐
5. ☺ 😐
6. ☺ 😐
7. ☺ 😐
8. ☺ 😐

___ / 8 Total

NAME: ______________________

DIRECTIONS Solve each problem.

SCORE

1. ☺ 😐
2. ☺ 😐
3. ☺ 😐
4. ☺ 😐
5. ☺ 😐
6. ☺ 😐
7. ☺ 😐
8. ☺ 😐

____ / 8 Total

1. Write the numeral for eighty-five.

____

2. $6 + 6 = \square$

3.
$$\begin{array}{r} 6 \\ -\ 1 \\ \hline \square \end{array}$$

4. $6 + \square = 7$

5. Count the sides.

______________ sides

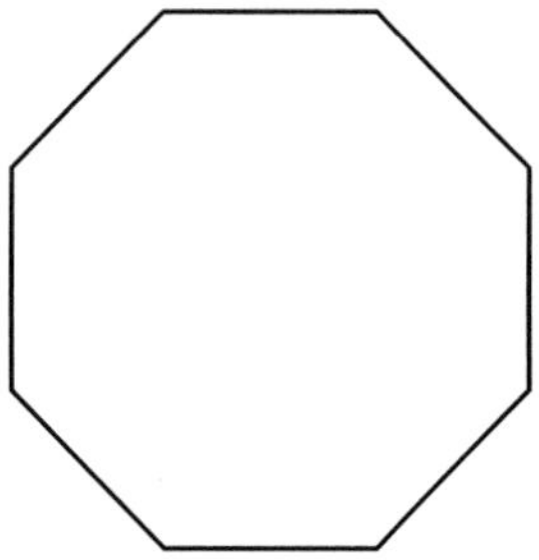

6. Record the area.

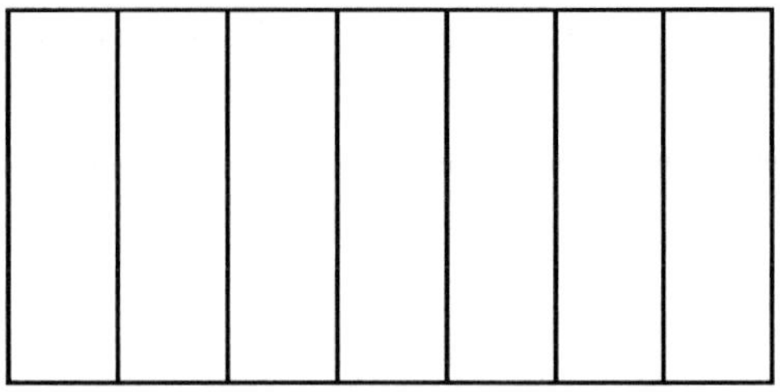

______ rectangles

7.

Children in Class

Boys	Girls
7	10

The teacher wants to put boys and girls together in pairs. Does she have enough boys for each girl to have a partner?

____

8. I am 10 less than 60. What number am I?

____

NAME: ____________________

DIRECTIONS Solve each problem.

1. Write the number before and after 77.

Before	Number	After
	77	

2.

$$\begin{array}{r} 10 \\ +\ \ 9 \\ \hline \square \end{array}$$

3. $8 - 7 = \square$

4. Write the missing sign.

$$\begin{array}{r} 11 \\ \square\ 5 \\ \hline 6 \end{array}$$

5. Will the object stack?

Circle: yes no

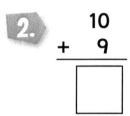

6. Write the day that comes after Sunday.

____

7. Record the data in the chart. Use tally marks.

- Four girls like dolls.
- Seven girls like sticker books.
- Two girls like paper dolls.

Favorite Types of Toys

Dolls	
Sticker Books	
Paper Dolls	

8. Dad builds 15 birdhouses to sell. Then he builds 5 more. How many birdhouses did Dad build?

____

SCORE

1. ☺ 😐
2. ☺ 😐
3. ☺ 😐
4. ☺ 😐
5. ☺ 😐
6. ☺ 😐
7. ☺ 😐
8. ☺ 😐

____ / 8 Total

DAY

84

NAME: ____________________

DIRECTIONS Solve each problem.

SCORE

1. ☺ 😐
2. ☺ 😐
3. ☺ 😐
4. ☺ 😐
5. ☺ 😐
6. ☺ 😐
7. ☺ 😐
8. ☺ 😐

____ / 8

Total

1. Circle the larger number.

34   43

2. 3 + 9 = ☐

3.

$$\begin{array}{r} 9 \\ -\ 9 \\ \hline \square \end{array}$$

4. Continue the pattern.

1 2 3 1 2 ____

5. Draw a line of symmetry.

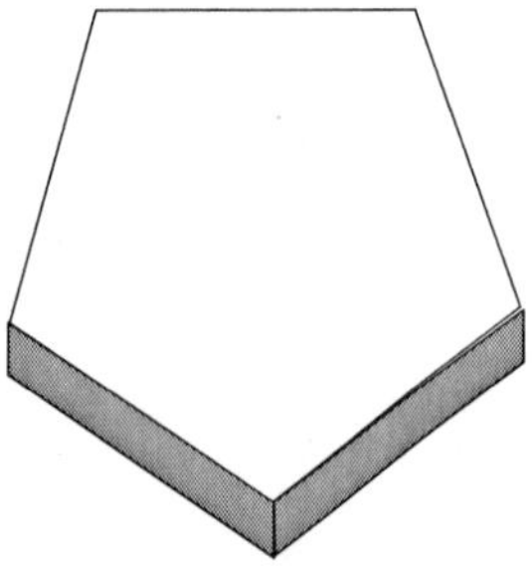

6. Is the object longer than your finger?

Circle: yes no

7. Count the tally marks. Write the numeral.

____

8. Faye goes to bed at 7:30. She watches TV for 1 hour before she goes to bed. What time does she start watching TV?

____

NAME: ____________________

DIRECTIONS Solve each problem.

1. Write the numeral.

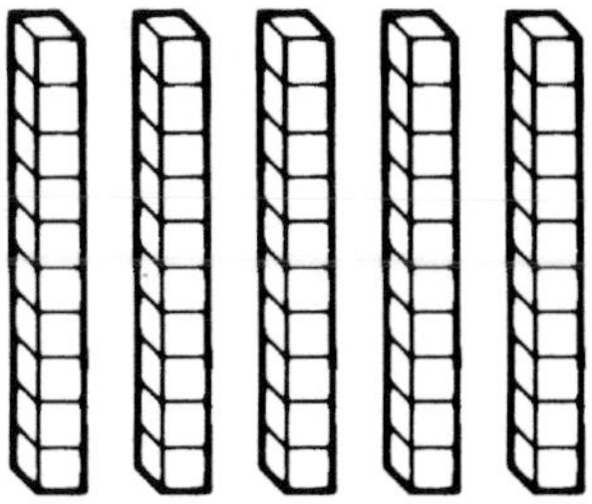

____

2.

$$\begin{array}{r} 5 \\ +\ 5 \\ \hline \square \end{array}$$

3. 10 – 7 = ☐

4. Circle the ways to make 4.

1 + 3

2 + 2

4 – 3

7 – 3

5. Circle the rectangular prism.

6. Write the month that comes after June.

____

7.

Favorite Animal

Cats	Dogs	Birds
7	9	4

Write a question about cats and birds using the data above.

____

____

8. Tammy has 5 quarters in her piggy bank. Grandpa gives her 2 quarters. How many quarters does Tammy have now?

____

SCORE

1.

2.

3.

4.

5.

6.

7.

8.

___ / 8

Total

NAME: ____________________

DIRECTIONS Solve each problem.

SCORE

1. ☺ 😐
2. ☺ 😐
3. ☺ 😐
4. ☺ 😐
5. ☺ 😐
6. ☺ 😐
7. ☺ 😐
8. ☺ 😐

____ / 8 Total

1. Write the numeral.

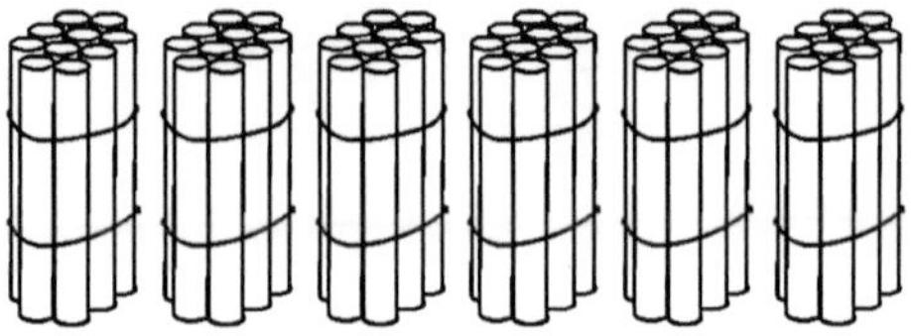

____

2. 4 + 10 = ☐

3.

$$\begin{array}{r} 7 \\ -\ 5 \\ \hline \square \end{array}$$

4. Write the missing number.

10 – ☐ = 4

5. Draw a cookie close to the milk.

6. How many cubes make this solid?

____________ cubes

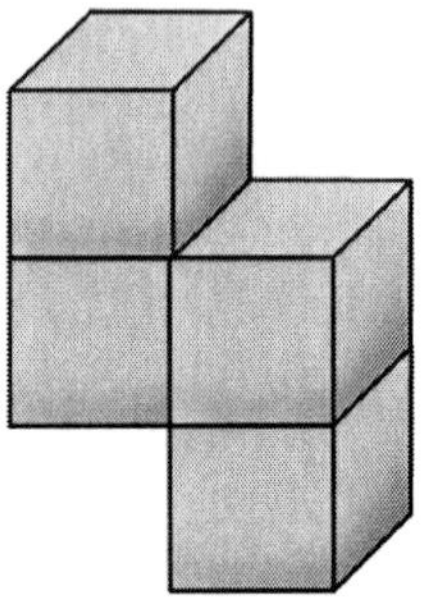

7. What question would you ask to find out about your friends' favorite ice cream flavors?

____

____

8. There are 12 children playing on a playground. Three of the children have to go home. How many children are still playing?

____

NAME: ____________________

DIRECTIONS Solve each problem.

SCORE

1. Write the numeral for the ordinal number eighty-second.

____

2.

$$\begin{array}{r} 6 \\ +\ 9 \\ \hline \square \end{array}$$

3. 11 – 2 = ☐

4.

$$\begin{array}{r} \square \\ +\ 5 \\ \hline 7 \end{array}$$

5. How many flat surfaces does the solid have?

____

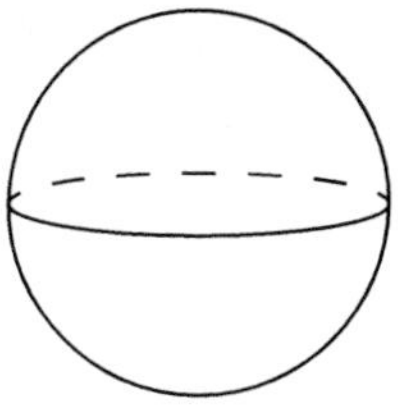

6. Record the line length.

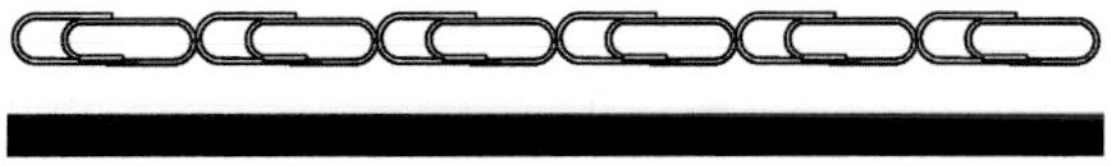

_____ paper clips

7. **Favorite Subject**

Math	☺☺☺☺☺☺
Reading	☺☺☺☺
Science	☺☺☺☺☺☺☺

Which subject was chosen by the fewest children?

____

8. Write a subtraction number sentence using the numbers 4, 5, and 9.

____

1. ☺ 😐
2. ☺ 😐
3. ☺ 😐
4. ☺ 😐
5. ☺ 😐
6. ☺ 😐
7. ☺ 😐
8. ☺ 😐

____ / 8
Total

DAY 88

NAME: ____________________

DIRECTIONS Solve each problem.

SCORE

1. ☺ 😐
2. ☺ 😐
3. ☺ 😐
4. ☺ 😐
5. ☺ 😐
6. ☺ 😐
7. ☺ 😐
8. ☺ 😐

____ / 8 Total

1. Write the number before and after 81.

Before	Number	After
	81	

2. 9 + 4 = ☐

3.

$$\begin{array}{r} 6 \\ -\ 6 \\ \hline \square \end{array}$$

4. ☐ − 4 = 1

5. Sonny has 3 balls. Can he stack them?

Circle: yes no

6. Show 5 o'clock.

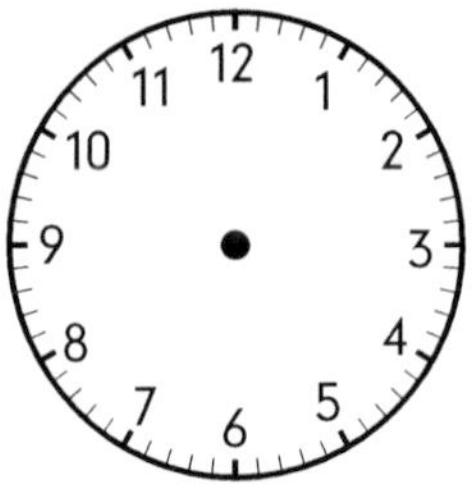

7. Favorite Activity

Swings	Slide	Monkey Bars	Balance Beam
8	5	7	2

Which activity did the fewest children like?

____

8. Write the number sentence using numerals.

Seventeen minus six equals eleven.

____

NAME: ____________________________

DIRECTIONS Solve each problem.

1. Draw dots to finish the ten frame. How many more dots are needed to make ten?

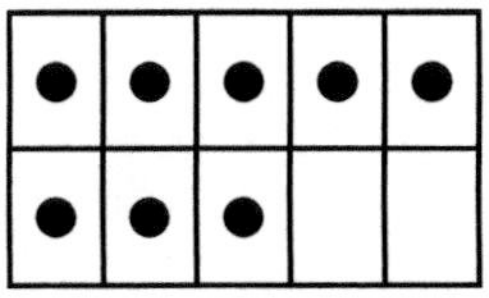

____

2.

$$\begin{array}{r} 10 \\ +\ \ 0 \\ \hline \square \end{array}$$

3. $8 - 0 = \square$

4. Write the missing sign.

$$\begin{array}{r} 13 \\ \square\ \ 2 \\ \hline 15 \end{array}$$

5. Draw a rhombus.

6. Record the area.

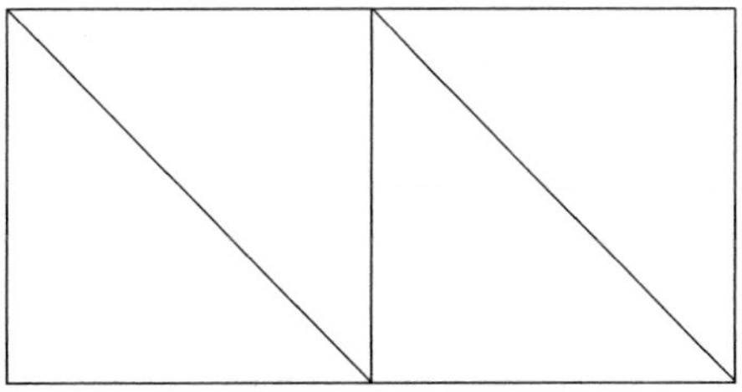

_____ triangles

7. Favorite Type of Movie

Funny	Cartoon	Scary	3-D
III	卌 III	I	卌

Which type of movie is liked least?

____

8. How many days are in 2 weeks?

____

SCORE

1. ☺ 😐
2. ☺ 😐
3. ☺ 😐
4. ☺ 😐
5. ☺ 😐
6. ☺ 😐
7. ☺ 😐
8. ☺ 😐

___ / 8 Total

DAY
90

NAME: ______________________________

DIRECTIONS Solve each problem.

SCORE

1. ☺ 😐
2. ☺ 😐
3. ☺ 😐
4. ☺ 😐
5. ☺ 😐
6. ☺ 😐
7. ☺ 😐
8. ☺ 😐

___ / 8
Total

1. Count the triangles. Draw 2 more. Write how many triangles there are now.

____

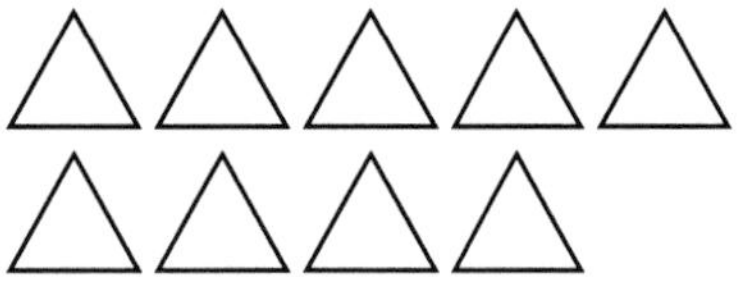

2. 6 + 4 = ☐

3.

$$\begin{array}{r} 9 \\ -\ 1 \\ \hline \square \end{array}$$

4. Write the missing number.

☐ − 5 = 5

5. Is the train on the right or on the left?

____

6. Write the day that comes after Wednesday.

____

7. What would be a good symbol to use in a picture graph that shows favorite ice cream flavors?

____

8. Today is Thursday, June 16th. Trudy's birthday is in 1 week. What is the date of Trudy's birthday?

____

NAME: ______________________

DIRECTIONS Solve each problem.

SCORE

1. Put these numbers in order from least to greatest.

54 45 61

_____ _____ _____

2.

$$\begin{array}{r} 1 \\ +\ 9 \\ \hline \square \end{array}$$

3. 10 – 2 = ☐

4. Complete the pattern.

↑↓ ___ ↓↑↓

5. Name the shape.

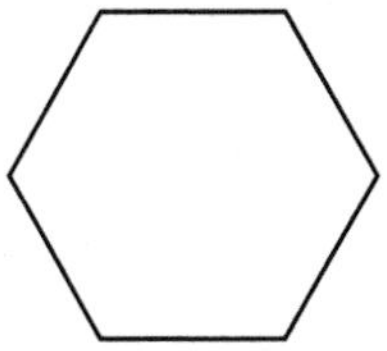

____

6. What tool would you use to measure weight: a clock or a scale?

____

7. Count how many. Record the numbers on the chart.

Stars	
Moons	

8. Write a matching subtraction problem using the same numerals.

4 + 4 = 8

____

1. ☺ 😐
2. ☺ 😐
3. ☺ 😐
4. ☺ 😐
5. ☺ 😐
6. ☺ 😐
7. ☺ 😐
8. ☺ 😐

___ / 8
Total

DAY 92

NAME: ____________________

DIRECTIONS Solve each problem.

SCORE

1. ☺ 😐
2. ☺ 😐
3. ☺ 😐
4. ☺ 😐
5. ☺ 😐
6. ☺ 😐
7. ☺ 😐
8. ☺ 😐

____ / 8
Total

1. Write the numeral for the ordinal number fifty-third.

____

2. 3 +10 = ☐

3.

$$\begin{array}{r} 7 \\ -\ 7 \\ \hline \square \end{array}$$

4. ☐ + 4 = 8

5. How many angles?

____

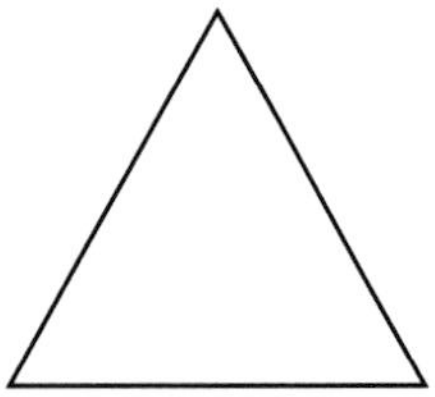

6. How many months are in a year?

____

7. Use the data from the chart. Write a statement about how many kids ride the bus to school.

Ways We Get to School

Car	Bike	Bus	Walk
6	2	10	7

____

____

8. I am a number you say when you count by 2s. I am more than 56 and less than 60. What number am I?

____

NAME: ______________________________

DIRECTIONS Solve each problem.

1. Write the number before and after 90.

Before	Number	After
	90	

2.

$$\begin{array}{r} 6 \\ +\ 8 \\ \hline \square \end{array}$$

3. $7 - 5 = \square$

4.

$$\begin{array}{r} \square \\ -\ 6 \\ \hline 2 \end{array}$$

5. Will the object roll?

Circle: yes no

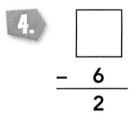

6. Write the time.

__________ o'clock

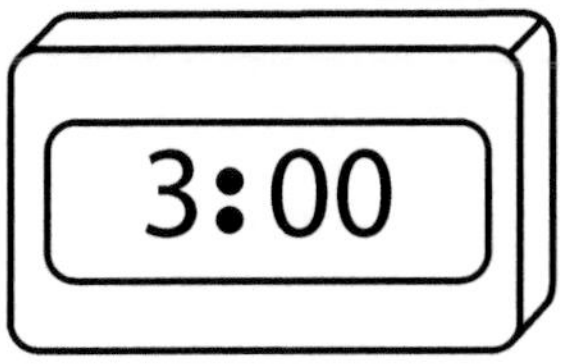

7. Pencil Colors

Red	𝍸
Green	𝍸 |||
Blue	|||

What is the least popular pencil color?

____

8. There are 15 frogs on a log. Six of the frogs jump in the water. How many frogs are left on the log?

____

SCORE

1. ☺ 😐

2. ☺ 😐

3. ☺ 😐

4. ☺ 😐

5. ☺ 😐

6. ☺ 😐

7. ☺ 😐

8. ☺ 😐

____ / 8 Total

DAY
94

NAME: ____________________

DIRECTIONS Solve each problem.

SCORE

1.

2.

3.

4.

5.

6.

7.

8.

____ / 8
Total

1. Write the numeral.

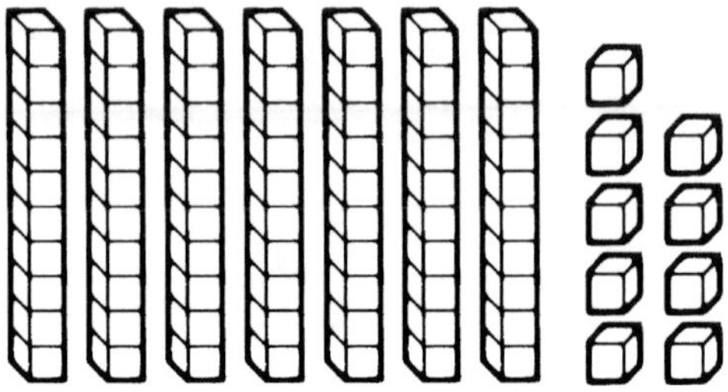

____

2. 10 + 2 = ☐

3.
$$\begin{array}{r} 8 \\ -\ 1 \\ \hline \square \end{array}$$

4. Write the missing numbers.

☐ + 4 = 8

8 − ☐ = 4

5. Draw a line of symmetry.

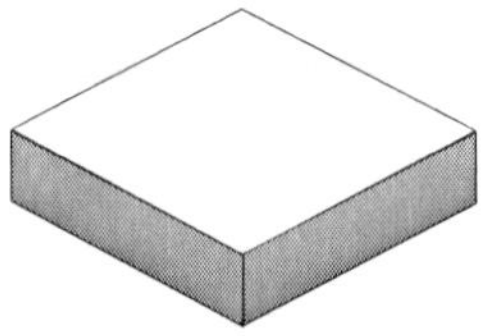

6. What month comes after November?

____

7. Favorite Recess Game

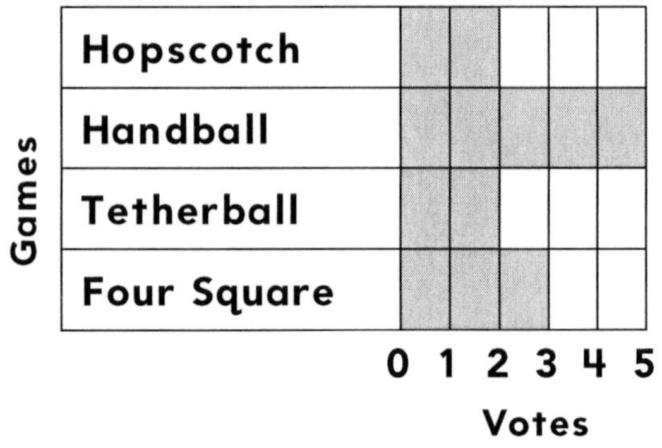

How many more votes did handball get than tetherball?

____

8. Evan was 36 inches tall. He grew 3 inches. How tall is he now?

____

NAME: ____________________

DIRECTIONS Solve each problem.

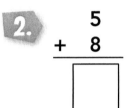

1. Write the missing number.

88, ____, 90

2.

$$\begin{array}{r} 5 \\ +\ 8 \\ \hline \square \end{array}$$

3. 9 – 0 = ☐

4. Write the missing sign.

$$\begin{array}{r} 5 \\ \square\ 3 \\ \hline 8 \end{array}$$

5. Circle the name of the solid.

cylinder   cone

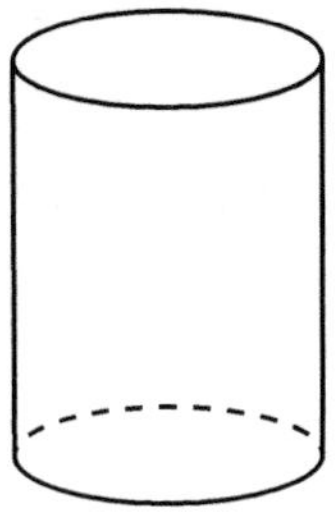

6. Would you use a scale or a thermometer to weigh a book?

____

7.

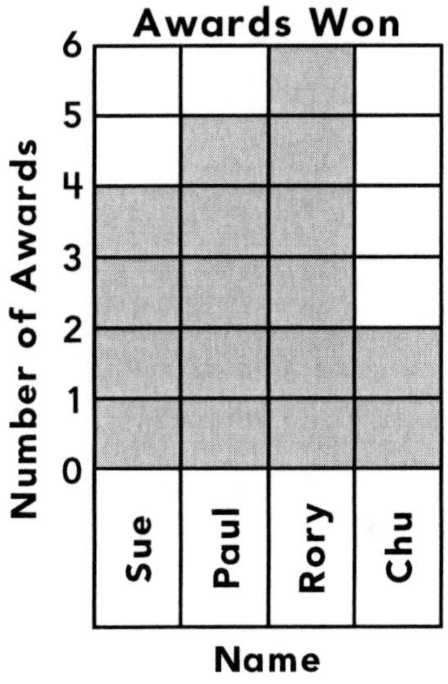

How many more awards does Rory have than Chu?

____

8. How many wheels are on 3 cars?

____

SCORE

1. ☺ 😐

2. ☺ 😐

3. ☺ 😐

4. ☺ 😐

5. ☺ 😐

6. ☺ 😐

7. ☺ 😐

8. ☺ 😐

____ / 8

Total

DAY
96

NAME: ____________________

DIRECTIONS Solve each problem.

SCORE

1. ☺ 😐
2. ☺ 😐
3. ☺ 😐
4. ☺ 😐
5. ☺ 😐
6. ☺ 😐
7. ☺ 😐
8. ☺ 😐

____ / 8
Total

1. Draw dots to fill the ten frame. How many more dots are needed to make ten?

●	●	●	●	

____

2. 2 + 9 = ☐

3.

$$\begin{array}{r} 11 \\ -\ \ 3 \\ \hline \square \end{array}$$

4. Circle the ways to make 8.

6 + 3   4 + 4

10 – 2   12 – 4

5. Is the pail behind the ball?

Circle: yes no

6. What is the area?

________ squares

7.

Favorite Weekend Activity

Play Video Games	𝍸 |
Read	𝍸 |||
Play with Toys	𝍸

How many more children preferred to read than to play video games?

____

8. Colin has 14 stuffed animals. He gets 2 more for his birthday. How many stuffed animals does Colin have in all?

____

DAY 97

NAME: ______________________________

DIRECTIONS Solve each problem.

1. Circle the seventh star.

★ ★ ★ ★ ★ ★ ★

2.
$$\begin{array}{r} 8 \\ +\ 7 \\ \hline \square \end{array}$$

3. 11 – 4 = ☐

4. Continue the pattern.

50 60 70 80 ____

5. Draw a shape with 5 sides.

6. Write the day that comes after Monday.

____

7. Count the tally marks. Write the numeral.

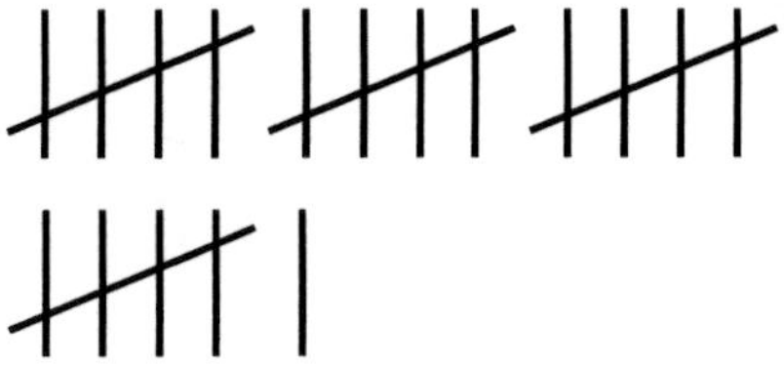

____

8. Name a shape that has 4 sides.

____

SCORE

1. ☺ 😐

2. ☺ 😐

3. ☺ 😐

4. ☺ 😐

5. ☺ 😐

6. ☺ 😐

7. ☺ 😐

8. ☺ 😐

____ / 8

Total

DAY 98

NAME: ____________________

DIRECTIONS Solve each problem.

SCORE

1. ☺ 😐
2. ☺ 😐
3. ☺ 😐
4. ☺ 😐
5. ☺ 😐
6. ☺ 😐
7. ☺ 😐
8. ☺ 😐

____ / 8 Total

1. Write the numeral for one hundred.

____

2. 9 + 7 = ☐

3. 12 − 5 = ☐

4. 7 + ☐ = 8

5. What smaller shapes are used to make this rhombus?

____

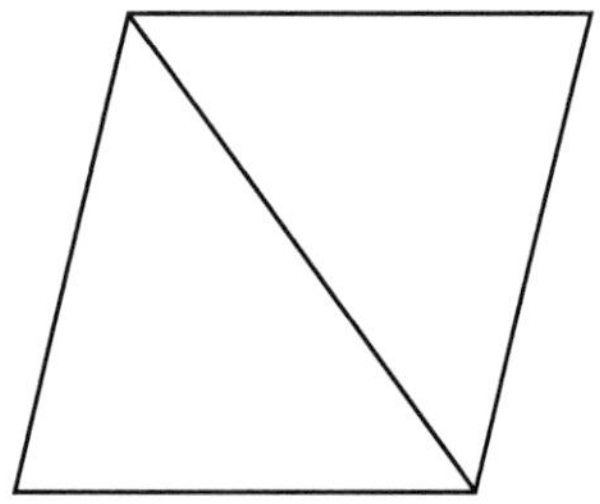

6. What month comes after May?

____

7. Number of Home Runs

Marc	Ramon	Jamal
7	4	15

How many more home runs did Jamal hit than Ramon?

____

8. Write the ice cream flavor next to the boy who likes it.

- Ralph does not like chocolate.
- Ian likes vanilla.
- Isaac does not like strawberry.

Ralph ____________________

Ian ____________________

Isaac ____________________

DAY 99

NAME: ____________________

DIRECTIONS Solve each problem.

1. Write the number before and after 76.

Before	Number	After
	76	

2.

$$\begin{array}{r} 3 \\ +\ 8 \\ \hline \square \end{array}$$

3. 10 – 8 = ☐

4. Write the missing numbers.

9 + 5 = ☐

☐ – 5 = 9

5. Draw a shape with 3 sides.

6. Show 7 o'clock.

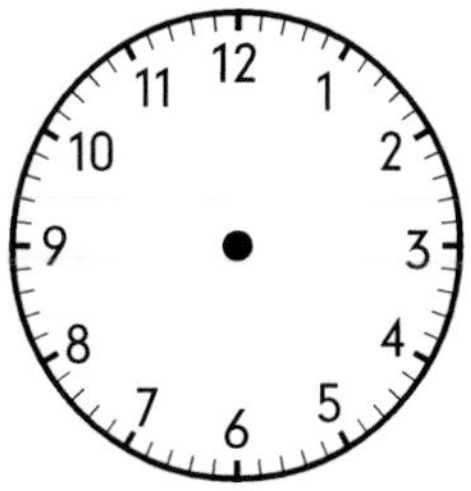

7.

Children in Class

Boys	Girls
7	10

How many more girls are there than boys?

____

8. Tina is only allowed to watch TV on the weekend. On what days can she watch TV?

____

____

SCORE

1. ☺ 😐

2. ☺ 😐

3. ☺ 😐

4. ☺ 😐

5. ☺ 😐

6. ☺ 😐

7. ☺ 😐

8. ☺ 😐

____ / 8

Total

NAME: ______________________________

DIRECTIONS Solve each problem.

SCORE

1. ☺ ☹
2. ☺ ☹
3. ☺ ☹
4. ☺ ☹
5. ☺ ☹
6. ☺ ☹
7. ☺ ☹
8. ☺ ☹

____ / 8 Total

1. Write the numeral.

____

2.

$$\begin{array}{r} 8 \\ +\ 8 \\ \hline \square \end{array}$$

3.

$$\begin{array}{r} 12 \\ -\ 7 \\ \hline \square \end{array}$$

4. $8 - \square = 1$

5. Draw a triangle below the oval.

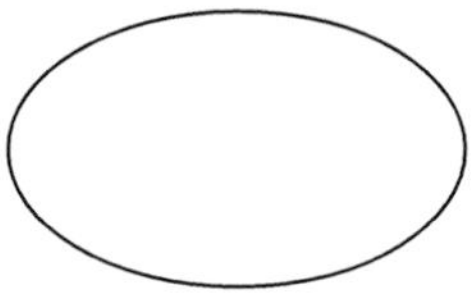

6. Record the line length.

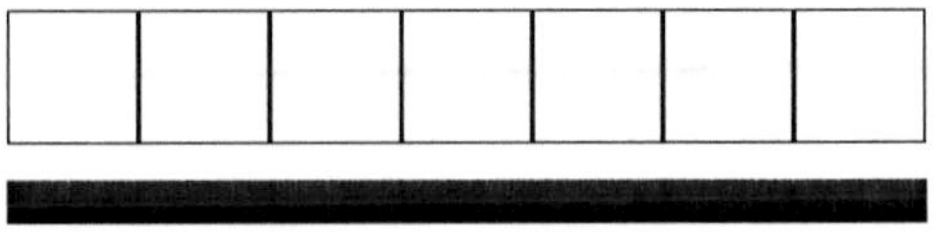

_____ blocks

7. Favorite Ice Cream

How many more children like chocolate ice cream than strawberry ice cream?

____

8. It is March 12. Terri's birthday is in 3 months. In what month is her birthday?

____

NAME: ______________________________

DIRECTIONS Solve each problem.

1. Put these numbers in order from least to greatest.

29 35 27

_____ _____ _____

2.

$$\begin{array}{r} 8 \\ +\ 9 \\ \hline \square \end{array}$$

3. $11 - 10 = \square$

4. Continue the pattern.

14 16 18 20 _____

5. Name the shape.

____

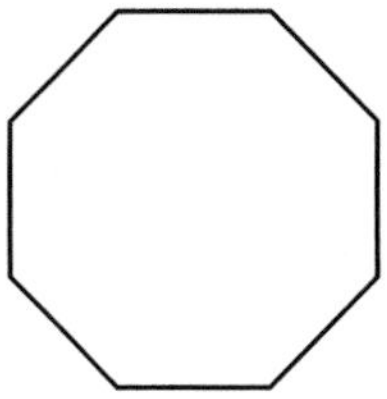

6. What weighs more: an apple or a watermelon?

____

7.

Favorite Animal

Cats	Dogs	Birds
7	9	4

Write a question about dogs and birds using the data above.

____

____

____

____

8. It is 7:00 right now. What time will it be in 2 hours?

____

SCORE

1. ☺ 😐

2. ☺ 😐

3. ☺ 😐

4. ☺ 😐

5. ☺ 😐

6. ☺ 😐

7. ☺ 😐

8. ☺ 😐

____ / 8

Total

DAY 102

NAME: ______________________________

DIRECTIONS Solve each problem.

SCORE

1.

2.

3.

4.

5.

6.

7.

8.

____ / 8

Total

1. Circle the smaller number.

50 49

2. 6 + 10 = ☐

3.

$$\begin{array}{r} 13 \\ -\ 4 \\ \hline \square \end{array}$$

4. ☐ + 4 = 7

5. Record the angles.

____

6. Write the time.

_____ : _____

7. Draw 4 tally marks.

8. I have 7 in the ones place and 8 in the tens place. What number am I?

____

NAME: ______________________________

DIRECTIONS Solve each problem.

1. Write the ordinal number.

The crossed out mouse is

____________________.

2.

$$\begin{array}{r} 5 \\ +\ 9 \\ \hline \square \end{array}$$

3. 11 – 5 = ☐

4. True or false?

5 + 3 = 6 + 2

____

5. Will the object stack?

____

6. Circle the object that is shorter than a pencil.

7. **Favorite Activity**

Swings	Slide	Monkey Bars	Balance Beam
8	5	7	2

How many more children liked the swings than the slide?

____

8. Makenzie has 3 dogs and 15 fish. How many pets does she have in all?

____

SCORE

1. ☺ 😐
2. ☺ 😐
3. ☺ 😐
4. ☺ 😐
5. ☺ 😐
6. ☺ 😐
7. ☺ 😐
8. ☺ 😐

____ / 8

Total

NAME: ______________________________

DIRECTIONS Solve each problem.

SCORE

1. ☺ 😐
2. ☺ 😐
3. ☺ 😐
4. ☺ 😐
5. ☺ 😐
6. ☺ 😐
7. ☺ 😐
8. ☺ 😐

____ / 8 Total

1. Write the number before and after 90.

Before	Number	After
	90	

2. 2 + 8 = ☐

3.

$$\begin{array}{r} 12 \\ -\ \ 8 \\ \hline \square \end{array}$$

4. Write the missing sign.

8 ☐ 2 = 10

5. Draw a line of symmetry.

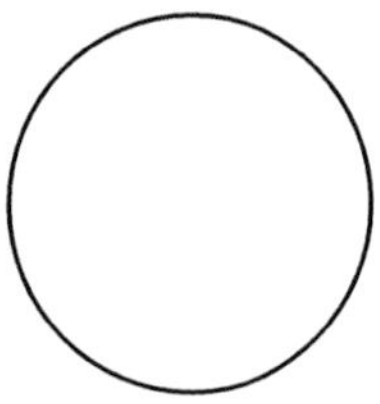

6. What is the first month of the year?

____

7. **Favorite Type of Movie**

<table>
<tr><th>Funny</th><th>Cartoon</th><th>Scary</th><th>3-D</th></tr>
<tr><td>|||</td><td>卌 |||</td><td>|</td><td>卌</td></tr>
</table>

How many more children like funny movies than scary movies?

____

8. What is the smallest 2-digit number you can make with the numbers 7, 2, and 5?

____

NAME: ______________________

DIRECTIONS Solve each problem.

1. Count the dots in the frame. How many more dots are needed to make twenty?

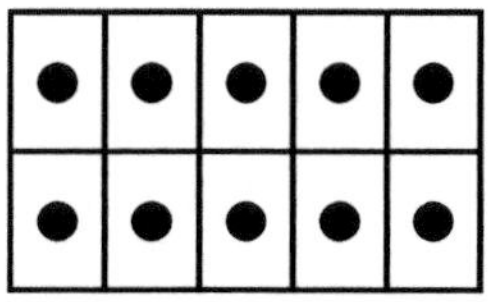

____

2.

$$\begin{array}{r} 10 \\ +\ 10 \\ \hline \square \end{array}$$

3. $13 - 8 = \square$

4.

$$\begin{array}{r} \square \\ -\ 5 \\ \hline 1 \end{array}$$

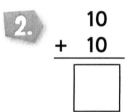

5. Name the solid.

____

6. Write the day that comes after Thursday.

____

7. Record the data in the chart with tally marks.

- Ten children like to swim.
- Six children like to run through the sprinklers.
- Five children like to stay inside.
- Three children like to play with water toys.

Favorite Summer Activity

Water Toys	
Sprinklers	
Stay Inside	
Swim	

8. There are 4 children. How many ears are there?

____

SCORE

1. ☺ 😐
2. ☺ 😐
3. ☺ 😐
4. ☺ 😐
5. ☺ 😐
6. ☺ 😐
7. ☺ 😐
8. ☺ 😐

____ / 8
Total

DAY 106

NAME: ____________________

DIRECTIONS Solve each problem.

SCORE

1. ☺ ☹
2. ☺ ☹
3. ☺ ☹
4. ☺ ☹
5. ☺ ☹
6. ☺ ☹
7. ☺ ☹
8. ☺ ☹

___ / 8 Total

1. Write the number word for 11.

____

2. $3 + 7 = \square$

3. $\begin{array}{r} 10 \\ -\ \ 4 \\ \hline \square \end{array}$

4. True or false?
$8 + 0 = 4 + 2$

____

5. Draw a ball far from the bear.

6. Would you use a ruler or a thermometer to find the temperature outside today?

____

7. What question would you ask to find out about your friend's favorite sports?

____

____

8. Dad has 16 model cars in a collection. He gives 3 of the models to his son. How many models does Dad still have?

____

NAME: ______________________________

DIRECTIONS Solve each problem.

1. 37 has _____ tens and _____ ones.

2.

$$\begin{array}{r} 9 \\ +\ 8 \\ \hline \square \end{array}$$

3. 12 – 6 = $\square$

4.

$$\begin{array}{r} 7 \\ +\ \square \\ \hline 9 \end{array}$$

5. Can you stack a cylinder on top of a rectangular prism?

Circle: yes no

6. Show 10 o'clock.

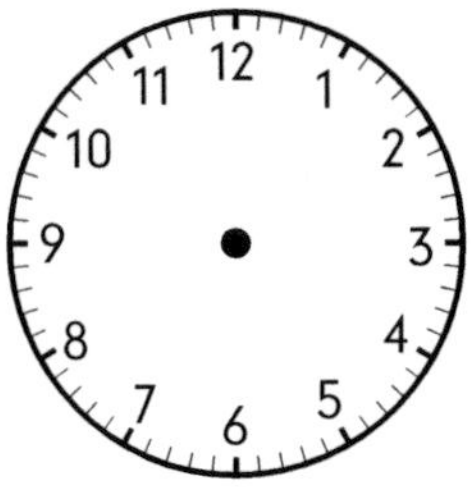

7. Favorite Subject

Math	☺ ☺ ☺ ☺ ☺ ☺
Reading	☺ ☺ ☺ ☺
Science	☺ ☺ ☺ ☺ ☺ ☺ ☺

How many more children like math than reading?

____

8. Write a subtraction number sentence using the numbers 3, 6, and 9.

____

SCORE

1. ☺ 😐
2. ☺ 😐
3. ☺ 😐
4. ☺ 😐
5. ☺ 😐
6. ☺ 😐
7. ☺ 😐
8. ☺ 😐

____ / 8
Total

DAY 108

NAME: ______________________

DIRECTIONS Solve each problem.

SCORE

1. ☺ 😐
2. ☺ 😐
3. ☺ 😐
4. ☺ 😐
5. ☺ 😐
6. ☺ 😐
7. ☺ 😐
8. ☺ 😐

___ /8
Total

1. Draw 5 squares. Draw a circle around the second square.

2. 7 + 10 = ☐

3.

$$\begin{array}{r} 13 \\ -\ \ 7 \\ \hline \square \end{array}$$

4. Complete the pattern.

_____ 58 59 60 61

5. Will the solid roll?

Circle: yes no

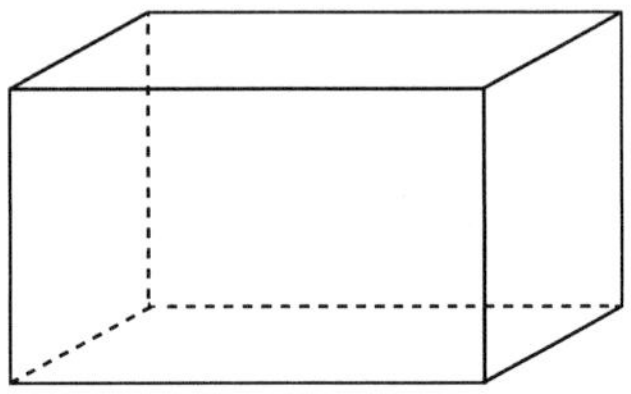

6. How many cubes make this solid?

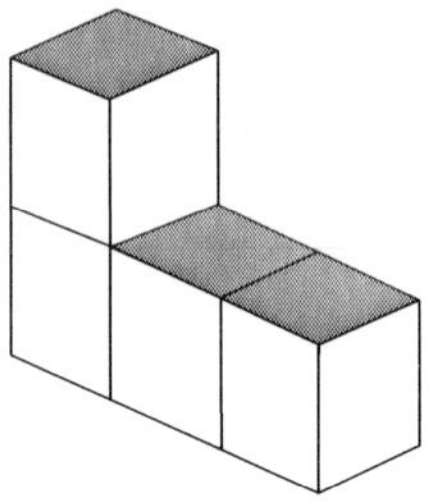

_____ cubes

7. Number of Home Runs

Marc	Ramon	Jamal
7	4	15

Sammy hit two more home runs than Ramon. How many home runs did Sammy hit?

____

8. There are 7 wheels. There is 1 tricycle. The rest are wagons. How many wagons are there?

____

NAME: ______________________________

DIRECTIONS Solve each problem.

1. Draw tens rods and ones cubes to show the number 14.

2.

$$\begin{array}{r} 8 \\ +\ 4 \\ \hline \square \end{array}$$

3. 10 – 9 = ☐

4. Write the missing number.

13 – ☐ = 7

5. Draw a shape with 4 equal sides.

6. Record the area.

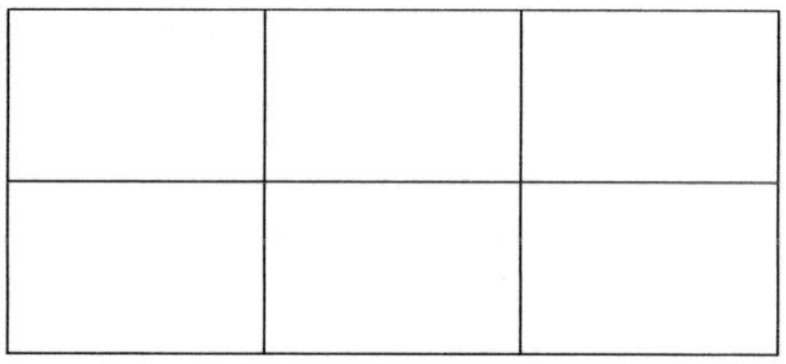

_____ rectangles

7. Favorite Recess Game

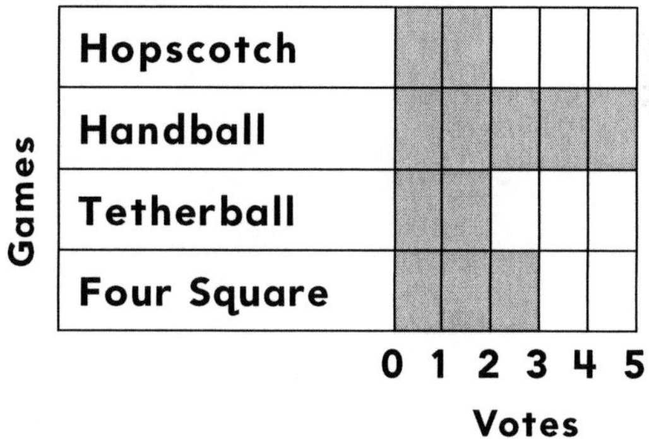

How many more children like four square than hopscotch?

____

8. There are 12 children playing basketball. There are 6 on one team. How many are on the other team?

____

SCORE

1.

2.

3.

4.

5.

6.

7.

8.

____ /8 Total

DAY 110

NAME: ____________________

DIRECTIONS Solve each problem.

SCORE

1. ☺☹
2. ☺☹
3. ☺☹
4. ☺☹
5. ☺☹
6. ☺☹
7. ☺☹
8. ☺☹

____ / 8
Total

1. About how many children are in a classroom? Circle one:

   20   80

2. 7 + 9 = ☐

3. $\begin{array}{r} 12 \\ -\ \ 4 \\ \hline \end{array}$ ☐

4. 8 − ☐ = 5

5. Draw a flower to the right of the dog.

6. Write the month that comes after April.

   ____

7. Favorite Weekend Activity

Play Video Games	卌 I
Read	卌 III
Play with Toys	卌

How many more children like to read than to play with toys?

____

8. Which weighs more: a school book or a bathtub?

____

NAME: ____________________

DIRECTIONS Solve each problem.

1. Put these numbers in order from least to greatest.

32   23   63

_____ _____ _____

2.

$$\begin{array}{r} 10 \\ +\ \ 3 \\ \hline \square \end{array}$$

3. $11 - 7 = \square$

4. True or false?

$9 + 1 = 6 + 4$

____

5. Circle the name of the shape.

hexagon   pentagon

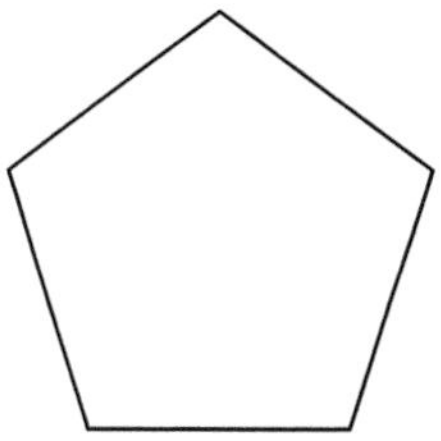

6. Write the time.

__________ o'clock

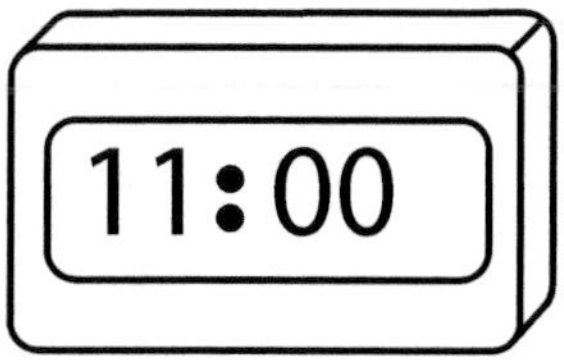

7. Use the data from the chart. Write a statement about how many children ride their bikes to school.

Ways We Get to School

Car	Bike	Bus	Walk
6	2	10	7

____

____

____

8. What is the largest 2-digit number you can make with the numbers 3, 5, and 1?

____

SCORE

1. ☺ 😐
2. ☺ 😐
3. ☺ 😐
4. ☺ 😐
5. ☺ 😐
6. ☺ 😐
7. ☺ 😐
8. ☺ 😐

____ / 8

Total

DAY
112

NAME: ____________________

DIRECTIONS Solve each problem.

SCORE

1. ☺ 😐
2. ☺ 😐
3. ☺ 😐
4. ☺ 😐
5. ☺ 😐
6. ☺ 😐
7. ☺ 😐
8. ☺ 😐

____ / 8

Total

1. What is the largest number that can be made with 3 and 7?

____

2. $6 + 7 = \square$

3.

$$\begin{array}{r} 13 \\ -\ \ 9 \\ \hline \square \end{array}$$

4. $\square - 5 = 5$

5. Count the angles.

____

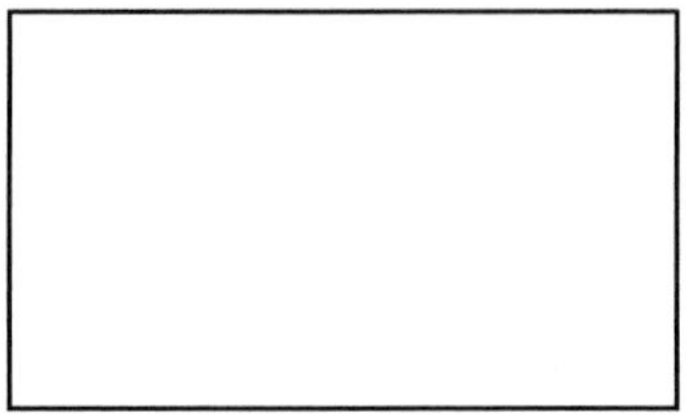

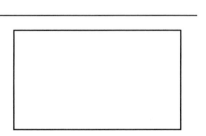

6. Write the day that comes after Saturday.

____

7. Make 13 tally marks.

8. I am 10 less than 82. What number am I?

____

NAME: ____________________

DIRECTIONS Solve each problem.

1. Circle the fourth pencil.

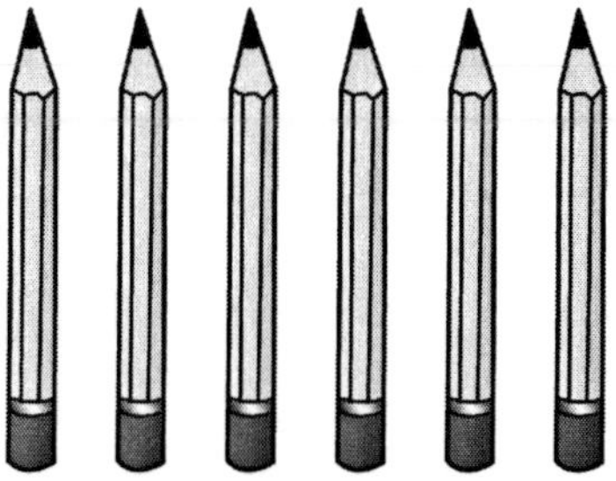

2.

$$\begin{array}{r} 10 \\ +\ \ 8 \\ \hline \square \end{array}$$

3. $12 - 3 = \square$

4.

$$\begin{array}{r} \square \\ +\ \ 6 \\ \hline 8 \end{array}$$

5. Will the object roll?

Circle: yes no

6. How many cubes make this solid?

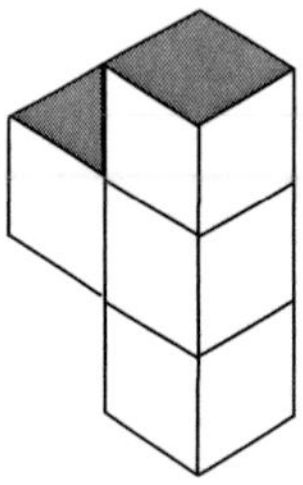

_____ cubes

7. **Pencil Colors**

Red	~~||||~~
Green	~~||||~~ |||
Blue	|||

How many more green pencils are there than red pencils?

____

8. There are 16 horses in a field. 10 of the horses go into the barn. How many horses are still in the field?

____

SCORE

1. ☺ 😐

2. ☺ 😐

3. ☺ 😐

4. ☺ 😐

5. ☺ 😐

6. ☺ 😐

7. ☺ 😐

8. ☺ 😐

____ / 8 Total

DAY **114**

NAME: ____________________

DIRECTIONS Solve each problem.

SCORE

1.
2.
3.
4.
5.
6.
7.
8.

____ / 8
Total

1. Draw dots to fill the frame. How many more dots are needed to make twenty?

●	●	●							

____

2. 7 + 7 = ☐

3.
$$\begin{array}{r} 10 \\ -\ 6 \\ \hline \square \end{array}$$

4. Continue the pattern.

10 15 20 25 ______

5. Draw a line of symmetry.

6. What tool would you use to measure time: a clock or a thermometer?

____

7. Children in Class

Boys	Girls
7	10

How many more girls are there than boys?

____

8. Lauren has a vase with 7 flowers in it. She added 5 flowers yesterday and 5 flowers today. How many flowers does Lauren have now?

____

NAME: ______________________

DIRECTIONS Solve each problem.

1. Draw 1 row of 5 apples.

2.
$$\begin{array}{r} 10 \\ +\ \ 1 \\ \hline \square \end{array}$$

3. 13 − 6 = ☐

4. Write the missing sign.
$$\begin{array}{r} 8 \\ \square\ 4 \\ \hline 4 \end{array}$$

5. Name the solid.

____

6. Which is longer: your hand or a 12-inch ruler?

____

7. Record the data in the chart. Use numbers.

- Yon did 35 minutes of homework.
- Joe did 23 minutes of homework.
- Lexi did 29 minutes of homework.

Time Spent on Homework

Yon	Joe	Lexi

8. How many legs are on 2 dogs?

____

SCORE

1. ☺ 😐
2. ☺ 😐
3. ☺ 😐
4. ☺ 😐
5. ☺ 😐
6. ☺ 😐
7. ☺ 😐
8. ☺ 😐

____ / 8 Total

NAME: ____________________

DIRECTIONS Solve each problem.

SCORE

1.
2.
3.
4.
5.
6.
7.
8.

____ / 8

Total

1. Write the number word for 16.

____

2. $7 + 4 = \square$

3. $\begin{array}{r} 11 \\ -\ \ 9 \\ \hline \square \end{array}$

4. $10 + \square = 10$

5. Is the plate beside the knife?

Circle: yes no

6. Show 2 o'clock.

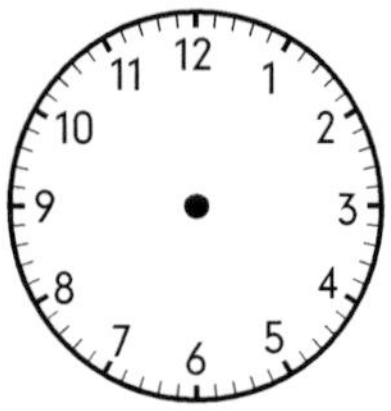

7.

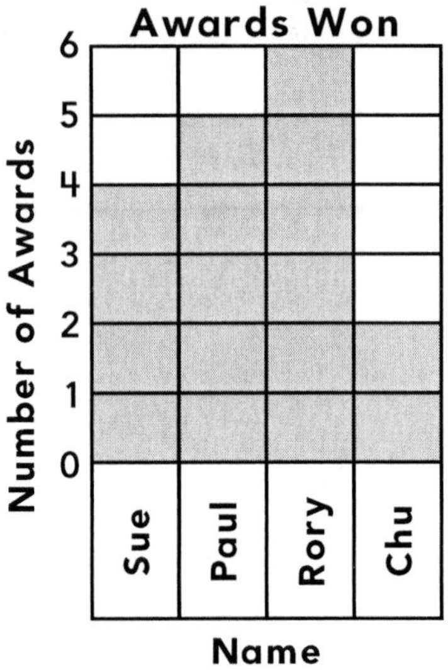

How many more awards does Paul have than Chu?

____

8. Jack picked 5 flowers for his mom. His mom already has 13 flowers. How many flowers does she have now?

____

NAME: ______________________________

DIRECTIONS Solve each problem.

1. 59 has ______ tens and ______ ones.

2.

$$\begin{array}{r} 5 \\ + \ 6 \\ \hline \square \end{array}$$

3. $14 - 8 = \square$

4.

$$\begin{array}{r} 9 \\ - \ \square \\ \hline 2 \end{array}$$

5. How many flat faces does the solid have?

____

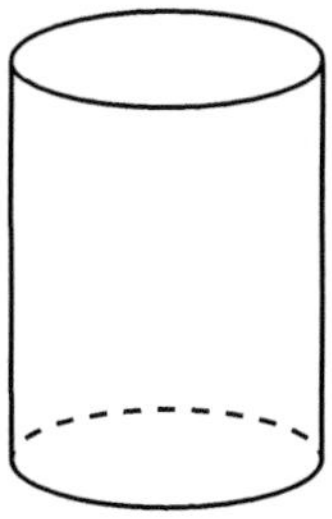

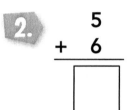

6. Write the month that comes after September.

____

7.

Favorite Animal

Cats	Dogs	Birds	Lizards
7	9	4	

Two less people like lizards than like cats. Record the data in the chart.

8. What shape has more than 4 sides, but less than 6 sides?

____

SCORE

1.

2.

3.

4.

5.

6.

7.

8.

___ / 8

Total

NAME: ____________________

DIRECTIONS Solve each problem.

SCORE

1. ☺ 😐
2. ☺ 😐
3. ☺ 😐
4. ☺ 😐
5. ☺ 😐
6. ☺ 😐
7. ☺ 😐
8. ☺ 😐

___ / 8
Total

1. Fill in the circle with <, >, or =.

18 ◯ 24

2. 8 + 4 = ☐

3.

$$\begin{array}{r} 10 \\ -\ 10 \\ \hline \square \end{array}$$

4. Complete the number sentence.

0 + 7 = 7

☐ − ☐ = 0

5. What smaller shapes are used to make this rectangle?

____

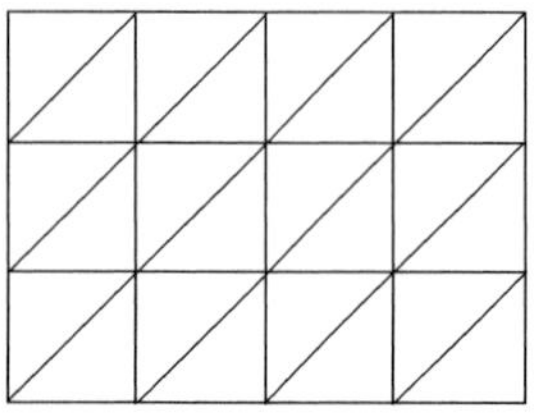

6. Would you use a clock or a ruler to tell what time you go to bed?

____________________.

7. Favorite Activity

Swings	Slide	Monkey Bars	Balance Beam
8	5	7	2

How many more children like the monkey bars than the balance beam?

____

8. There are 7 flowers. Simi wants to put one flower in each vase. How many vases does she need?

____

NAME: ______________________________

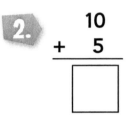

DIRECTIONS Solve each problem.

1. Draw 4 triangles. Circle the last triangle.

2.

$$\begin{array}{r} 10 \\ +\ \ 5 \\ \hline \square \end{array}$$

3. $12 - 1 = \square$

4. True or false?

$6 + 6 = 7 + 5$

____

5. Draw a closed shape with no straight sides.

6. Record the area.

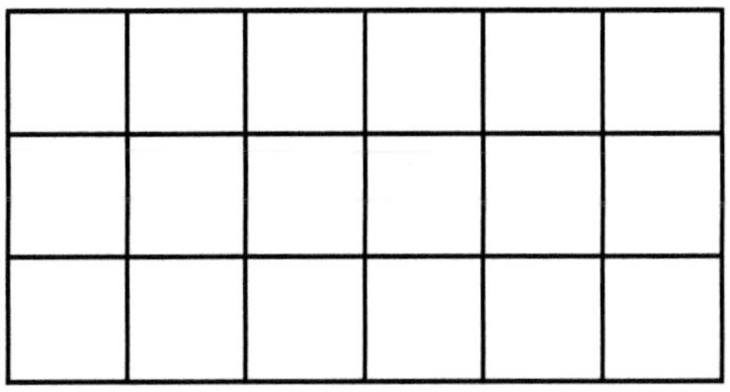

_____ squares

7. **Favorite Type of Movie**

Funny	Cartoon	Scary	3-D
|||	𝍸 |||	|	𝍸

How many more children like cartoons than 3-D movies?

____

8. The Rockets have 16 players. The Super Stars have 14 players. How many more players are on the Rockets than on the Super Stars?

____

SCORE

1. ☺ 😐
2. ☺ 😐
3. ☺ 😐
4. ☺ 😐
5. ☺ 😐
6. ☺ 😐
7. ☺ 😐
8. ☺ 😐

____ / 8 Total

NAME: ______________________

DIRECTIONS Solve each problem.

SCORE

1. ☺ ☹
2. ☺ ☹
3. ☺ ☹
4. ☺ ☹
5. ☺ ☹
6. ☺ ☹
7. ☺ ☹
8. ☺ ☹

____ / 8 Total

1. Write the missing number.

77, ______, 79

2. 5 + 7 = ☐

3.
$$\begin{array}{r} 14 \\ -\ \ 5 \\ \hline \square \end{array}$$

4. Complete the pattern.

90 80 70 60 ____ 40

5. Draw a plate below the pie.

6. Circle the object that is taller than you.

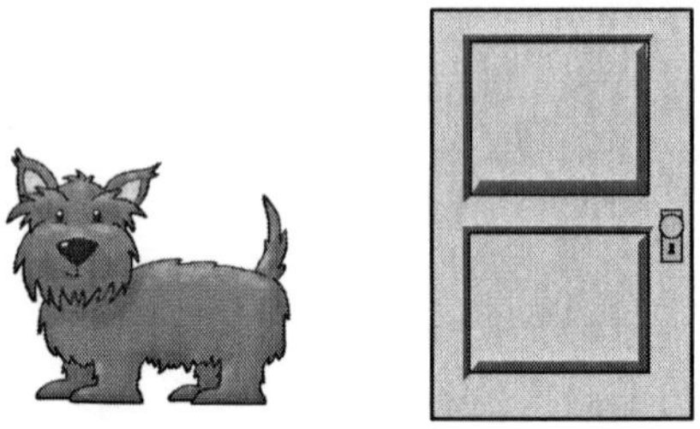

7. What question would you ask to find out about your friends' favorite winter activities?

____

____

____

8. Rick is going on vacation in 5 days. Today is Tuesday. What day of the week will Rick leave for vacation?

____

NAME: ______________________

DIRECTIONS Solve each problem.

1. Put these numbers in order from least to greatest.

65 56 76

_____ _____ _____

2.

$$\begin{array}{r} 7 \\ +\ 3 \\ \hline \square \end{array}$$

3. $13 - 3 = \square$

4. True or false?

$7 + 8 = 7 + 7$

____

5. Circle the name of the shape.

hexagon rhombus

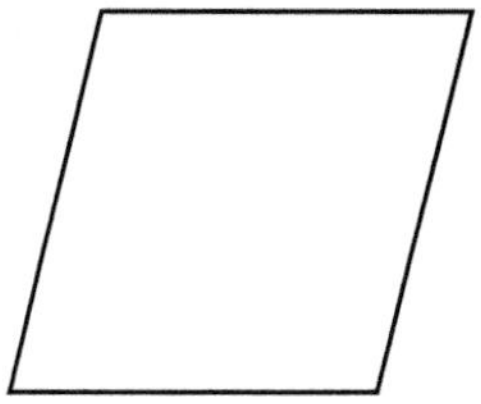

6. What is the 4th month of the year?

____

7. What would be a good symbol for a picture graph showing data for the number of miles run?

____

8. Carl does 5 pages of math each day in a workbook. How many math pages will Carl do in 4 days?

____

Day 1	
Day 2	
Day 3	
Day 4	

SCORE

1. ☺ 😐
2. ☺ 😐
3. ☺ 😐
4. ☺ 😐
5. ☺ 😐
6. ☺ 😐
7. ☺ 😐
8. ☺ 😐

____ / 8 Total

DAY 122

NAME: ______________________

DIRECTIONS Solve each problem.

SCORE

1. ☺ ☹
2. ☺ ☹
3. ☺ ☹
4. ☺ ☹
5. ☺ ☹
6. ☺ ☹
7. ☺ ☹
8. ☺ ☹

____ / 8 Total

1. Circle the larger number.

63 36

2. 2 + 9 = ☐

3.

$$\begin{array}{r} 15 \\ -\ 6 \\ \hline \square \end{array}$$

4. 12 − ☐ = 10

5. Count the angles.

____

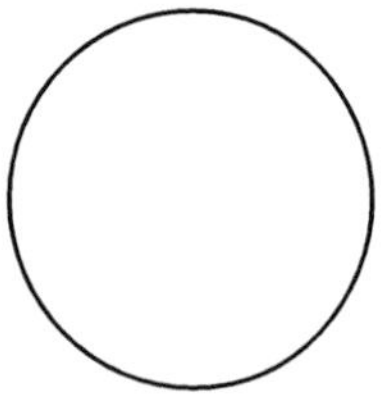

6. How many cubes make this solid?

_______ cubes

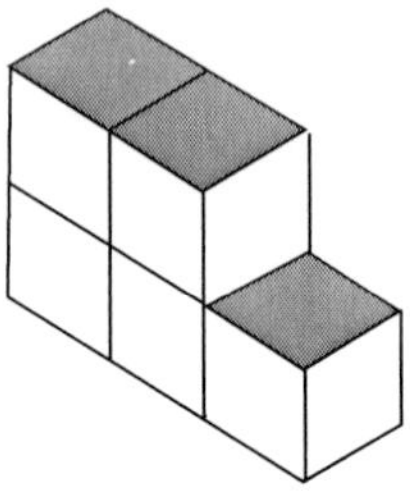

7. Make 9 tally marks.

8. I have 4 in the ones place and 9 in the tens place. What number am I?

____

NAME: ______________________

DIRECTIONS Solve each problem.

1. Write the ordinal number.

The marked tree is

______________________.

2.

$$\begin{array}{r} 9 \\ +\ 4 \\ \hline \square \end{array}$$

3. $12 - 9 = \square$

4.

$$\begin{array}{r} \square \\ +\ 6 \\ \hline 7 \end{array}$$

5. Will the object stack?

____

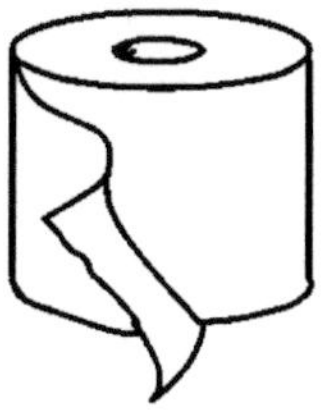

6. Record the area.

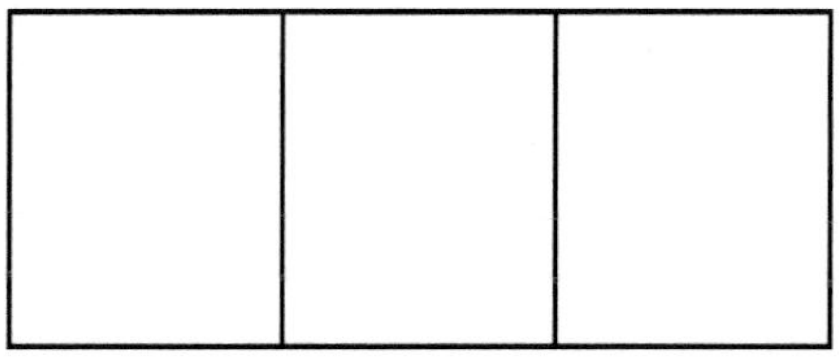

_____ rectangles

7. Favorite Recess Game

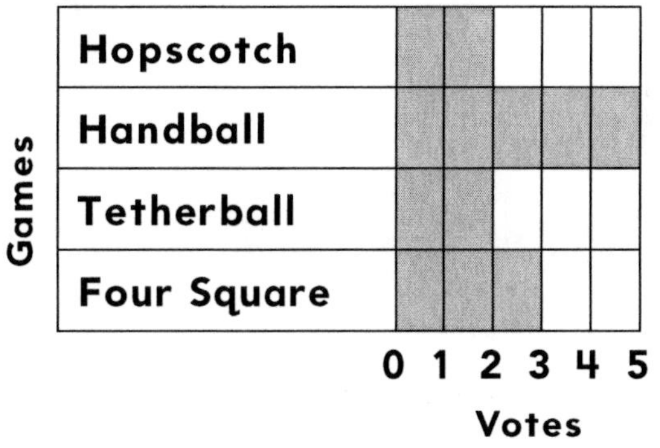

Which activities are liked by the same number of students?

____

____

8. There are 17 students in a class. The class gets a new student. How many students are in the class now?

____

SCORE

1. ☺ 😐
2. ☺ 😐
3. ☺ 😐
4. ☺ 😐
5. ☺ 😐
6. ☺ 😐
7. ☺ 😐
8. ☺ 😐

___ / 8 Total

NAME: ____________________

DIRECTIONS Solve each problem.

SCORE

1. ☺ 😐
2. ☺ 😐
3. ☺ 😐
4. ☺ 😐
5. ☺ 😐
6. ☺ 😐
7. ☺ 😐
8. ☺ 😐

____ / 8
Total

1. Draw dots to fill the ten frame. How many more dots are needed to make ten?

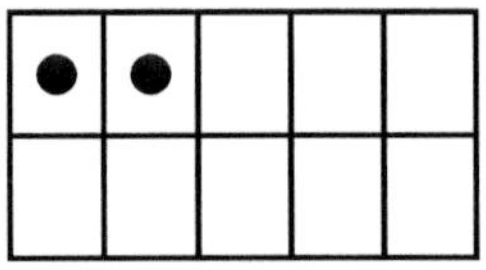

____

2. 7 + 6 = ☐

3.

$$\begin{array}{r} 15 \\ -\ \ 6 \\ \hline \square \end{array}$$

4. Write the missing number.

4 + ☐ = 8

5. Draw a line of symmetry.

6. What tool would you use to measure temperature: a clock or thermometer?

____

7. Favorite Ice Cream

Chocolate Ice Cream	
Strawberry Ice Cream	

How many fewer children like strawberry ice cream than chocolate ice cream?

____

8. Sue gets up every morning at 7:00. School begins 1 hour later. What time does school begin?

____

NAME: ____________________

DIRECTIONS Solve each problem.

1. Draw tens rods and ones cubes to show the number 25.

2.

$$\begin{array}{r} 9 \\ +\ 3 \\ \hline \square \end{array}$$

3. $14 - 7 = \square$

4. Write the missing sign.

$5 \ \square \ 7 = 12$

5. Name the solid.

____

6. What is a good time to go to bed: 1:00 P.M. or 8:00 P.M.?

____

7. Favorite Weekend Activity

Play Video Games	𝍸 |
Read	𝍸 |||
Play with Toys	𝍸

How many more children like to play video games than play with toys?

____

8. Sandra drinks a glass of milk for breakfast and a glass of milk for dinner. How many glasses of milk does she drink in 2 days?

____

SCORE

1. ☺ 😐
2. ☺ 😐
3. ☺ 😐
4. ☺ 😐
5. ☺ 😐
6. ☺ 😐
7. ☺ 😐
8. ☺ 😐

___ / 8
Total

DAY 126

NAME: ______________________

DIRECTIONS Solve each problem.

SCORE

1. ☺ 😐
2. ☺ 😐
3. ☺ 😐
4. ☺ 😐
5. ☺ 😐
6. ☺ 😐
7. ☺ 😐
8. ☺ 😐

____ / 8 Total

1. Write the number word for 37.

____

2. 7 + 8 = ☐

3. 11 – 6 = ☐

4. Complete the pattern.

46 48 50 52 54 ____

5. Draw a piece of paper near the scissors.

6. How many cubes make this solid?

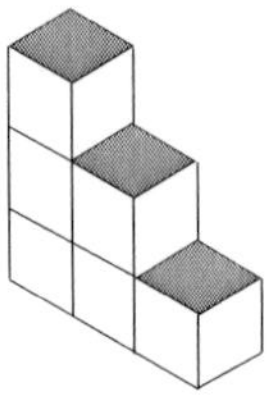

______ cubes

7. Record the data in the chart using numbers.

- Five kids play soccer after school.
- Two more kids play basketball than play soccer.
- Six kids play tennis.
- Three more kids play baseball than tennis.

After-School Sports

Tennis	Soccer	Baseball	Basketball

8. Andrew builds a tower with 15 blocks. Nine of the blocks fall over. How many blocks did not fall over?

____

NAME: ______________________________

DIRECTIONS Solve each problem.

1. 32 has ______ tens

and ______ ones.

2. 9 + 6 = ☐

3. 15 − 8 = ☐

4.

```
   ☐
−  5
----
   6
```

5. Can you stack a cone on top of a cube?

____

6. Write the digital time.

______ : ______

7.

Favorite Subject

Math	☺☺☺☺☺☺
Reading	☺☺☺☺
Science	☺☺☺☺☺☺☺

How many more children picked science than math?

____

8. Write two addition number sentences with the numbers 4, 6, and 10.

____

____

SCORE

1. ☺ 😐
2. ☺ 😐
3. ☺ 😐
4. ☺ 😐
5. ☺ 😐
6. ☺ 😐
7. ☺ 😐
8. ☺ 😐

____ / 8
Total

DAY 128

NAME: ______________________

DIRECTIONS Solve each problem.

SCORE

1. ☺ ☹
2. ☺ ☹
3. ☺ ☹
4. ☺ ☹
5. ☺ ☹
6. ☺ ☹
7. ☺ ☹
8. ☺ ☹

____ / 8 Total

1. Fill in the circle with <, >, or =.

23 ◯ 23

2. 5 + 8 = ☐

3.

$$\begin{array}{r} 10 \\ -\ 0 \\ \hline \square \end{array}$$

4. ☐ + 5 = 9

5. Sonya has 4 cans of soup. Can she roll them?

____

6. What is the 12th month?

____

7. Number of Home Runs

Marc	Ramon	Jamal
7	4	15

Trae hit one home run less than Jamal. How many home runs did Trae hit?

____

8. Fill in the blank with the correct pet. Use the pets named.

- The boys do not have a cat.
- Tim does not have a turtle.
- Amy does not have a dog.

Tim has a ________.

Amy has a ________.

Dave has a ________.

NAME: ____________________

DIRECTIONS Solve each problem.

1. Circle about how many pennies will fit in one hand.

20 80

2.

$$\begin{array}{r} 7 \\ +\ 5 \\ \hline \square \end{array}$$

3. 15 – 0 = ☐

4. True or false?
5 + 6 = 10 + 1

____

5. Draw 2 different shapes with 4 sides.

6. Record the area.

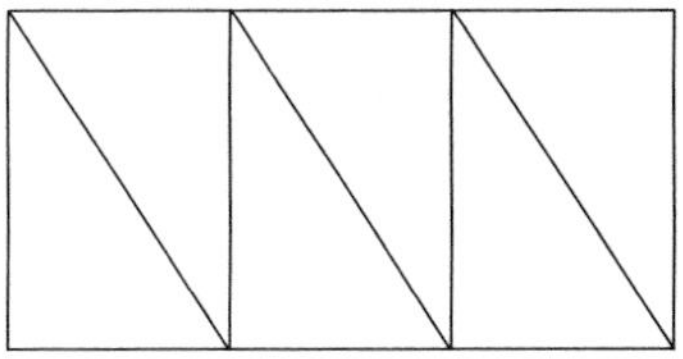

______ triangles

7. Number of Students

Mrs. Garcia	23
Mr. Ream	21
Mrs. Stein	24
Mr. Miller	22

Which teacher has the most students?

____

8. Maggie has swim practice on Monday and Wednesday. She has piano lessons on Tuesday. She practices the piano on Saturday, Thursday, and Friday. What day of the week does she have free?

____

SCORE

1. ☺ 😐
2. ☺ 😐
3. ☺ 😐
4. ☺ 😐
5. ☺ 😐
6. ☺ 😐
7. ☺ 😐
8. ☺ 😐

____ / 8
Total

DAY 130

NAME: ____________________

DIRECTIONS Solve each problem.

SCORE

1. ☺ 😐
2. ☺ 😐
3. ☺ 😐
4. ☺ 😐
5. ☺ 😐
6. ☺ 😐
7. ☺ 😐
8. ☺ 😐

____ / 8 Total

1. What is the largest number that can be made with the numerals 8 and 9?

____

2. 8 + 6 = ☐

3.

$$\begin{array}{r} 12 \\ -\ 10 \\ \hline \square \end{array}$$

4. Write the matching subtraction sentence.

9 + 8 = 17

☐ – ☐ = ☐

5. Draw 3 bubbles to the left of the fish.

6. Would you use a ruler or a thermometer to measure how long your foot is?

____

7. Children in Class

Boys	Girls
7	10

The class can have a total of 20 students. How many more students can be in the class?

____

8. School ends one month from today. Today is May 4th. On what date will school end?

____

NAME: ______________________

DIRECTIONS Solve each problem.

1. Put these numbers in order from least to greatest.

89 75 77

_____ _____ _____

2.

$$\begin{array}{r} 4 \\ +\ 7 \\ \hline \square \end{array}$$

3. $15 - 9 = \square$

4.

$$\begin{array}{r} \square \\ +\ 9 \\ \hline 22 \end{array}$$

5. Color the shape with straight lines.

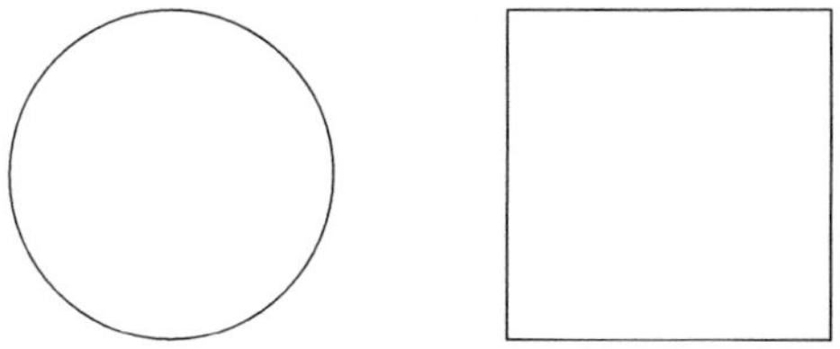

6. Circle the object that is heavier than a watermelon.

7. Use the data from the chart below. Write a statement about how many children ride in a car to school.

Ways We Get to School

Car	Bike	Bus	Walk
6	2	10	7

____

____

____

8. I am 10 more than 47. What number am I?

____

SCORE

1. ☺ 😐

2. ☺ 😐

3. ☺ 😐

4. ☺ 😐

5. ☺ 😐

6. ☺ 😐

7. ☺ 😐

8. ☺ 😐

____ / 8 Total

DAY 132

NAME: ____________________

DIRECTIONS Solve each problem.

SCORE

1. ☺ 😐
2. ☺ 😐
3. ☺ 😐
4. ☺ 😐
5. ☺ 😐
6. ☺ 😐
7. ☺ 😐
8. ☺ 😐

____ / 8 Total

1. Draw 2 rows with 6 circles in each row. Write how many there are in all.

____

2. 6 + 5 = ☐

3.

$$\begin{array}{r} 13 \\ -\ \ 5 \\ \hline \square \end{array}$$

4. Continue the pattern.

45 50 55 60 ____

5. Count the angles.

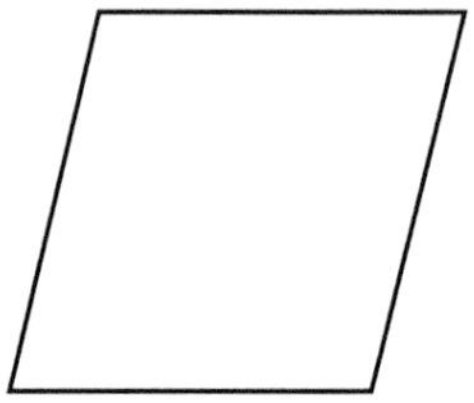

____

6. How many minutes are in 1 hour?

____

7. Make 19 tally marks.

8. Ally has 30 pennies in her piggy bank. Each day she puts 5 more pennies in her piggy bank. How many pennies will she have after 4 days?

____

Start	Day 1	Day 2	Day 3	Day 4
30				

NAME: ____________________

DIRECTIONS Solve each problem.

1. Circle the first ice cream cone.

2.

$$\begin{array}{r} 3 \\ +\ 8 \\ \hline \square \end{array}$$

3. $15 - 5 = \square$

4.

$$\begin{array}{r} 15 \\ -\ \square \\ \hline 7 \end{array}$$

5. Will the object roll?

Circle: yes no

6. What is the 6th month of the year?

____

7.

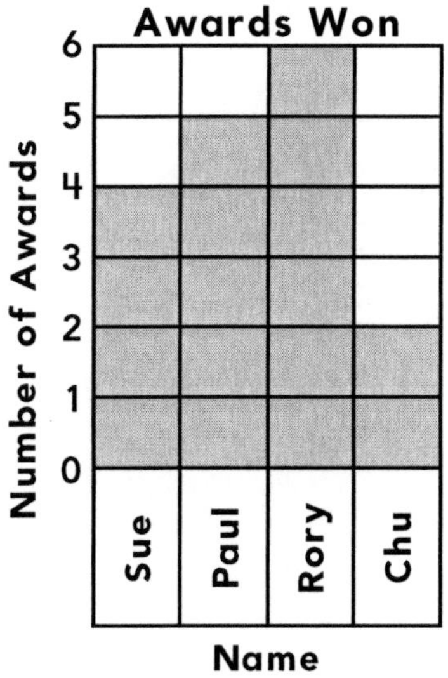

How many more awards does Rory have than Sue?

____

8. There are 18 children playing soccer. Nine are on one team. How many children are on the other team?

____

SCORE

1.

2.

3.

4.

5.

6.

7.

8.

___ / 8 Total

NAME: ____________________

DIRECTIONS Solve each problem.

SCORE

1. ☺ 😐
2. ☺ 😐
3. ☺ 😐
4. ☺ 😐
5. ☺ 😐
6. ☺ 😐
7. ☺ 😐
8. ☺ 😐

____ /8 Total

1. Draw dots to fill the frame. How many more dots are needed to make ten?

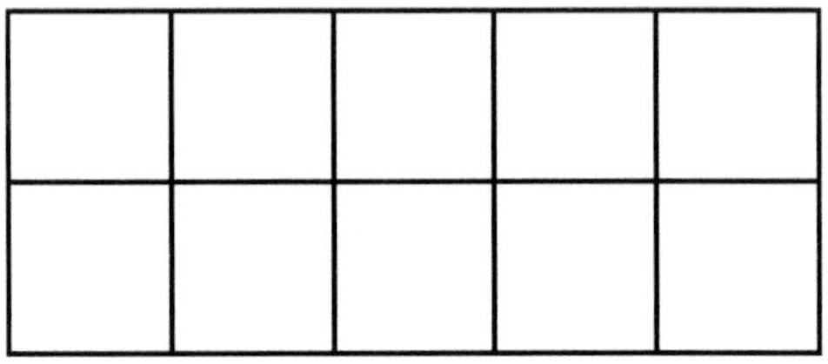

____

2. 7 + 10 = ☐

3.

$$\begin{array}{r} 12 \\ -\ \ 2 \\ \hline \square \end{array}$$

4. Write the missing sign.

14 ☐ 5 = 9

5. Draw a line of symmetry.

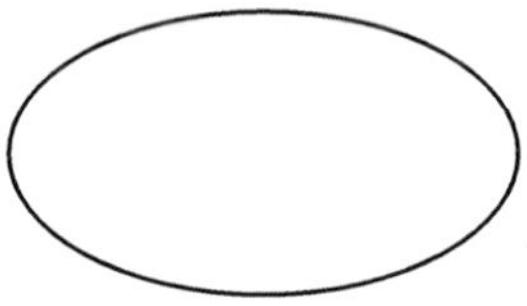

6. Show 11 o'clock.

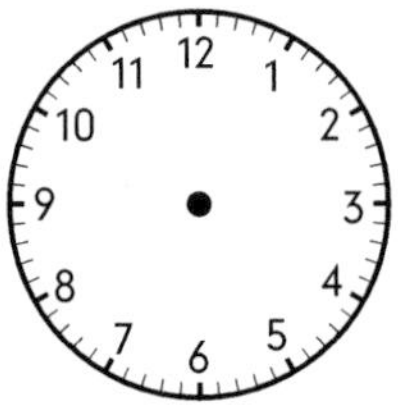

7. Favorite Activity

Swings	Slide	Monkey Bars	Balance Beam
8	5	7	2

How many children like the swings and slide?

____

8. I have 3 in the ones place and 7 in the tens place. What number am I?

____

NAME: ____________________

DIRECTIONS Solve each problem.

1. Draw 8 circles. Color in the 6th circle.

2. $\begin{array}{r} 8 \\ + \quad 4 \\ \hline \square \end{array}$

3. $14 - 9 = \square$

4. True or false?
$8 + 3 = 6 + 7$

____

5. Name the solid.

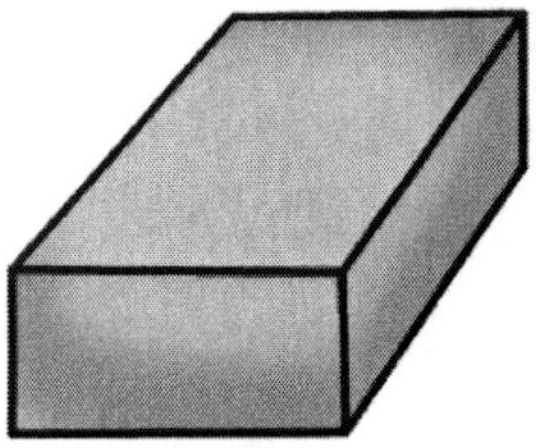

____

6. What tool would you use to measure length: a ruler or a thermometer?

____

7. **Favorite Type of Movie**

Funny	Cartoon	Scary	3-D
𝍷𝍷𝍷	𝍸 𝍷𝍷𝍷	𝍷	𝍸

How many more children preferred 3-D than both funny and scary movies?

____

8. It is a 10 minute walk from Maria's house to her school. How many minutes does it take her to walk to and from school each day?

____

SCORE

1. ☺ 😐
2. ☺ 😐
3. ☺ 😐
4. ☺ 😐
5. ☺ 😐
6. ☺ 😐
7. ☺ 😐
8. ☺ 😐

____ / 8
Total

DAY 136

NAME: ____________________

DIRECTIONS Solve each problem.

SCORE

1.

2.

3.

4.

5.

6.

7.

8.

___ / 8

Total

1. Write the number word for 21.

____

2. 3 + 9 = ☐

3.

$$\begin{array}{r} 15 \\ -\ 10 \\ \hline \square \end{array}$$

4. Write the missing sign.

15 ☐ 8 = 7

5. Draw a cup next to the pitcher.

6. Record the area.

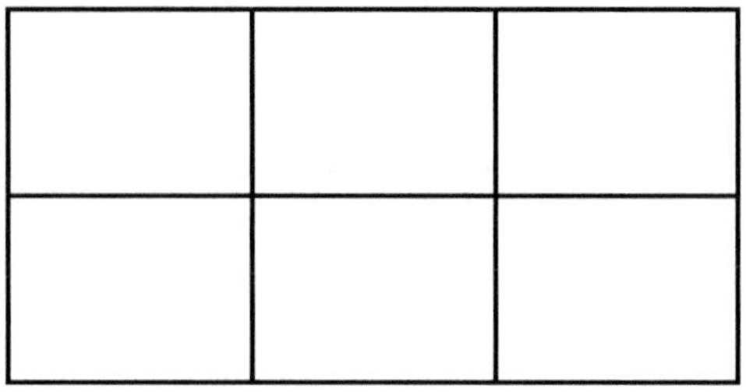

______ rectangles

7.

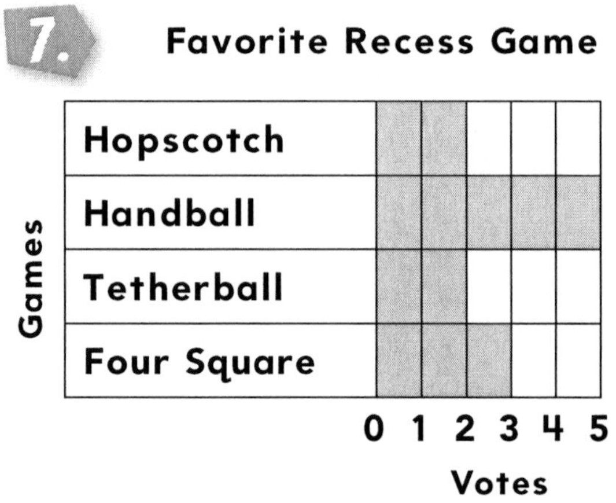

How many students like hopscotch and tetherball?

____

8. Rachel ate 18 grapes. Then she ate 6 more. How many grapes did Rachel eat?

____

NAME: ____________________

DIRECTIONS Solve each problem.

1. 79 has ______ tens and ______ ones.

2.
$$\begin{array}{r} 10 \\ +\ 1 \\ \hline \square \end{array}$$

3. $11 - 8 = \square$

4. Write the matching addition sentence.

   $13 - 6 = 7$

   $\square + \square = \square$

5. How many flat surfaces does a cube have?

   ____

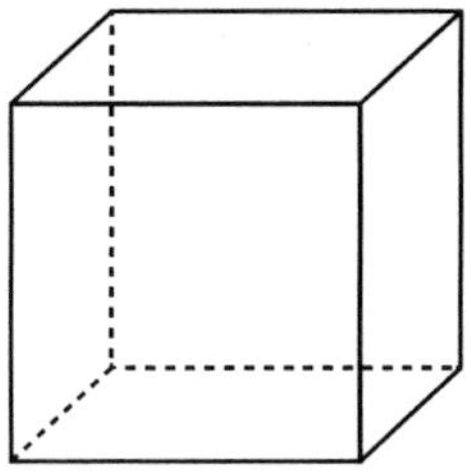

6. How many hours are in one day?

   ____

7. Favorite Animal

Cats	Dogs	Birds	Lizards
7	9	4	5

How many people were asked about their favorite animal?

____

8. Which shape has more than 7 sides but less than 9?

   ____

SCORE

1. ☺ 😐
2. ☺ 😐
3. ☺ 😐
4. ☺ 😐
5. ☺ 😐
6. ☺ 😐
7. ☺ 😐
8. ☺ 😐

____ / 8 Total

DAY
138

NAME: ____________________

DIRECTIONS Solve each problem.

SCORE

1. ☺ ☹
2. ☺ ☹
3. ☺ ☹
4. ☺ ☹
5. ☺ ☹
6. ☺ ☹
7. ☺ ☹
8. ☺ ☹

____ / 8
Total

1. Fill in the circle with <, >, or =.

37 ◯ 43

2. 7 + 8 = ☐

3.
$$\begin{array}{r} 14 \\ -\ \ 4 \\ \hline \square \end{array}$$

4. 2 + ☐ = 9

5. Count how many sides are on a cube. How many sides are on 3 cubes?

____

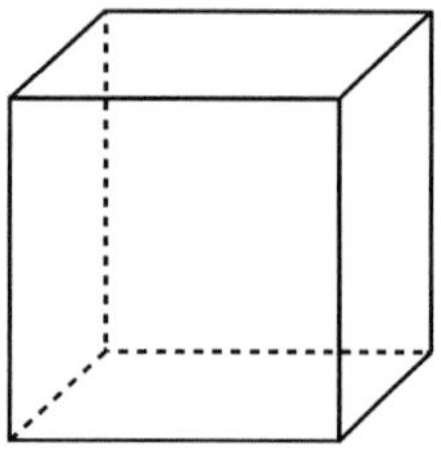

6. Show 8 o'clock.

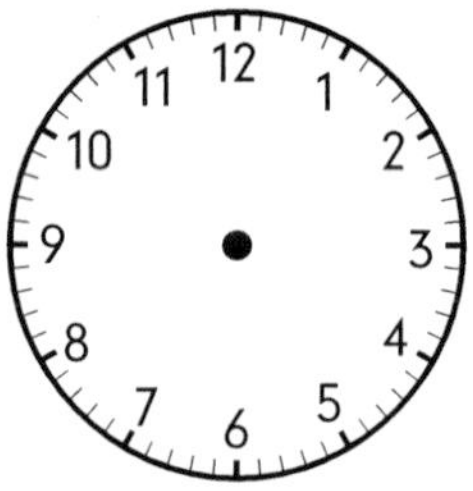

7. What question would you ask to find out about how many brothers and sisters your friends have?

____

____

____

____

8. If you add 4 to me, you get 7. What number am I?

____

NAME: ____________________________

DIRECTIONS Solve each problem.

1. Draw tens rods and ones cubes to show the number 50.

2. 1 + 9 = ☐

3. 15 – 7 = ☐

4. Continue the pattern.

77 79 81 83 ____

5. Draw a shape with 5 sides.

6. Write the time.

_____ : _____

7. Complete the chart to show the following data. Include each name and the time

- Tammi goes to bed at 8:00.
- Marco goes to bed at 8:30.
- Shavon goes to bed at 7:30.

Bedtimes

Tammi		
		7:30

8. There are 19 children in Mrs. Hutah's class. There are 17 children in Mrs. Zyke's class. How many fewer children are in Mrs. Zyke's class?

____

SCORE

1. ☺ 😐

2. ☺ 😐

3. ☺ 😐

4. ☺ 😐

5. ☺ 😐

6. ☺ 😐

7. ☺ 😐

8. ☺ 😐

____ / 8
Total

DAY
140

NAME: ______________________________

DIRECTIONS Solve each problem.

SCORE

1. ☺ 😐
2. ☺ 😐
3. ☺ 😐
4. ☺ 😐
5. ☺ 😐
6. ☺ 😐
7. ☺ 😐
8. ☺ 😐

____ / 8
Total

1. Write the missing numbers.

68, ____, ____, 71

2. 10 + 9 = ☐

3.

$$\begin{array}{r} 12 \\ -\ 11 \\ \hline \square \end{array}$$

4. ☐ – 6 = 7

5. Draw a piece of paper above the scissors.

6. What is the 3rd month of the year?

____

7.

Favorite Weekend Activity

Play Video Games	卌 |
Read	卌 |||
Play with Toys	卌

How many people were surveyed?

____

8. Which is longer: a car or a tricycle?

____

NAME: ______________________

DIRECTIONS Solve each problem.

1. Put these numbers in order from least to greatest.

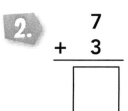

92 97 89

_____ _____ _____

2.

$$\begin{array}{r} 7 \\ +\ 3 \\ \hline \square \end{array}$$

3. 16 – 0 = ☐

4. True or false?

7 + 9 = 10 + 7

____

5. Color the shape with curved sides.

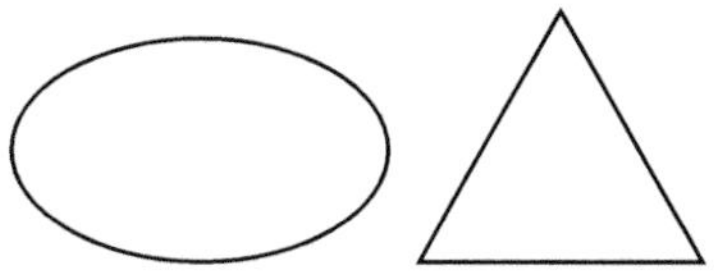

6. Are these objects equal in weight?

Circle: yes no

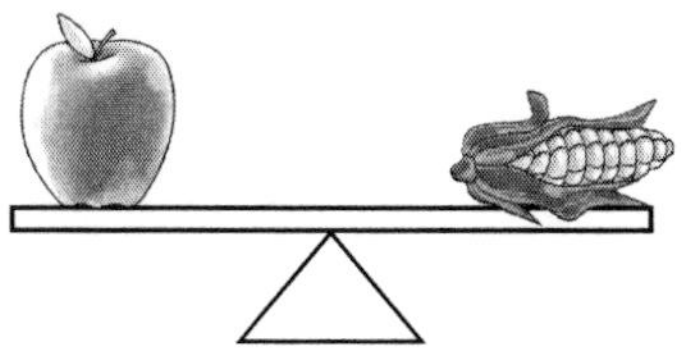

7.

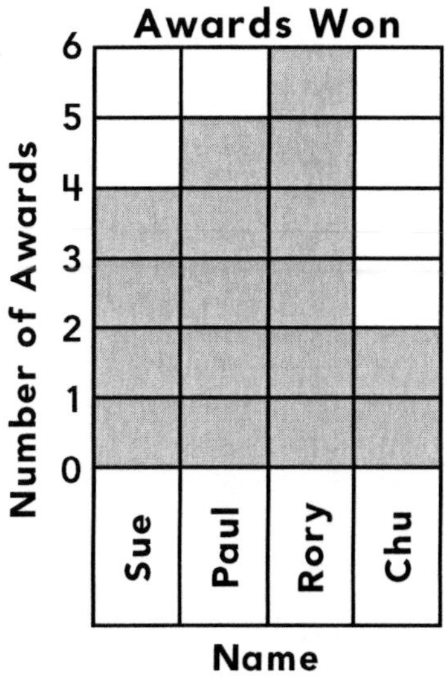

How many more awards does Sue have than Chu?

____

8. Linda has soccer practice on Monday, Wednesday, and Friday. She has a game on Saturday. Which days does Linda have free?

____

____

SCORE

1. ☺ 😐
2. ☺ 😐
3. ☺ 😐
4. ☺ 😐
5. ☺ 😐
6. ☺ 😐
7. ☺ 😐
8. ☺ 😐

____ / 8 Total

DAY
142

NAME: ____________________

DIRECTIONS Solve each problem.

SCORE

1. ☺ 😐
2. ☺ 😐
3. ☺ 😐
4. ☺ 😐
5. ☺ 😐
6. ☺ 😐
7. ☺ 😐
8. ☺ 😐

____ / 8
Total

1. Circle the smaller number.

43 82

2. 9 + 6 = ☐

3.

  12
– 10
☐

4. Write a matching addition sentence.

15 – 5 = 10

☐ + ☐ = ☐

5. How many angles?

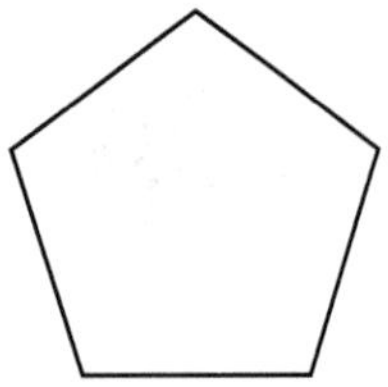

____

6. Show 9 o'clock.

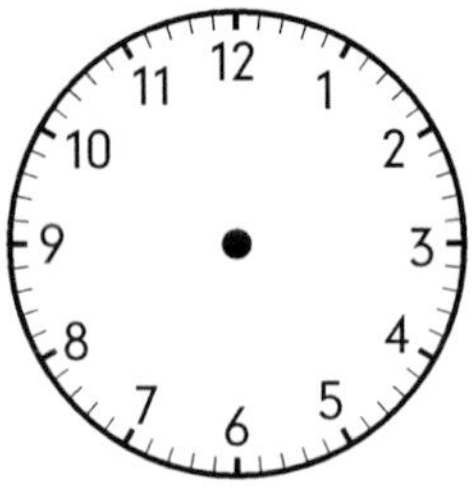

7. Make 25 tally marks.

8. Marcy made 5 ice cream sundaes. She put 2 cherries on each sundae. Draw a picture to show how many cherries Marcy used.

____

NAME: ______________________

DIRECTIONS Solve each problem.

1. Write the ordinal number.

The marked ice cream cone is

______________________.

2.

$$\begin{array}{r} 0 \\ + \quad 4 \\ \hline \square \end{array}$$

3. $17 - 8 = \square$

4.

$$\begin{array}{r} \square \\ + \quad 6 \\ \hline 8 \end{array}$$

5. Will the object stack?

Circle: yes no

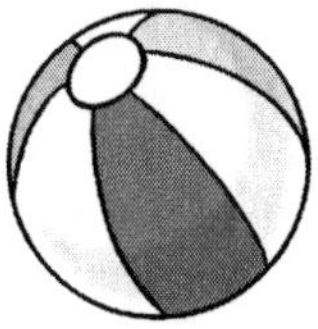

6. Would you use a ruler or a scale to weigh an apple?

____

7. Record the data in the chart. Use numbers.

- Fifteen kids like strawberry, and seven more kids like chocolate.
- Twelve kids like vanilla, but six fewer kids like banana.

Favorite Ice Cream Flavors

Banana	
Chocolate	
Vanilla	
Strawberry	

8. Landon read 43 books in 3 weeks. Then he read 10 more books. How many books did Landon read?

____

SCORE

1. ☺ 😐
2. ☺ 😐
3. ☺ 😐
4. ☺ 😐
5. ☺ 😐
6. ☺ 😐
7. ☺ 😐
8. ☺ 😐

___ / 8 Total

DAY 144

NAME: ____________________

DIRECTIONS Solve each problem.

SCORE

1. ☺ 😐
2. ☺ 😐
3. ☺ 😐
4. ☺ 😐
5. ☺ 😐
6. ☺ 😐
7. ☺ 😐
8. ☺ 😐

____ / 8

Total

1. Circle about how many people will fit in a van.

10 50

2. 7 + 5 = ☐

3.

$$\begin{array}{r} 16 \\ -\ \ 6 \\ \hline \square \end{array}$$

4. 18 − ☐ = 9

5. Draw a line of symmetry.

6. Record the area.

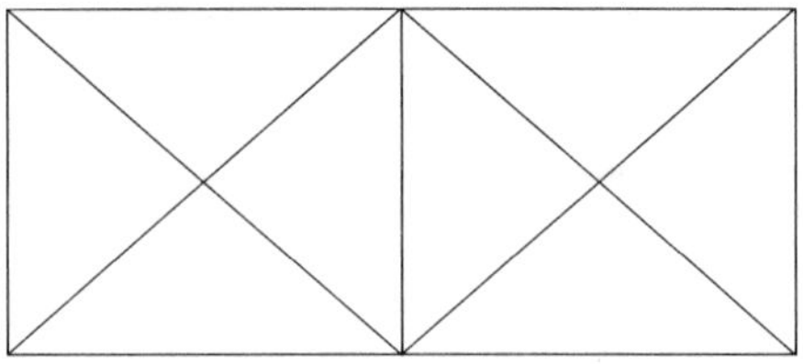

_____ triangles

7.

Number of Students

Mrs. Garcia	23
Mr. Ream	21
Mrs. Stein	24
Mr. Miller	22

Which teacher had the fewest students?

____

8. There are 7 teacups. There are 2 teapots. How many more teacups are there than teapots?

____

NAME: ______________________________

DIRECTIONS Solve each problem.

1. Draw dots to fill the frame. How many more dots were needed to make ten?

●	●	●	●	●

____

2.
$$\begin{array}{r} 10 \\ +\ \ 5 \\ \hline \square \end{array}$$

3. $18 - 9 = \square$

4. Complete the pattern.

75 70 65 60 ____

5. Color the shape that you would see from the top.

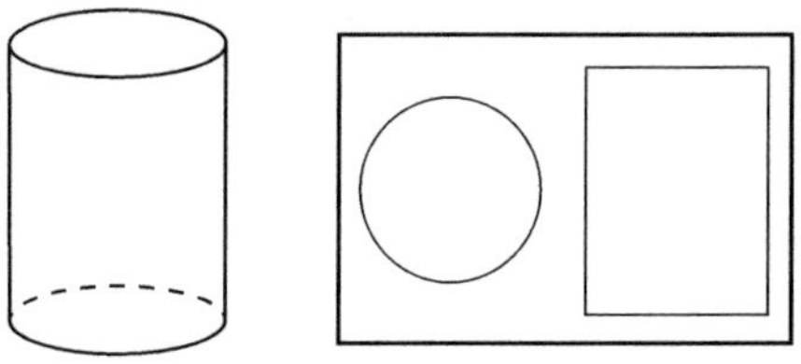

6. What is the 10th month of the year?

____

7. Create a tally chart with the data.

- Twenty-three dogs were sold.
- Twelve cats were sold.

Animals Sold

Dogs	
Cats	

8. Marvin's mom bakes cookies. Marvin eats 3 of the cookies every day. How many cookies will Marvin eat in 2 days?

____

SCORE

1. ☺ 😐

2. ☺ 😐

3. ☺ 😐

4. ☺ 😐

5. ☺ 😐

6. ☺ 😐

7. ☺ 😐

8. ☺ 😐

____ / 8

Total

DAY
146

NAME: ____________________________

DIRECTIONS Solve each problem.

SCORE

1. ☺ 😐
2. ☺ 😐
3. ☺ 😐
4. ☺ 😐
5. ☺ 😐
6. ☺ 😐
7. ☺ 😐
8. ☺ 😐

____ / 8
Total

1. Write the number word for 58.

____

2. 7 + 6 = ☐

3.

$$\begin{array}{r} 16 \\ -\ \ 7 \\ \hline \square \end{array}$$

4. Write the missing sign.

12 ☐ 5 = 7

5. Draw toothpaste on top of the toothbrush.

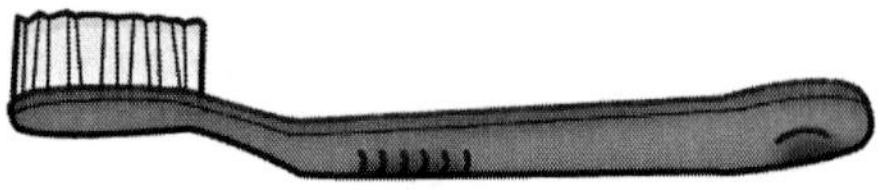

6. Write the time.

half past ______

7.

Children in Class

Boys	Girls
7	10

How many more boys are needed to equal the number of girls?

____

8. There are 20 questions on a test. Mark missed 3 questions. How many questions did Mark get correct?

____

NAME: ______________________________

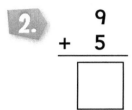

DIRECTIONS Solve each problem.

1. 80 has ______ tens and ______ ones.

2.

$$\begin{array}{r} 9 \\ +\ 5 \\ \hline \square \end{array}$$

3. 19 – 0 = $\square$

4. True or false?

6 + 8 = 7 + 7

____

5. Can you stack a cube on top of a sphere?

Circle: yes no

6. Circle the months that have 31 days.

January

February

March

7. Favorite Subject

Math	☺☺☺☺☺☺
Reading	☺☺☺☺
Science	☺☺☺☺☺☺☺

How many more children like math than reading?

____

8. Write two different subtraction number sentences with the numbers 3, 5, and 8.

____

____

SCORE

1. ☺ 😐

2. ☺ 😐

3. ☺ 😐

4. ☺ 😐

5. ☺ 😐

6. ☺ 😐

7. ☺ 😐

8. ☺ 😐

____ / 8

Total

DAY 148

NAME: ____________________

DIRECTIONS Solve each problem.

SCORE

1. ☺ ☹

2. ☺ ☹

3. ☺ ☹

4. ☺ ☹

5. ☺ ☹

6. ☺ ☹

7. ☺ ☹

8. ☺ ☹

____ / 8 Total

1. Fill in the circle with <, >, or =.

45 ◯ 64

2. 3 + 1 + 0 = ☐

3. 16
− 8
☐

4. 9 − ☐ = 5

5. Draw a rectangle. Draw a line of symmetry.

6. Is this object longer than your pencil?

Circle: yes no

7. Use the data from the chart. Write a statement about how many more children come to school by bus than by bike.

Ways We Get to School

Car	Bike	Bus	Walk
6	2	10	7

____

____

____

____

8. Add two 10s to the number 62.

____

NAME: ____________________

DIRECTIONS Solve each problem.

SCORE

1. What is the largest number that can be made with the numerals 5 and 6?

____

2.
$$\begin{array}{r} 2 \\ 2 \\ +\ 1 \\ \hline \square \end{array}$$

3. $17 - 9 = \square$

4.
$$\begin{array}{r} \square \\ -\ 7 \\ \hline 6 \end{array}$$

5. Draw a shape with six sides.

6. You have 2 pencils that are the same length.
If 1 pencil measures 5 cubes, how long are 2 pencils?

__________ cubes

7. Favorite Activity

Swings	Slide	Monkey Bars	Balance Beam
8	5	7	2

How many children like the monkey bars and balance beam?

____

8. It is 5:00 right now. What time was it an hour ago?

____

1. ☺ 😐
2. ☺ 😐
3. ☺ 😐
4. ☺ 😐
5. ☺ 😐
6. ☺ 😐
7. ☺ 😐
8. ☺ 😐

____ / 8 Total

NAME: ____________________

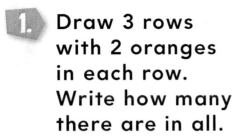

DIRECTIONS Solve each problem.

SCORE

1. ☺ 😐
2. ☺ 😐
3. ☺ 😐
4. ☺ 😐
5. ☺ 😐
6. ☺ 😐
7. ☺ 😐
8. ☺ 😐

____ / 8
Total

1. Draw 3 rows with 2 oranges in each row. Write how many there are in all.

____

2. 1 + 4 + 1 = ☐

3.

$$\begin{array}{r} 16 \\ -\ 10 \\ \hline \square \end{array}$$

4. 5 + 3 = 6 + ☐

5. Draw a square to the right of the circle.

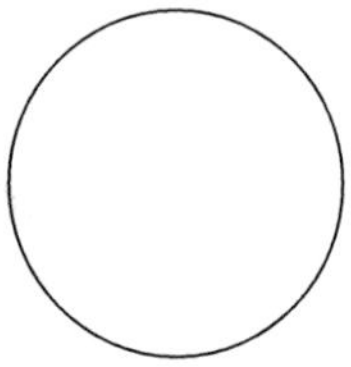

6. Write down the time school begins.

____

7. Favorite Type of Movie

Funny	Cartoon	Scary	3-D
|||	𝍸 |||	|	𝍸

How many people were asked about their favorite type of movie?

____

8. Rita's piano recital was the day before yesterday. Today is Monday. On what day of the week was the piano recital?

____

NAME: ____________________

DIRECTIONS Solve each problem.

1. Put these numbers in order from least to greatest.

73   37   72

____ ____ ____

2.

$$\begin{array}{r} 2 \\ 3 \\ +\ 1 \\ \hline \square \end{array}$$

3. $19 - 9 = \square$

4. Continue the pattern.

82 84 86 88 ____

5. Color the shape with straight sides.

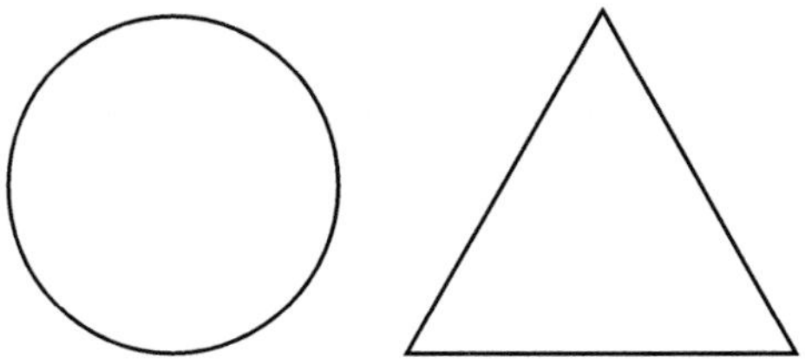

6. Write the time.

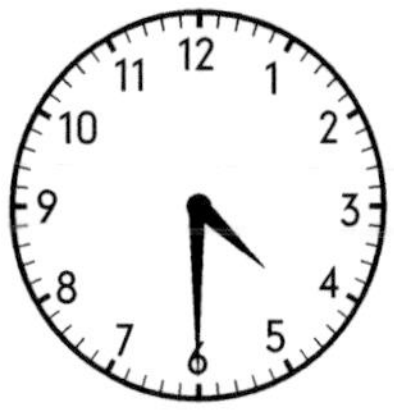

____ : ____

7. What would be a good symbol to use in a picture graph showing data for the number of apples eaten each day for a week?

____

8. Bryan reads 2 books each day. How many books will he read in 4 days?

Day 1	Day 2	Day 3	Day 4

SCORE

1. ☺ 😐
2. ☺ 😐
3. ☺ 😐
4. ☺ 😐
5. ☺ 😐
6. ☺ 😐
7. ☺ 😐
8. ☺ 😐

____ / 8 Total

DAY 152

NAME: ______________________

DIRECTIONS Solve each problem.

SCORE

1. ☺ ☹
2. ☺ ☹
3. ☺ ☹
4. ☺ ☹
5. ☺ ☹
6. ☺ ☹
7. ☺ ☹
8. ☺ ☹

____ / 8 Total

1. Draw tens rods and ones cubes to show the number 62.

2. $3 + 2 + 1 = \square$

3.

$$\begin{array}{r} 16 \\ -\ \ 9 \\ \hline \square \end{array}$$

4. $\square + 5 = 10$

5. Count the angles.

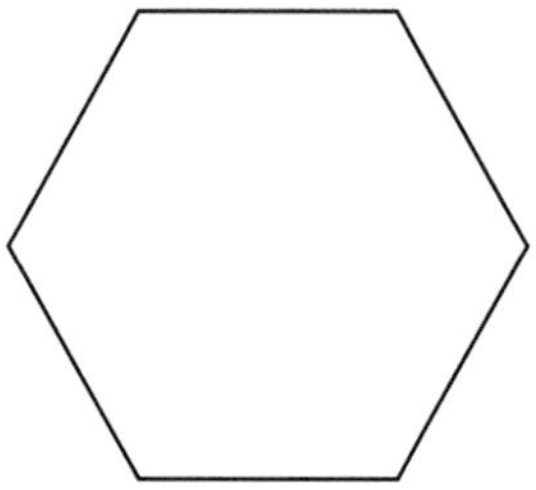

____

6. Would you use a thermometer or a clock to measure the temperature outside today?

____

7. Make 21 tally marks.

8. I am 1 less than 87. What number am I?

____

NAME: ____________________

DIRECTIONS Solve each problem.

1. Circle the 5th car.

2.

$$\begin{array}{r} 2 \\ 4 \\ +\ 2 \\ \hline \square \end{array}$$

3. $17 - 7 = \square$

4.

$$\begin{array}{r} \square \\ -\ 9 \\ \hline 8 \end{array}$$

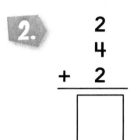

5. Will the object roll?

Circle: yes no

6. Write down the time school ends.

____

7.

Pencil Colors

Red	卌
Green	卌 |||
Blue	|||

How many more green pencils are there than blue pencils?

____

8. There are 25 children in a class. Two children are absent. How many children are not absent?

____

SCORE

1. ☺ 😐

2. ☺ 😐

3. ☺ 😐

4. ☺ 😐

5. ☺ 😐

6. ☺ 😐

7. ☺ 😐

8. ☺ 😐

____ / 8

Total

DAY 154

NAME: ______________________

DIRECTIONS Solve each problem.

SCORE

1.
2.
3.
4.
5.
6.
7.
8.

____ / 8
Total

1. What is the smallest number that can be made with the numerals 6 and 1?

____

2. 1 + 1 + 1 = ☐

3.
$$\begin{array}{r} 20 \\ -\ 10 \\ \hline \square \end{array}$$

4. Write the missing number.

13 – ☐ = 9

5. Draw a line of symmetry.

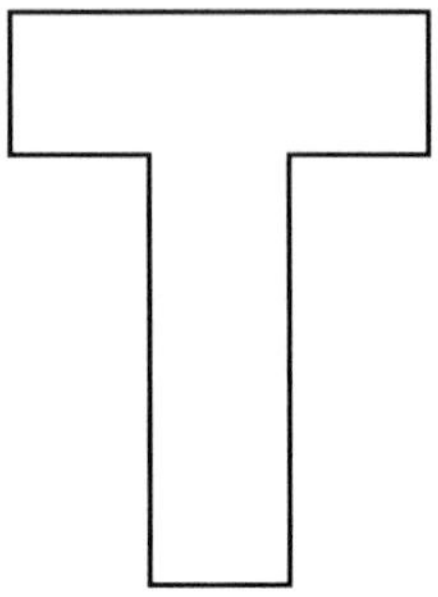

6. What is the first month of the year?

____

7. Favorite Recess Game

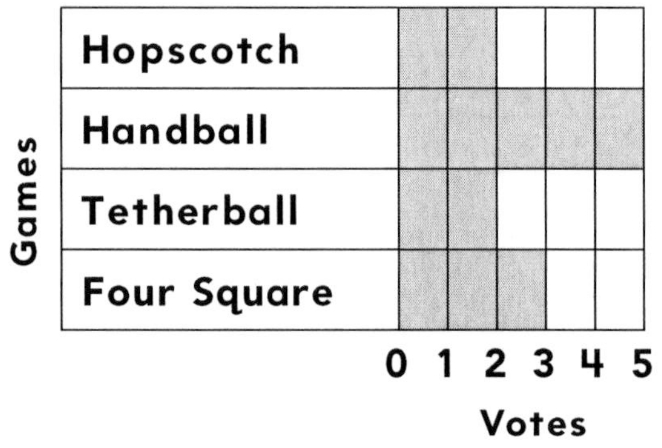

How many students like tetherball and four square?

____

8. Helen has 4 pairs of mittens. How many mittens does she have in all?

____

NAME: ______________________

DIRECTIONS Solve each problem.

1. Write the number that comes after 34.

____

2.

$$\begin{array}{r} 1 \\ 0 \\ +\ 5 \\ \hline \square \end{array}$$

3. $17 - 0 = \square$

4. $6 + 5 = 11 + \square$

5. Color the shape that you would see from the top.

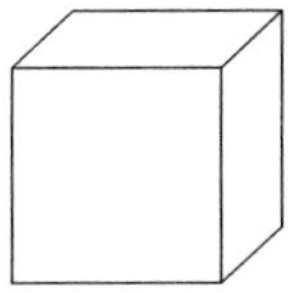

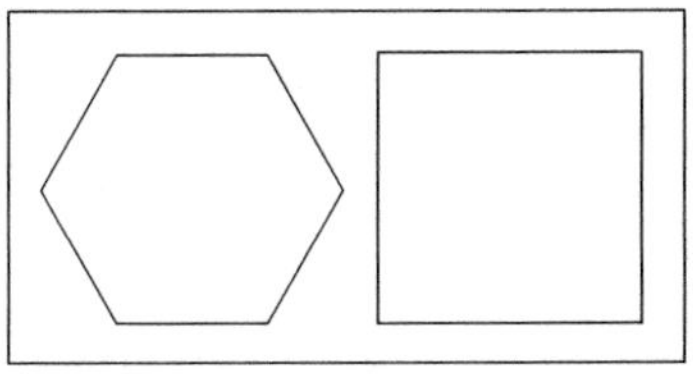

6. Record the area.

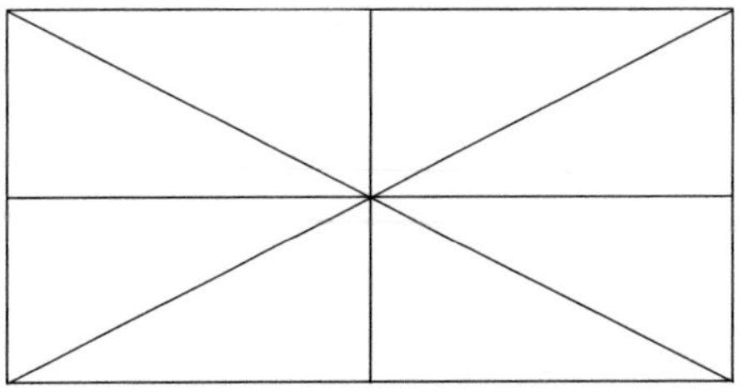

______ triangles

7. Favorite Animal

Cats	Dogs	Birds	Lizards
7	9	4	5

How many more people like dogs than birds?

____

8. A pack of gum has 6 pieces in it. Mom chews one piece of gum each day. How many days will it take her to eat the whole pack of gum?

____

SCORE

1. ☺ 😐

2. ☺ 😐

3. ☺ 😐

4. ☺ 😐

5. ☺ 😐

6. ☺ 😐

7. ☺ 😐

8. ☺ 😐

____ / 8 Total

DAY
156

NAME: ____________________

DIRECTIONS Solve each problem.

SCORE

1. ☺ 😐
2. ☺ 😐
3. ☺ 😐
4. ☺ 😐
5. ☺ 😐
6. ☺ 😐
7. ☺ 😐
8. ☺ 😐

____ / 8
Total

1. Write the number word for 72.

____

2. 5 + 5 + 0 = ☐

3.

$$\begin{array}{r} 19 \\ -\ 10 \\ \hline \square \end{array}$$

4. True or false?
7 + 0 = 6 + 1

____

5. Draw a bat near the baseball.

6. Is the animal longer than your pencil?
Circle: yes no

7. Favorite Activity on the Weekend

Play Video Games	𝍸 |
Read	𝍸 |||
Play with Toys	𝍸

Two more children were asked their favorite activities. One said reading and one said playing with toys. Now how many children prefer reading?

____

8. Meg picked 67 blueberries. Then she picked 10 more. How many blueberries did Meg pick in all?

____

NAME: ______________________

DIRECTIONS Solve each problem.

1. 99 has ______ tens and ______ ones.

2.

$$\begin{array}{r} 6 \\ 1 \\ +\ 1 \\ \hline \square \end{array}$$

3. 17 – 9 = ☐

4. Complete the pattern.

52 50 48 ____ 44

5. How many curved surfaces does the object have?

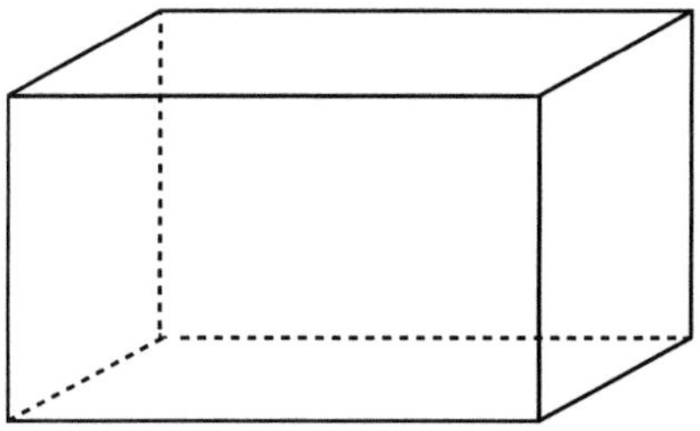

____

6. Circle the months that have 31 days.

June

July

August

7. Number of Students

Mrs. Garcia	23
Mr. Ream	21
Mrs. Stein	24
Mr. Miller	22

How many more students are in Mrs. Garcia's class than in Mr. Miller's class?

____

8. Write one addition number sentence and one subtraction number sentence with the numbers 1, 6, and 7.

____

____

SCORE

1. ☺ 😐

2. ☺ 😐

3. ☺ 😐

4. ☺ 😐

5. ☺ 😐

6. ☺ 😐

7. ☺ 😐

8. ☺ 😐

____ / 8 Total

DAY
158

NAME: ______________________________

DIRECTIONS Solve each problem.

SCORE

1. ☺ 😐
2. ☺ 😐
3. ☺ 😐
4. ☺ 😐
5. ☺ 😐
6. ☺ 😐
7. ☺ 😐
8. ☺ 😐

____ / 8
Total

1. Fill in the circle with <, >, or =.

52 ◯ 52

2. $6 + 5 + 2 = \square$

3.

$$\begin{array}{r} 18 \\ -\;\;8 \\ \hline \square \end{array}$$

4. Write the missing number.

$16 - \square = 7$

5. What smaller shapes make this hexagon?

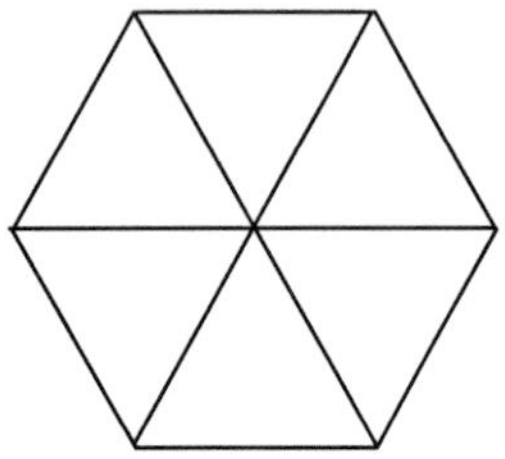

____

6. Write the time.

______ : ______

7. What question would you ask to find out about the color of your friend's bike?

____

____

8. Write the children in order. Will is second. Trish is before Will. Mark is not before Trish.

1. ______________________
2. ______________________
3. ______________________

NAME: ______________________

DIRECTIONS Solve each problem.

1. About how many chairs are in a classroom? Circle one:

20 100

2.

$$\begin{array}{r} 1 \\ 3 \\ +\ 8 \\ \hline \square \end{array}$$

3. $20 - 0 = \square$

4.

$$\begin{array}{r} 8 \\ +\ \square \\ \hline 10 \end{array}$$

5. Draw a shape with 8 sides.

6. Record the length.

__________ crayons

7.

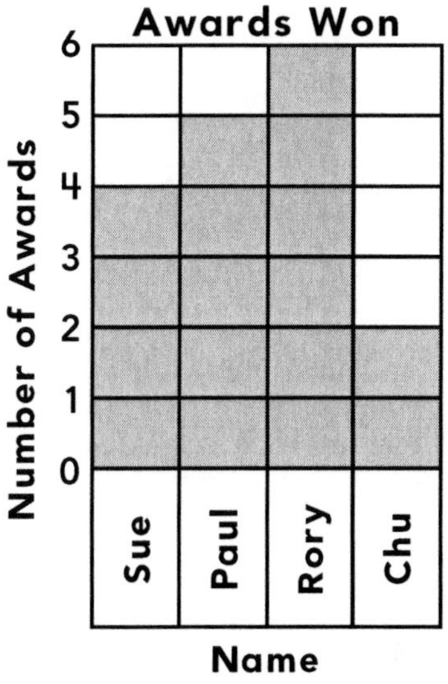

If Paul wins 2 more awards, who will have won the most awards?

____

8. Randy will be 10 in 4 years. How old is Randy now?

____

SCORE

1.

2.

3.

4.

5.

6.

7.

8.

___ / 8 Total

DAY
160

NAME: ______________________________

DIRECTIONS Solve each problem.

SCORE

1. ☺ 😐
2. ☺ 😐
3. ☺ 😐
4. ☺ 😐
5. ☺ 😐
6. ☺ 😐
7. ☺ 😐
8. ☺ 😐

____ / 8
Total

1. Write the missing numbers.

53, ____, ____, 56

2. 7 + 5 + 7 = ☐

3.

$$\begin{array}{r} 17 \\ -\ \ 0 \\ \hline \square \end{array}$$

4. 16 – ☐ = 8

5. Draw a road below the car.

6. Is a door taller or shorter than a child?

____

7. Create a chart showing the following data.

- Tom scored 5 goals, but Tony scored 4 more goals than Tom.
- Jacqueline scored 8 goals.
- Nikki scored 5 more goals than Tony.

Number of Goals Scored This Season

Tom	
Tony	
Jacqueline	
Nikki	

8. Today is September 27th. Dean's birthday was one month ago. In what month was Dean's birthday?

____

DAY
161

NAME: ______________________________

DIRECTIONS Solve each problem.

1. Put the numbers in order from least to greatest.

79 76 81

______ ______ ______

2.

$$\begin{array}{r} 5 \\ 6 \\ +\ 6 \\ \hline \square \end{array}$$

3. $18 - 10 = \square$

4. Write the missing sign.

$$\begin{array}{r} 9 \\ \square\ 7 \\ \hline 16 \end{array}$$

5. Color the shape with curved sides.

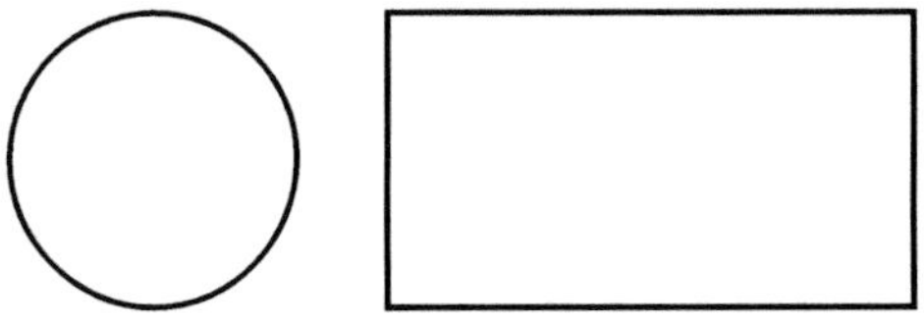

6. Write the time.

______ : ______

7. How many tally marks are there?

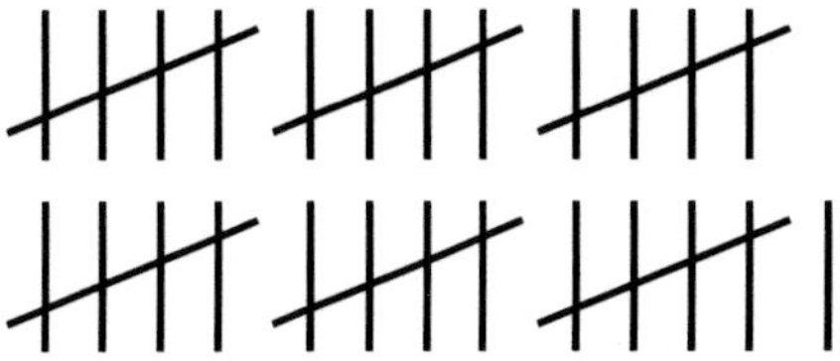

____

8. Mom wants to double a recipe that calls for 2 cups of sugar. How many cups of sugar does she need?

____

SCORE

1. ☺ 😐

2. ☺ 😐

3. ☺ 😐

4. ☺ 😐

5. ☺ 😐

6. ☺ 😐

7. ☺ 😐

8. ☺ 😐

____ / 8
Total

NAME: ____________________

DIRECTIONS Solve each problem.

SCORE

1. ☺ 😐
2. ☺ 😐
3. ☺ 😐
4. ☺ 😐
5. ☺ 😐
6. ☺ 😐
7. ☺ 😐
8. ☺ 😐

____ / 8 Total

1. Circle the larger number.

   83 93

2. 4 + 4 + 4 = ☐

3. 19 − 7 = ☐

4. 10 − 4 = 3 + ☐

5. Count the angles.

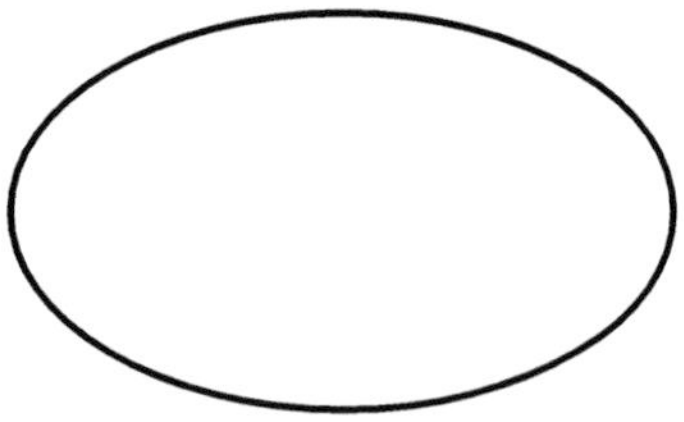

____

6. What is the 8th month of the year?

____

7. Make 41 tally marks.

8. I have 8 in the ones place and 2 in the tens place. What number am I?

____

NAME: ____________________

DIRECTIONS Solve each problem.

1. Write the ordinal number.

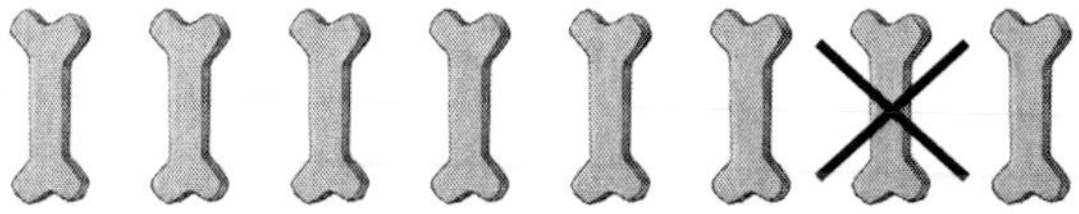

The marked bone is

____________________.

2.

$$\begin{array}{r} 7 \\ 2 \\ +\ 5 \\ \hline \square \end{array}$$

3. 17 – 10 = ☐

4. ☐ + 9 = 8 + 10

5. Will the object stack?

____

6. Would you use a ruler or a thermometer to measure the length of a book?

____

7. Favorite Activity

Swings	Slide	Monkey Bars	Balance Beam
8	5	7	2

How many children were surveyed?

____

8. Dawn has a rock collection with 72 rocks. A friend gives her 10 more rocks. How many rocks are in Dawn's collection now?

____

SCORE

1. ☺ 😐
2. ☺ 😐
3. ☺ 😐
4. ☺ 😐
5. ☺ 😐
6. ☺ 😐
7. ☺ 😐
8. ☺ 😐

____ / 8
Total

NAME: ____________________

DIRECTIONS Solve each problem.

SCORE

1. ☺ 😐
2. ☺ 😐
3. ☺ 😐
4. ☺ 😐
5. ☺ 😐
6. ☺ 😐
7. ☺ 😐
8. ☺ 😐

____ / 8
Total

1. What is the largest number that can be made with the numerals 7 and 4?

____

2. 6 + 7 + 3 = ☐

3.

$$\begin{array}{r} 18 \\ -\ \ 0 \\ \hline \square \end{array}$$

4. Complete the pattern.

81   79   77   ____   73

5. Draw a line of symmetry.

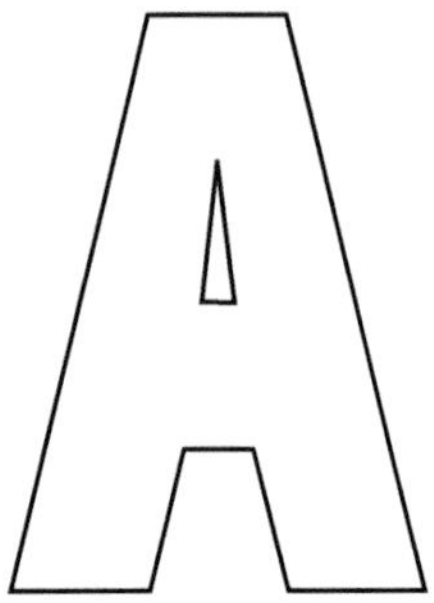

6. Circle the object that is taller than you.

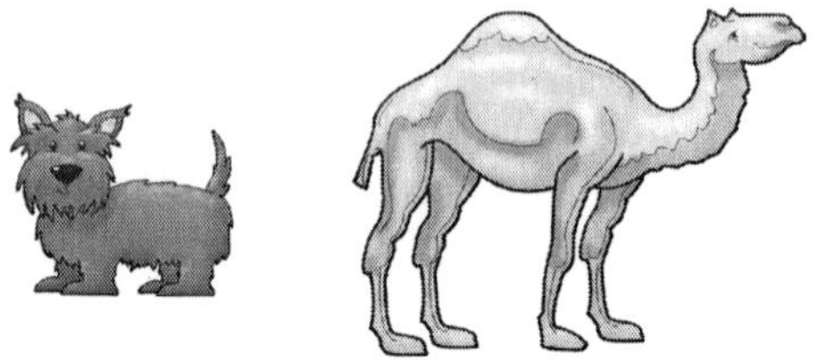

7. Devon has 30 toy cars, Marshall has 23 toy cars, and Travis has 27 toy cars. Make a tally chart with the data.

Toy Cars in a Collection

Devon	
Marshall	
Travis	

8. Sally sees 6 bluebirds, 4 seagulls, and 5 pigeons. How many birds does she see in all?

____

DAY 165

NAME: ______________________________

DIRECTIONS Solve each problem.

1. Draw tens rods and ones cubes to show the number 42.

2.

$$\begin{array}{r} 6 \\ 6 \\ +\ 7 \\ \hline \square \end{array}$$

3. $13 - 8 = \square$

4.

$$\begin{array}{r} 17 \\ -\ \square \\ \hline 8 \end{array}$$

5. Color the shape that you see on the base of the cone.

6. Write the time you went to bed last night.

____

7. Record the data in the chart.

- Three children like colored pencils.
- Two more children like clay than colored pencils.
- The number of children who like paints equals the total number of children who like clay and colored pencils.

Favorite Art Material

Paints	
Clay	
Colored Pencils	

8. Mom bought a dozen eggs. She uses 2 eggs for a cake. How many eggs are left?

____

SCORE

1. ☺ 😐
2. ☺ 😐
3. ☺ 😐
4. ☺ 😐
5. ☺ 😐
6. ☺ 😐
7. ☺ 😐
8. ☺ 😐

____ / 8 Total

DAY

166

NAME: ____________________________

DIRECTIONS Solve each problem.

SCORE

1. ☺ 😐
2. ☺ 😐
3. ☺ 😐
4. ☺ 😐
5. ☺ 😐
6. ☺ 😐
7. ☺ 😐
8. ☺ 😐

____ / 8

Total

1. Write the number word for 43.

____

2. 4 + 5 + 4 = ☐

3.

$$\begin{array}{r} 15 \\ -\ \ 6 \\ \hline \square \end{array}$$

4. Write the missing number.

☐ + 8 = 18

5. Draw a hat on the bear.

6. Write the time.

____ : ____

7. Favorite Recess Game

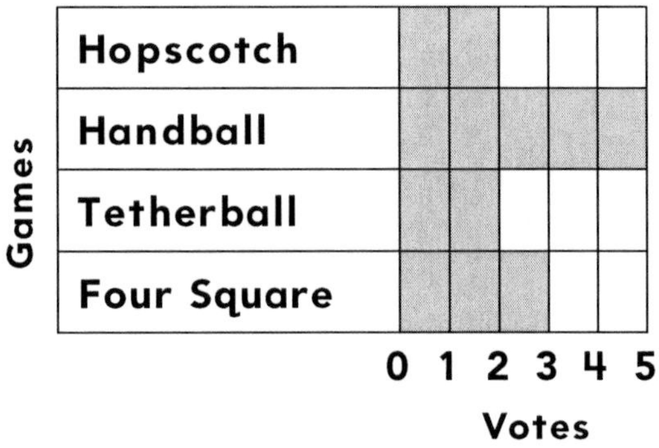

How many students were surveyed?

____

8. There are 10 pieces of candy in a bowl. After the party, there are only 2 pieces left. How many pieces of candy were eaten?

____

NAME: ____________________

DIRECTIONS Solve each problem.

1. 65 has ______ tens and ______ ones.

2.

$$\begin{array}{r} 6 \\ 2 \\ +\ 2 \\ \hline \square \end{array}$$

3. $14 - 5 = \square$

4. Complete the pattern.

____ 75 70 65 60

5. Would a box of crackers slide?

Circle: yes no

6. Record the area.

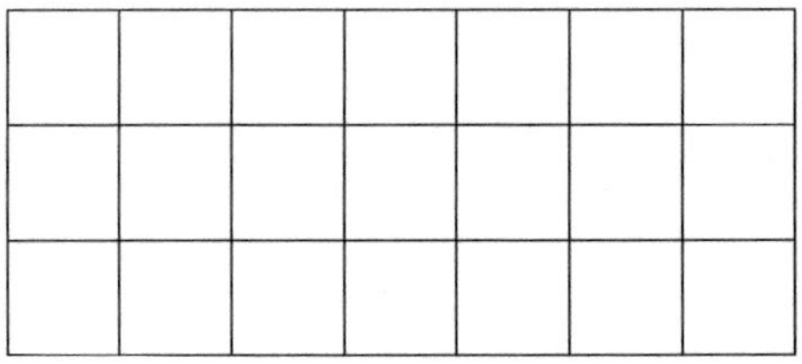

__________ squares

7. Favorite Type of Movie

Funny	Cartoon	Scary	3-D
III	𝍸 III	I	𝍸

How many more children like cartoons than 3-D movies?

____

8. Write two addition and two subtraction number sentences with the numbers 2, 7, and 9.

____

____

____

____

SCORE

1. ☺ 😐
2. ☺ 😐
3. ☺ 😐
4. ☺ 😐
5. ☺ 😐
6. ☺ 😐
7. ☺ 😐
8. ☺ 😐

____ / 8

Total

NAME: ______________________________

DIRECTIONS Solve each problem.

SCORE

1. ☺ 😐
2. ☺ 😐
3. ☺ 😐
4. ☺ 😐
5. ☺ 😐
6. ☺ 😐
7. ☺ 😐
8. ☺ 😐

____ / 8
Total

1. Fill in the circle with <, >, or =.

78 ◯ 68

2. 7 + 4 + 3 = ☐

3.

$$\begin{array}{r} 12 \\ -\ \ 7 \\ \hline \square \end{array}$$

4. ☐ – 3 = 2 + 2

5. Draw an oval. Draw a line of symmetry.

6. Is this object longer than your pencil?

Circle: yes no

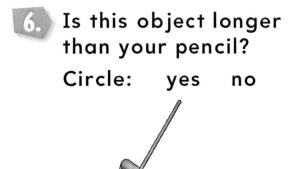

7. Favorite Subject

Math	☺☺☺☺☺☺
Reading	☺☺☺☺
Science	☺☺☺☺☺☺☺

How many children were asked about their favorite subject?

____

8. I am 3 more ones and 4 more tens than the number 24. What number am I?

____

DAY 169

NAME: ____________________

DIRECTIONS Solve each problem.

1. Write the number that comes after 52.

____

2.

$$\begin{array}{r} 5 \\ 2 \\ +\ 3 \\ \hline \square \end{array}$$

3. 15 – 9 = $\square$

4.

$$\begin{array}{r} \square \\ +\ 5 \\ \hline 14 \end{array}$$

5. Draw a shape with less than 4 sides.

6. What is the 2nd month of the year?

____

7.

Children in Class

Boys	Girls
7	10

The boys want to challenge the girls in kickball. How many more boys are needed so the teams are even?

____

8. Max has 10 crayons, 8 markers, and 6 colored pencils in a box. How many markers and colored pencils does he have altogether?

____

SCORE

1. ☺ 😐
2. ☺ 😐
3. ☺ 😐
4. ☺ 😐
5. ☺ 😐
6. ☺ 😐
7. ☺ 😐
8. ☺ 😐

___ / 8
Total

DAY 170

NAME: ______________________

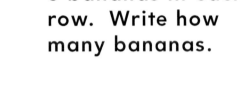

DIRECTIONS Solve each problem.

SCORE

1. ☺ ☹
2. ☺ ☹
3. ☺ ☹
4. ☺ ☹
5. ☺ ☹
6. ☺ ☹
7. ☺ ☹
8. ☺ ☹

____ / 8 Total

1. Draw 2 rows with 3 bananas in each row. Write how many bananas.

____

2. $6 + 7 + 2 = \square$

3.

$$\begin{array}{r} 13 \\ -\ \ 6 \\ \hline \square \end{array}$$

4. $\square - 3 = 7 + 5$

5. Draw a circle to the left of the triangle.

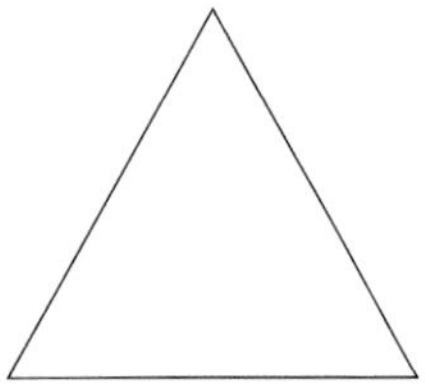

6. Write the time.

half past __________

7. Read the data in the chart. Write a statement about how many more children walk to school than come by car.

Ways We Get to School

Car	Bike	Bus	Walk
6	2	10	7

____

____

____

____

8. Which weighs more: a feather or a rock?

____

NAME: ______________________

DIRECTIONS Solve each problem.

1. Put these numbers in order from least to greatest.

   88 91 89

   ______ ______ ______

2. $8 + 4 + 1 = \square$

3. $14 - 9 = \square$

4. $\square - 5 = 8$

5. Color the shape with straight sides.

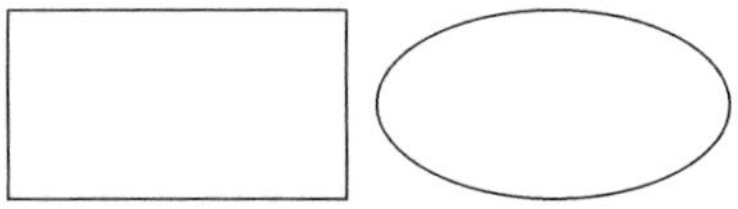

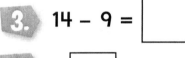

6. Circle the month that has 28 or 29 days in it.

   February

   March

   April

7. Favorite Weekend Activity

Play Video Games	𝍸 |
Read	𝍸 |||
Play with Toys	𝍸

Two more children were asked their favorite activities.

One said reading and one said playing with toys.

Now how many children prefer playing with toys?

____

8. There are 6 buckets, 5 shovels, and 2 balls. How many toys are there in all?

____

SCORE

1. ☺ 😐
2. ☺ 😐
3. ☺ 😐
4. ☺ 😐
5. ☺ 😐
6. ☺ 😐
7. ☺ 😐
8. ☺ 😐

___ / 8 Total

DAY
172

NAME: ______________________________

DIRECTIONS Solve each problem.

SCORE

1. ☺ 😐
2. ☺ 😐
3. ☺ 😐
4. ☺ 😐
5. ☺ 😐
6. ☺ 😐
7. ☺ 😐
8. ☺ 😐

____ / 8
Total

1. What is the largest number that can be made with the numerals 6 and 3?

____

2. 7 + 1 + 8 = ☐

3.

$$\begin{array}{r} 16 \\ -\ \ 7 \\ \hline \square \end{array}$$

4. 4 + ☐ = 10 + 0

5. Count the angles.

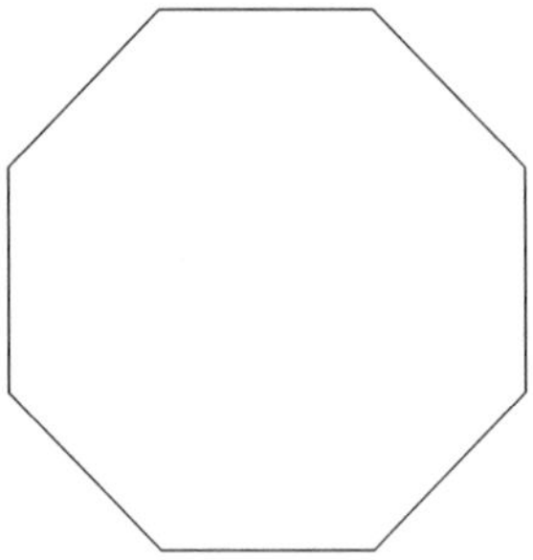

____

6. You have 3 books that are the same size. If 1 book is 5 inches long, how long are 3 books?

____________ inches

7. Make 10 tally marks.

8. I am 10 less than 62. What number am I?

____

NAME: ____________________

DIRECTIONS Solve each problem.

1. Circle the 4th tree.

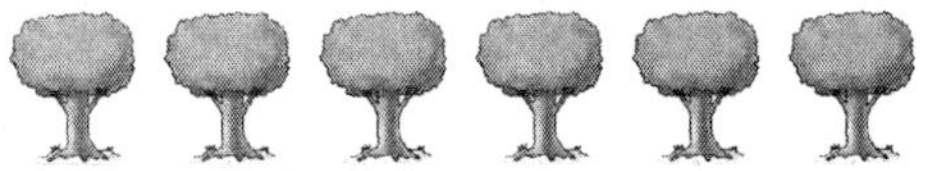

2.

$$\begin{array}{r} 6 \\ 7 \\ +\ 5 \\ \hline \square \end{array}$$

3. 11 – 3 = ☐

4. Complete the pattern.

_____ 92 90 88 86

5. Will the object roll?

Circle: yes no

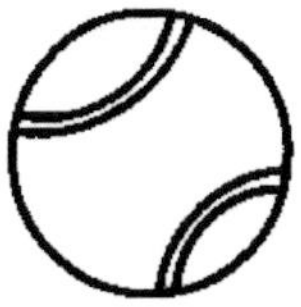

6. Write the time.

_____ : _____

7.

First Grade Students

Mrs. Garcia	23
Mr. Ream	21
Mrs. Stein	24
Mr. Miller	22

There can be a maximum of 25 students per class. How many more students can Mr. Ream have in his class?

____

8. Mrs. Jones made 14 hats. She gave away 7 of them. Then she made 4 more. How many hats does she have now?

____

SCORE

1.

2.

3.

4.

5.

6.

7.

8.

___ / 8

Total

NAME: ______________________________

DIRECTIONS Solve each problem.

SCORE

1. ☺ 😐
2. ☺ 😐
3. ☺ 😐
4. ☺ 😐
5. ☺ 😐
6. ☺ 😐
7. ☺ 😐
8. ☺ 😐

____ / 8 Total

1. Write the numeral.

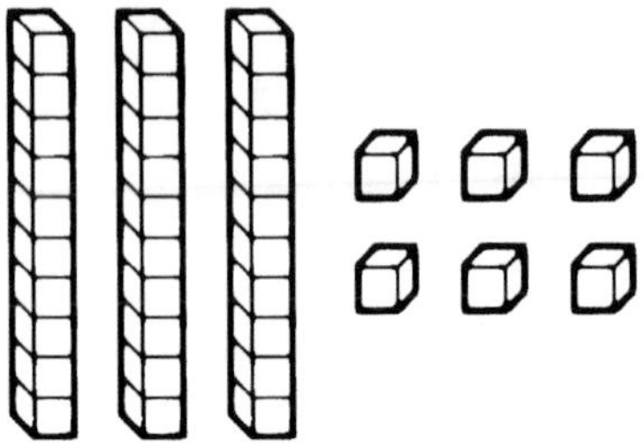

____

2. 8 + 4 + 0 = ☐

3.

$$\begin{array}{r} 12 \\ -\ \ 8 \\ \hline \square \end{array}$$

4. Write the missing sign.

18 ☐ 9 = 9

5. Draw a line of symmetry.

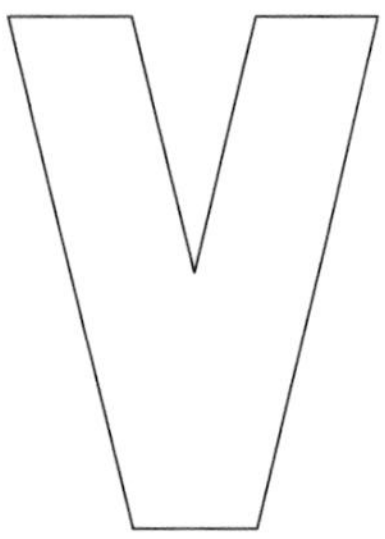

6. Would you use a scale or a clock to tell what time school starts?

____

7.

Pencil Colors

<table>
<tr><td>Red</td><td>卌</td></tr>
<tr><td>Green</td><td>卌 |||</td></tr>
<tr><td>Blue</td><td>|||</td></tr>
</table>

There are two more yellow pencils than red pencils. How many yellow pencils are there?

____

8. Amber has 7 stuffed teddy bears, 3 stuffed dogs, and 6 stuffed rabbits. How many stuffed animals does she have in all?

____

NAME: ____________________

DIRECTIONS Solve each problem.

SCORE

1. About how many kids are on a soccer team? Circle one.

   10   100

2. $$\begin{array}{r} 1 \\ 7 \\ +\ 6 \\ \hline \square \end{array}$$

3. $15 - 9 = \square$

4. $3 + 2 = \square - 4$

5. Color the shape that you would see from the top of this prism.

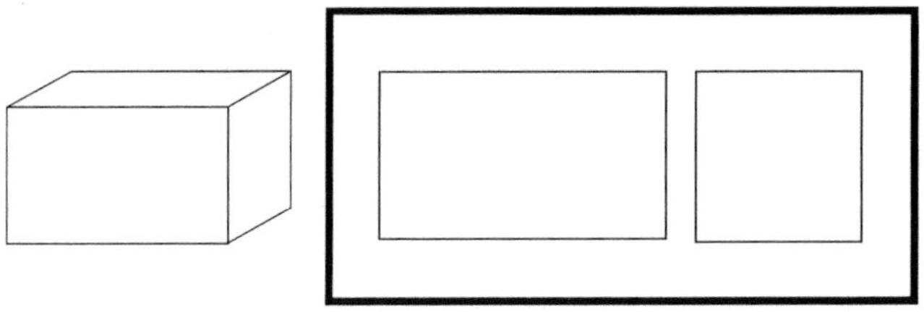

6. What is the 11th month of the year?

   ____

7. What would be a good symbol for a picture graph showing data for the number of home runs hit?

   ____

8. There are 8 bike wheels. How many bikes are there?

   ____

1. ☺ 😐
2. ☺ 😐
3. ☺ 😐
4. ☺ 😐
5. ☺ 😐
6. ☺ 😐
7. ☺ 😐
8. ☺ 😐

____ / 8
Total

DAY
176

NAME: ______________________

DIRECTIONS Solve each problem.

SCORE

1. ☺ 😐
2. ☺ 😐
3. ☺ 😐
4. ☺ 😐
5. ☺ 😐
6. ☺ 😐
7. ☺ 😐
8. ☺ 😐

____ / 8
Total

1. Write the number word for 95.

____

2. 5 + 5 + 5 = ☐

3.

   17
−   8
―――
  ☐

4. ☐ + 8 = 14

5. Draw a coin next to the piggy bank.

6. Circle the object that weighs less than a watermelon.

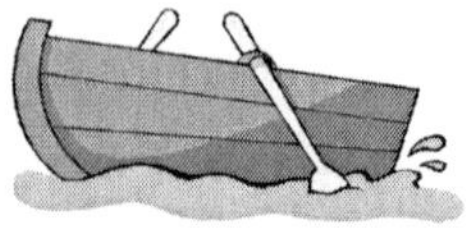

7. What question would you ask to find out about your friends' favorite foods?

____

____

____

____

8. Conner has seen 71 movies. If he sees 1 more, how many movies will Conner have seen?

____

NAME: ____________________

DIRECTIONS Solve each problem.

1. 74 has ______ tens and ______ ones.

2.

$$\begin{array}{r} 3 \\ 7 \\ +\ 9 \\ \hline \square \end{array}$$

3.

$$\begin{array}{r} \square \\ -\ 2 \\ \hline 11 \end{array}$$

4. $14 - 8 = 3 + \square$

5. Draw a square. Draw a line of symmetry.

6. Is the object longer than your pencil?

Circle: yes no

7.

Favorite Animal

Cats	Dogs	Birds	Lizards
7	9	4	5

Which two groups of animals added together equal the number of people who like dogs?

____

____

8. Write two addition and two subtraction number sentences with the numbers 7, 6, and 13.

____

____

____

____

SCORE

1. ☺ ☹
2. ☺ ☹
3. ☺ ☹
4. ☺ ☹
5. ☺ ☹
6. ☺ ☹
7. ☺ ☹
8. ☺ ☹

____ / 8 Total

NAME: ____________________

DIRECTIONS Solve each problem.

SCORE

1. ☺ 😐
2. ☺ 😐
3. ☺ 😐
4. ☺ 😐
5. ☺ 😐
6. ☺ 😐
7. ☺ 😐
8. ☺ 😐

____ / 8 Total

1. Fill in the circle with <, >, or =.

45 ◯ 64

2. 9 + 8 + 9 = ☐

3.
  12
− 5
☐

4. Complete the pattern.

54 52 ____ 48 46

5. Can you stack a cylinder on top of a cube?

Circle: yes no

6. Record the area.

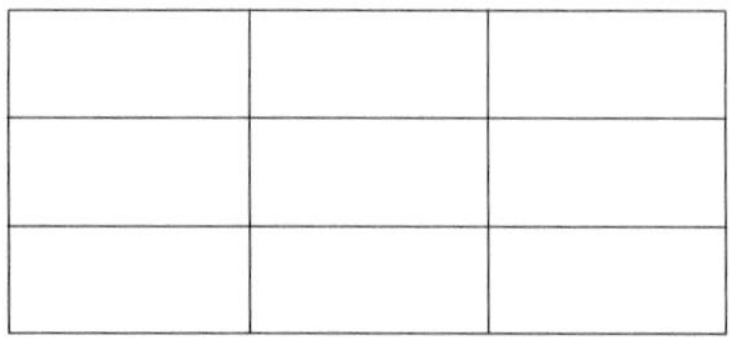

______ rectangles

7.

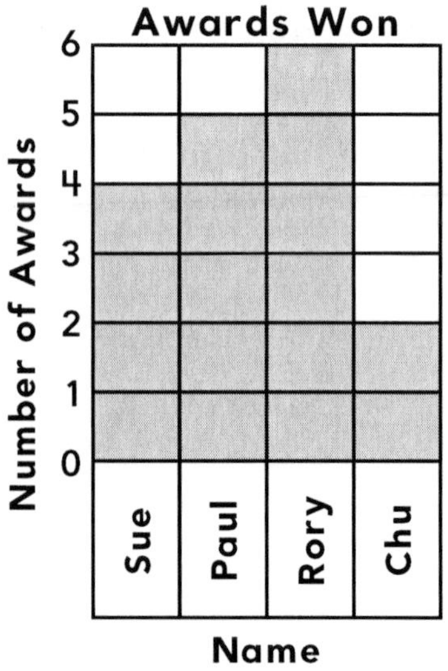

How many more awards does Sue have to win to tie with Paul?

____

8. Roy brings 2 shirts and 1 pair of shorts on a trip. How many different outfits can he make?

____

____

NAME: ______________________

DIRECTIONS Solve each problem.

SCORE

1. Write the numbers that come between.

46, ____, ____, 49

2.
$$\begin{array}{r} 4 \\ 8 \\ +\ 1 \\ \hline \square \end{array}$$

3. $11 - 8 = \square$

4. $7 + 2 = 14 - \square$

5. Draw a shape with more than 5 sides.

6. Write the time.

____ : ____

7. 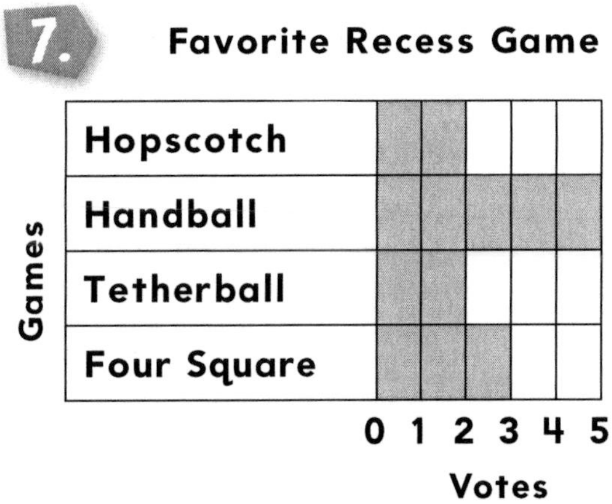

Two more students were surveyed. One liked hopscotch and the other liked four square. Now how many students like hopscotch?

____

8. In a parking lot there are 3 blue cars, 2 red cars, and 5 white cars. How many blue and red cars are there altogether?

____

1. ☺ 😐
2. ☺ 😐
3. ☺ 😐
4. ☺ 😐
5. ☺ 😐
6. ☺ 😐
7. ☺ 😐
8. ☺ 😐

____ / 8
Total

DAY
180

NAME: ______________________________

DIRECTIONS Solve each problem.

SCORE

1. ☺ 😐
2. ☺ 😐
3. ☺ 😐
4. ☺ 😐
5. ☺ 😐
6. ☺ 😐
7. ☺ 😐
8. ☺ 😐

____ / 8
Total

1. Circle the smaller number.

99 89

2. 7 + 3 + 7 = ☐

3.

$$\begin{array}{r} 12 \\ -\ 9 \\ \hline \square \end{array}$$

4. ☐ – 6 = 8

5. Draw a cloud next to the airplane.

6. What are two other ways to write the time twelve thirty?

half past __________

or

_____ : _____

7. Favorite Activity

Swings	Slide	Monkey Bars	Balance Beam
8	5	7	2

Two more kids are surveyed. Both like the monkey bars best. Now which activity is the favorite?

____

8. A team scored 8 runs in a baseball game. Three of the runs were made by Chan. How many runs were made by other teammates?

____

ANSWER KEY

Day 1

1. 16 stars
2. 6 baseballs
3. 2 flowers
4. 1
5. The circle should be colored.
6. The longer snake should be circled.
7. tea cups: 4 tally marks
   saucers: 3 tally marks
8. A circle should be drawn around the group of 2 happy faces.

Day 2

1. 5, 7
2. 7 flowers
3. 4 frogs
4. B, A
5. 4
6. The boot should be circled.
7. 4 home runs
8. 4

Day 3

1. 6
2. 7 fish
3. 7 cans
4. 2
5. yes
6. 2 or two
7. 3 pencils
8. 4 flowers

Day 4

1. The number 8 should be circled.
2. 9 pencils
3. 7 screws
4. +
5.  Any one line should be drawn.
6. The kettle should be circled.
7. 3 children
8. 3 cats

Day 5

1. 2nd
2. 9 squares
3. 3 ice cream cones
4. 1 + 3
   2 + 2
   4 + 0
5. The can should be circled.
6. yes
7. 5 awards
8. 6 wheels

Day 6

1. 12
2. 7
3. 3
4. 2, 1
5. A fish should be drawn in the box.
6. The shorter pants should be circled.
7. 5
8. 2 scoops

Day 7

1. 10
2. 8
3. 4
4. 0
5. no
6. The hamburger should be circled.
7. 7 children
8. 1 + 3 = 4 or 3 + 1 = 4

Day 8

1. 12, 14
2. 8
3. 2
4. 0
5. A square with a dot outside of it should be drawn.
6. 8 or eight
7. 8 children
8. 2, 3, 1

Day 9

1. 4
2. 6
3. 4
4. +
5. A circle should be drawn.
6. no
7. 2 children
8. a dog

Day 10

1. There should be 1 square drawn; 5 squares
2. 9
3. 4
4. 4
5. left
6. The bucket should be circled.
7. 3 children
8. Wednesday

Day 11

1. 15 stars
2. 2 + 4 = 6
3. 6 − 5 = 1
4. □○
5. The square should be colored.
6. The taller camel should be circled.
7. Boys: 4;
   Girls: 3
8. There should be a circle around the group of 10 stars.

Day 12

1. 0
2. 3 + 3 = 6
3. 5 − 3 = 2
4. 1
5. 3
6. The larger circle should be circled.
7. 15 home runs
8. 9

ANSWER KEY *(cont.)*

Day 13
1. 9
2. 5 + 2 = 7
3. 5 – 5 = 0
4. 2 + 3
   3 + 2
   4 + 1
5. yes
6. The bear should be circled.
7. 5 pencils
8. 4 stickers

Day 14
1. 19, 21
2. 4 + 2 = 6
3. 6 – 4 = 2
4. –
5. Either line is correct.

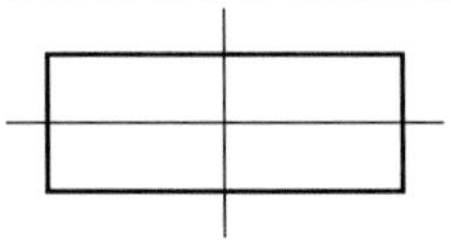

6. 5 or five
7. 8 people
8. 2 crackers

Day 15
1. 7th
2. 3 + 5 = 8
3. 8 – 2 = 6
4. 2
5. The cone should be circled.
6. yes
7. 2 awards
8. 6 years old

Day 16
1. 20
2. 4 + 3 = 7
3. 6 – 2 = 4
4. 3
5. yes
6. The bigger frog should be circled.
7. 13
8. 6 cars

Day 17
1. 14
2. 6 + 1 = 7
3. 5 – 1 = 4
4. 0
5. A tree should be drawn with a sun above it.
6. 3
7. 7 tally marks for cats; 9 tally marks for dogs
8. 1, 4, 7

Day 18
1. 9
2. 5 + 2 = 7
3. 6 – 2 = 4
4. B, A
5. yes
6. The trash can should be circled.
7. Water Parks: 3 tally marks; Amusement Parks: 5 tally marks
8. 2 bikes

Day 19
1. 34, 36
2. 1 + 6 = 7
3. 4 – 3 = 1
4. 1
5. A square should be drawn.
6. The longest line should be circled.
7. 5 children
8. add

Day 20
1. There should be two circles drawn; 5 circles
2. 5 + 4 = 9
3. 7 – 4 = 3
4. +
5. The square should have a circle drawn above it.
6. yes
7. Answers will vary. Possible answer: What is your favorite animal?
8. January

Day 21
1. 12 should be circled.
2. 5 + 5 = 10
3. 7 – 5 = 2
4. 4
5. The triangle should be colored.
6. yes
7. 3; 3
8. Both groups of three dots should be circled.

Day 22
1. 18 stars
2. 6 + 3 = 9
3. 8 – 5 = 3
4. 2
5. 0
6. 11:00
7. 7 home runs
8. 8

Day 23
1. 29, 31
2. 4 + 3 = 7
3. 8 – 4 = 4
4. sad face; happy face
5. yes
6. The larger square should be circled.
7. 8 pencils
8. 9 stickers

Day 24
1. 1
2. 3 + 7 = 10
3. 9 – 3 = 6
4. 0
5. 
6. The pitcher should be circled.
7. 8
8. 3 carrots

ANSWER KEY *(cont.)*

Day 25
1. 7
2. 6 + 4 = 10
3. 9 – 5 = 4
4. 1 + 1
   0 + 2
5. The ball should be circled.
6. 4
7. 4 awards
8. 9 sides

Day 26
1. 13
2. 2
3. 4 – 3 = 1
4. 2
5. A frog should be drawn on the lily pad.
6. yes
7. 6 children
8. 4 bones

Day 27
1. 50
2. 4
3. 7 – 5 = 2
4. 1
5. yes
6. The hen should be circled.
7. 6 children
8. 2 + 3 = 5 or 3 + 2 = 5

Day 28
1. 3 happy faces should be drawn; 8 happy faces
2. 1
3. 5 – 4 = 1
4. down arrow
5. yes
6. The pitcher should be circled.
7. 5 children
8. Jack: blue; Elly: red

Day 29
1. 10th
2. 5
3. 9 – 4 = 5
4. 0
5. A triangle should be drawn.
6. 1 or one
7. 5 children
8. a man

Day 30
1. 41, 43
2. 5
3. 7 – 5 = 2
4. +
5. right
6. The baseball should be circled.
7. more girls
8. 3:00

Day 31
1. 10
2. 3
3. 6 – 2 = 4
4. 1
5. The rectangle should be colored.
6. 7 or seven
7. Cats: 1
   Dogs: 3
   Birds: 2
8. 11, 12, 13, 14, 15

Day 32
1. 24
2. 2
3. 5 – 2 = 3
4. empty circle
5. 4
6. no
7. Jamal
8. 14

Day 33
1. 19 stars
2. 3
3. 7 – 6 = 1
4. 1
5. no
6. yes
7. yes
8. 6 birds

Day 34
1. 10
2. 4
3. 5 – 3 = 2
4. 5 + 0
   1 + 4
   3 + 2
5. The dress should have a vertical line down the center.
6. The quarter should be circled.
7. 10
8. Friday

Day 35
1. 22, 24
2. 5
3. 9 – 5 = 4
4. 4
5. The block should be circled.
6. The crayon should be circled.
7. 6 awards
8. 2 children

Day 36
1. 1
2. 4
3. 1
4. 1
5. no
6. February
7. 7 children
8. 5 stickers

ANSWER KEY *(cont.)*

Day 37
1. 16
2. 3
3. 0
4. 6
5. sphere
6. 4 or four
7. 6 children
8. 0, 3, 6, 8, (optional 9)

Day 38
1. 40
2. 5
3. 2
4. 2
5. no
6. The dog should be circled.
7. Answers will vary.
8. 1 car

Day 39
1. 48, 50
2. 2
3. 1
4. –
5. A rectangle should be drawn.
6. 5
7. Tacos: 4 faces; Pizza: 6 faces; For example

Tacos	☺☺ ☺☺
Pizza.	☺☺☺ ☺☺☺

8. legs on a spider

Day 40
1. There should be 2 triangles drawn; 7 triangles
2. 4
3. 1
4. 1
5. A square should be drawn below the triangle.
6. The car should be circled.
7. Answers will vary. Possible answer: What is your favorite color?
8. January

Day 41
1. 15
2. 4
3. 3
4. 6
5. circle
6. yes
7. Buckets: 6
   Shovels: 5
8. 4 apples

Day 42
1. 13
2. 1
3. 3
4. 1
5. 0
6. 1:00
7. Ramon
8. 15

Day 43
1. 13
2. 5
3. 1
4. 2
5. no
6. The caution sign should be circled.
7. no
8. 8 marbles

Day 44
1. 21 should be circled.
2. 3
3. 2
4. right arrow
5. 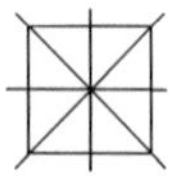 Any line is correct.
6. The yo-yo should be circled.
7. 2 children
8. 5 + 2 = 7

Day 45
1. The 5th star should be circled.
2. 2
3. 5
4. 4 + 4
   6 + 2
   10 – 2
5. The soap box should be circled.
6. 7
7. Rory
8. 8 sides

Day 46
1. 26, 28
2. 5
3. 0
4. +
5. A boy should be next to the pig.
6. no
7. 12
8. 4 marshmallows

Day 47
1. 30
2. 7
3. 3
4. 2
5. 6 flat surfaces
6. The die should be circled.
7. 4 children
8. 3 + 3 = 6

Day 48
1. 20 stars
2. 8
3. 2
4. A circle should be drawn.
5. rectangle
6. 3 blocks
7. 1 child
8. Brandon: apple
   Allison: orange
   Craig: banana

ANSWER KEY *(cont.)*

Day 49

1. There should be 5 shells drawn; 9 shells
2. 6
3. 0
4. 3 + 3
   2 + 4
   6 – 0
   8 – 2
5. An oval should be drawn.
6. yes
7. 17 children
8. 6 shoes

Day 50

1. 20th
2. 8
3. 0
4. 4
5. left
6. 12 or twelve
7. 8
8. swimming pool

Day 51

1. 5; 7; 9
2. 7
3. 1
4. 1
5. rectangle
6. 5
7. pencil: 4
   crayon: 2
   dictionary: 4
8. 3 + 2 = 5

Day 52

1. 60; 62
2. 8
3. 4
4. 50
5. 4
6. The cup should be circled.
7. 5 children
8. 30

Day 53

1. 28
2. 9
3. 0
4. 6
5. yes
6. yes
7. yes
8. 6 bananas

Day 54

1. 80
2. 6
3. 0
4. +
5. 
6. 5
7. 9 children
8. 10 cups

Day 55

1. 22
2. 7
3. 4
4. 7
5. The die should be circled.
6. 7 days
7. Chu
8. 10 fingers

Day 56

1. 39
2. 9
3. 2
4. 9 – 2
   7 – 0
5. the ball
6. 4
7. 20
8. 13 pieces

Day 57

1. There should be 1 dot drawn; 1 dot
2. 8
3. 3
4. A happy face should be drawn.
5. yes
6. no
7. 2 children
8. 2, 5, 9

Day 58

1. There should be 4 apples drawn; 8 apples
2. 7
3. 1
4. 2
5. yes
6. yes
7. 3 more home runs
8. 3 books

Day 59

1. 78; 80
2. 9
3. 4
4. 6
5. A hexagon should be drawn.
6. The bird should be circled.
7. Action Figures: 6;
   Robots: 5;
   Balls: 3
8. 9:00

Day 60

1. 21
2. 6
3. 4
4. +
5. A sun should be drawn above the dog.
6. 10:00
7. 8 children
8. door
   boy
   cat

ANSWER KEY *(cont.)*

Day 61

1. 12; 13; 18
2. 9
3. 5
4. 2
5. square
6. The box should be circled.
7. Oranges: 3;
   Bananas: 1;
   Apples: 2
8. 1 + 4 =5

Day 62

1. 15th
2. 6
3. 5
4. 26; 28
5. 6
6. yes
7. Answers will vary. Possible answer: What is your favorite TV show?
8. 30

Day 63

1. 23 should be circled.
2. 9
3. 10
4. 8
5. yes
6. 3
7. 46
8. 7 presents

Day 64

1. 42
2. 8
3. 5
4. 3
5. The shorts should have a vertical line drawn through the center.
6. November
7. handball
8. Friday

Day 65

1. 84, 86
2. 6
3. 1
4. 5 + 3, 10 – 2
5. The ball should be circled.
6. no
7. read
8. 8 wheels

Day 66

1. 43
2. 7
3. 0
4. 4
5. The pencil should be circled.
6. Saturday
7. 8 boys
8. 3 robots

Day 67

1. 70
2. 6
3. 2
4. 4
5. 1 flat surface
6. 1:00 should be shown on the clock.
7. science
8. 6 – 4 = 2 or 6 – 2 = 4

Day 68

1. The 3rd star should be circled.
2. 8
3. 4
4. 4
5. The cylinder should be circled.
6. The rooster should be circled.
7. 32
8. 4 sandwiches

Day 69

1. There should be 3 dots drawn; 3 dots
2. 7
3. 6
4. 8 – 6, 5 – 3
5. A pentagon should be drawn.
6. September
7. Answers will vary.
8. subtract

Day 70

1. There should be 6 circles drawn; 7 circles
2. 9
3. 6
4. A triangle should be drawn.
5. left
6. The small lizard should be circled.
7. Answers will vary.
8. December

Day 71

1. 17, 21, 25
2. 6
3. 4
4. 3
5. triangle
6. no
7. baseballs: 2 tally marks
   soccer balls: 1 tally mark
   footballs: 2 tally marks
8. 10 – 4 = 6

Day 72

1. 90, 92
2. 8
3. 6
4. 6
5. 5
6. 1 or one
7. swings
8. 35

ANSWER KEY *(cont.)*

Day 73
1. 31
2. 9
3. 6
4. 4
5. no
6. The apple should be circled.
7. green
8. 3 ears of corn

Day 74
1. 46
2. 7
3. 1
4. 10
5. 
6. 4
7. 23
8. 4 apples

Day 75
1. 90
2. 8
3. 7
4. +
5. The can of peaches should be circled.
6. December
7. cartoon
8. 20 corners

Day 76
1. 61
2. 9
3. 2
4. 4
5. yes
6. Wednesday
7. chocolate ice cream
8. 15 pictures

Day 77
1. 65, 67
2. 9
3. 3
4. 5
5. yes
6. yes
7. 1 more award
8. circle, oval, or sphere

Day 78
1. 45
2. 7
3. 7
4. 3 + 3
2 + 4
13 – 7
5. squares
6. 3:00 should be shown on the clock.
7. 8 more home runs
8. 3 + 3 = 6

Day 79
1. Four dots should be drawn; 4 dots
2. 8
3. 3
4. 10
5. An octagon should be drawn.
6. 6
7. hopscotch and tetherball
8. months in a year

Day 80
1. There should be 3 squares drawn; 10 squares
2. 9
3. 3
4. 5
5. A rock should be drawn below the turtle.
6. 5
7. play with toys
8. giraffe

Day 81
1. 14, 23, 36
2. 12
3. 7
4. 7
5. oval
6. 8:00
7. Flowers: 4
Worms: 2
Trees: 1
8. Saturday

Day 82
1. 85
2. 12
3. 5
4. 1
5. 8
6. 7
7. no
8. 50

Day 83
1. 76, 78
2. 19
3. 1
4. –
5. no
6. Monday
7. Dolls: 4 tally marks
Sticker Books: 7 tally marks
Paper Dolls: 2 tally marks
8. 20 birdhouses

Day 84
1. 43 should be circled.
2. 12
3. 0
4. 3
5.  Any line is correct.
6. no
7. 15
8. 6:30

ANSWER KEY *(cont.)*

Day 85

1. 50
2. 10
3. 3
4. 1 + 3
   2 + 2
   7 − 3
5. The box of detergent should be circled.
6. July
7. Answers will vary.
8. 7 quarters

Day 86

1. 60
2. 14
3. 2
4. 6
5. A cookie should be next to the milk.
6. 4
7. Answers will vary. Possible answer: What is your favorite ice cream flavor?
8. 9 children

Day 87

1. 82
2. 15
3. 9
4. 2
5. 0 flat surfaces
6. 6
7. reading
8. 9 − 4 = 5 or
   9 − 5 = 4

Day 88

1. 80, 82
2. 13
3. 0
4. 5
5. no
6. The clock should show 5:00.
7. balance beam
8. 17 − 6 = 11

Day 89

1. There should be 2 dots drawn; 2 dots
2. 10
3. 8
4. +
5. A rhombus should be drawn.
6. 4
7. scary
8. 14 days

Day 90

1. There should be 2 triangles drawn; 11 triangles
2. 10
3. 8
4. 10
5. right
6. Thursday
7. Answers will vary.
8. Thursday, June 23rd

Day 91

1. 45, 54, 61
2. 10
3. 8
4. up arrow
5. hexagon
6. a scale
7. Stars: 10
   Moons: 1
8. 8 − 4 = 4

Day 92

1. 53
2. 13
3. 0
4. 4
5. 3 angles
6. 12 months
7. Answers will vary. Possible answer: 10 children ride the bus to school.
8. 58

Day 93

1. 89, 91
2. 14
3. 2
4. 8
5. Yes
6. 3 or three
7. blue
8. 9 frogs

Day 94

1. 79
2. 12
3. 7
4. 4, 4
5. Any line is correct.

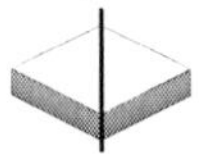

6. December
7. 3 more votes
8. 39 inches

Day 95

1. 89
2. 13
3. 9
4. +
5. The cylinder should be circled.
6. scale
7. 4 more awards
8. 12 wheels

Day 96

1. There should be 6 dots drawn; 6 dots
2. 11
3. 8
4. 4 + 4
   10 − 2
   12 − 4
5. no
6. 8
7. 2 more children
8. 16 stuffed animals

ANSWER KEY *(cont.)*

Day 97

1. The 7th star should be circled.
2. 15
3. 7
4. 90
5. A pentagon should be drawn. (Any 5-sided polygon is acceptable.)
6. Tuesday
7. 21
8. Answers will vary: square, rectangle, or rhombus,

Day 98

1. 100
2. 16
3. 7
4. 1
5. triangles
6. June
7. 11 more home runs
8. Ralph: strawberry;
   Ian: vanilla;
   Isaac: chocolate

Day 99

1. 75, 77
2. 11
3. 2
4. 14, 14
5. A triangle should be drawn.
6. The clock should show 7:00.
7. 3 more girls
8. Saturday and Sunday

Day 100

1. 100
2. 16
3. 5
4. 7
5. There should be a triangle drawn below the oval.
6. 7
7. 3 more children
8. June

Day 101

1. 27, 29, 35
2. 17
3. 1
4. 22
5. octagon
6. watermelon
7. Answers will vary.
8. 9:00

Day 102

1. 49 should be circled.
2. 16
3. 9
4. 3
5. 4 angles
6. 9:00
7. 4 tally marks should be drawn.
8. 87

Day 103

1. 3rd
2. 14
3. 6
4. true
5. yes
6. The paper clip should be circled.
7. 3 more children
8. 18 pets

Day 104

1. 89, 91
2. 10
3. 4
4. +
5. The circle can show any line drawn through the center point.
6. January
7. 2 more children
8. 25

Day 105

1. There are 10 dots in the frame; 10 more dots
2. 20
3. 5
4. 6
5. cube
6. Friday
7. Water Toys: 3 tally marks
   Sprinklers: 6 tally marks
   Stay Inside: 5 tally marks
   Swim: 10 tally marks
8. 8 ears

Day 106

1. eleven
2. 10
3. 6
4. false
5. The ball should be drawn far from the bear.
6. thermometer
7. Answers will vary. Possible answer: What is your favorite sport?
8. 13 models

Day 107

1. 3, 7
2. 17
3. 6
4. 2
5. yes
6. The clock should show 10:00.
7. 2 more children
8. 9 – 6 = 3 or 9 – 3 = 6

Day 108

1. The 2nd of 5 squares should be circled.
2. 17
3. 6
4. 57
5. no
6. 4
7. 6 home runs
8. 1 wagon

ANSWER KEY *(cont.)*

Day 109

1. 1 ten rod and 4 ones cubes should be drawn.
2. 12
3. 1
4. 6
5. A square should be drawn.
6. 6
7. 1 more child
8. 6 children

Day 110

1. 20
2. 16
3. 8
4. 3
5. A flower should be on the right side of the dog.
6. May
7. 3 more children
8. bathtub

Day 111

1. 23, 32, 63
2. 13
3. 4
4. true
5. pentagon
6. 11 or eleven
7. Answers will vary. Possible answer: 2 children ride their bikes to school.
8. 53

Day 112

1. 73
2. 13
3. 4
4. 10
5. 4 angles
6. Sunday
7. There should be 13 tally marks drawn.
8. 72

Day 113

1. The 4th pencil should be circled.
2. 18
3. 9
4. 2
5. yes
6. 4
7. 3 more green pencils
8. 6 horses

Day 114

1. There should be 17 dots; 17 dots
2. 14
3. 4
4. 30
5. The bow should have a vertical line drawn down the center.
6. a clock
7. 3 more girls
8. 17 flowers

Day 115

1. There should be 5 apples in one row.
2. 11
3. 7
4. –
5. sphere
6. a ruler
7. Yon: 35;
Joe: 23;
Lexi: 29
8. 8 legs

Day 116

1. sixteen
2. 11
3. 2
4. 0
5. yes
6. 2:00 should be shown on the clock.
7. 3 more awards
8. 18 flowers

Day 117

1. 5, 9
2. 11
3. 6
4. 7
5. 2 flat surfaces
6. October
7. Lizards: 5
8. pentagon

Day 118

1. $<$
2. 12
3. 0
4. $7 - 7 = 0$
5. triangles
6. a clock
7. 5 more children
8. 7 vases

Day 119

1. The 4th triangle should be circled.
2. 15
3. 11
4. true
5. A circle, oval, or non-polygon with curved sides should be drawn.
6. 18
7. 3 more children
8. 2 more players

Day 120

1. 78
2. 12
3. 9
4. 50
5. There should be a plate drawn below the pie.
6. The door should be circled.
7. Answers will vary. Possible answer: What is your favorite winter activity?
8. Sunday

ANSWER KEY *(cont.)*

Day 121
1. 56, 65, 76
2. 10
3. 10
4. false
5. rhombus
6. April
7. Answers will vary. Possible answers include running shoes or a person running.
8. 20 pages;
   Day 1: 5,
   Day 2: 10,
   Day 3: 15,
   Day 4: 20

Day 122
1. 63 should be circled.
2. 11
3. 9
4. 2
5. 0 angles
6. 5
7. 9 tally marks should be drawn.
8. 94

Day 123
1. 1st
2. 13
3. 3
4. 1
5. yes
6. 3
7. hopscotch and tetherball
8. 18 students

Day 124
1. 8 dots should be drawn; 8 dots
2. 13
3. 9
4. 4
5. The butterfly should have a line drawn vertically down the middle of it.
6. a thermometer
7. 3 fewer students
8. 8:00

Day 125
1. 2 tens rods and 5 ones cubes should be drawn.
2. 12
3. 7
4. +
5. cube
6. 8:00 P.M.
7. 1 more child
8. 4 glasses

Day 126
1. thirty-seven
2. 15
3. 5
4. 56
5. There should be a piece of paper drawn near the scissors.
6. 6
7. Tennis: 6;
   Soccer: 5;
   Baseball: 9;
   Basketball: 7
8. 6 blocks

Day 127
1. 3, 2
2. 15
3. 7
4. 11
5. yes
6. 6:00
7. 1 more child
8. 4 + 6 = 10 and 6 + 4 = 10

Day 128
1. =
2. 13
3. 10
4. 4
5. yes
6. December
7. 14 home runs
8. Tim has a dog, Amy has a cat, and Dave has a turtle.

Day 129
1. 20
2. 12
3. 15
4. true
5. 2 shapes with 4 sides should be drawn. (Possible answers include: square, rectangle, or rhombus)
6. 6
7. Mrs. Stein
8. Sunday

Day 130
1. 98
2. 14
3. 2
4. 17 – 9 = 8 or 17 – 8 = 9
5. There should be 3 bubbles drawn to the left of the fish.
6. a ruler
7. 3 more students
8. June 4th

Day 131
1. 75, 77, 89
2. 11
3. 6
4. 13
5. The square should be colored.
6. The car should be circled.
7. Answers will vary. Possible answer: 6 children ride in a car to school.
8. 57

ANSWER KEY *(cont.)*

Day 132

1. 2 rows with 6 circles in each row should be drawn; 12 circles
2. 11
3. 8
4. 65
5. 4 angles
6. 60 minutes
7. 19 tally marks should be drawn.
8. 50 pennies;
   Day 1: 35,
   Day 2: 40,
   Day 3: 45,
   Day 4: 50

Day 133

1. The 1st ice cream cone should be circled.
2. 11
3. 10
4. 8
5. no
6. June
7. 2 more awards
8. 9 children

Day 134

1. 10 dots should be drawn; 10 dots
2. 17
3. 10
4. –
5. 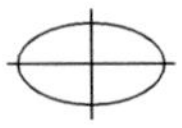 Any one line of symmetry should be drawn.
6. 11:00 should be shown on the clock.
7. 13 children
8. 73

Day 135

1. The 6th circle of 8 circles should be colored.
2. 12
3. 5
4. false
5. rectangular prism
6. a ruler
7. 1 more child
8. 20 minutes

Day 136

1. twenty-one
2. 12
3. 5
4. –
5. There should be a cup drawn next to the pitcher.
6. 6
7. 4 students
8. 24 grapes

Day 137

1. 7, 9
2. 11
3. 3
4. 7 + 6 = 13 or 6 + 7 = 13
5. 6 flat surfaces
6. 24 hours
7. 25 people
8. an octagon

Day 138

1. <
2. 15
3. 10
4. 7
5. 18 sides are on 3 cubes.
6. 8:00 should be shown on the clock.
7. Answers will vary. Possible answer: How many brothers and sisters do you have?
8. 3

Day 139

1. There should be 5 tens rods and 0 ones cubes drawn.
2. 10
3. 8
4. 85
5. There should be a pentagon drawn.
6. 5:00
7. Tammi: 8:00
   Marco: 8:30
   Shavon: 7:30
8. 2 fewer children

Day 140

1. 69, 70
2. 19
3. 1
4. 13
5. There should be a piece of paper drawn above the scissors.
6. March
7. 19 people
8. a car

Day 141

1. 89, 92, 97
2. 10
3. 16
4. false
5. The oval should be colored.
6. yes
7. 2 more awards
8. Tuesday, Thursday, and Sunday

ANSWER KEY *(cont.)*

Day 142

1. 43 should be circled.
2. 15
3. 2
4. 5 + 10 = 15 or 10 + 5 = 15
5. 5 angles
6. 9:00 should be shown on the clock.
7. There should be 25 tally marks drawn.
8. There should be a drawing of 5 ice cream sundaes with 2 cherries on each, totaling to 10 cherries.

Day 143

1. 5th
2. 4
3. 9
4. 2
5. no
6. a scale
7. banana: 6;
chocolate: 22;
vanilla: 12;
strawberry: 15
8. 53 books

Day 144

1. 10
2. 12
3. 10
4. 9
5. The mushroom should have a line drawn vertically down the middle of it.
6. 8
7. Mr. Ream
8. 5 more teacups

Day 145

1. 5 dots should be drawn;
5 dots
2. 15
3. 9
4. 55
5. The circle should be colored.
6. October
7. The tally chart should show 23 tally marks for dogs and 12 tally marks for cats.
8. 6 cookies

Day 146

1. fifty-eight
2. 13
3. 9
4. –
5. There should be toothpaste drawn on top of the toothbrush.
6. 1 or one
7. 3 more boys
8. 17 questions

Day 147

1. 8, 0
2. 14
3. 19
4. true
5. no
6. January and March
7. 2 more children
8. 8 – 5 = 3 and 8 – 3 = 5

Day 148

1. <
2. 4
3. 8
4. 4
5. There should be a rectangle drawn with a line through the center of it, either vertically or horizontally.
6. yes
7. Answers will vary. Possible answer: 8 more children come by bus than by bike.
8. 82

Day 149

1. 65
2. 5
3. 8
4. 13
5. A hexagon should be drawn.
6. 10
7. 9 children
8. 4:00

Day 150

1. 3 rows with 2 oranges in each row should be drawn;
6 oranges
2. 6
3. 6
4. 2
5. A square should be drawn to the right of the circle.
6. Answers will vary.
7. 17 people
8. Saturday

Day 151

1. 37, 72, 73
2. 6
3. 10
4. 90
5. The triangle should be colored.
6. 4:30
7. Answers will vary. Possible answer: an apple
8. 8 books
Day 1: 2
Day 2: 4
Day 3: 6
Day 4: 8

ANSWER KEY *(cont.)*

Day 152
1. There should be 6 tens rods and 2 ones cubes drawn.
2. 6
3. 7
4. 5
5. 6 angles
6. a thermometer
7. There should be 21 tally marks drawn.
8. 86

Day 153
1. The 5th car should be circled.
2. 8
3. 10
4. 17
5. no
6. Answers will vary.
7. 5 more green pencils
8. 23 children

Day 154
1. 16
2. 3
3. 10
4. 4
5. 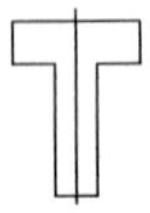
6. January
7. 5 students
8. 8 mittens

Day 155
1. 35
2. 6
3. 17
4. 0
5. The square should be colored.
6. 8
7. 5 more people
8. 6 days

Day 156
1. seventy-two
2. 10
3. 9
4. true
5. There should be a bat drawn near the baseball.
6. no
7. 9 children
8. 77 blueberries

Day 157
1. 9, 9
2. 8
3. 8
4. 46
5. 0
6. July and August should be circled.
7. 1 more student
8. $1 + 6 = 7$ or $6 + 1 = 7$; $7 - 6 = 1$ or $7 - 1 = 6$

Day 158
1. =
2. 13
3. 10
4. 9
5. triangles
6. 8:30
7. Answers will vary. Possible answer: What color is your bike?
8. 1. Trish
   2. Will
   3. Mark

Day 159
1. 20
2. 12
3. 20
4. 2
5. An octagon should be drawn.
6. 4
7. Paul
8. 6 years old

Day 160
1. 54, 55
2. 19
3. 17
4. 8
5. A road should be drawn below the car.
6. taller
7. Tom: 5
   Tony: 9
   Jacqueline: 8
   Nikki: 14
8. August

Day 161
1. 76, 79, 81
2. 17
3. 8
4. +
5. The circle should be colored.
6. 9:30
7. 31
8. 4 cups

Day 162
1. 93 should be circled.
2. 12
3. 12
4. 3
5. 0 angles
6. August
7. There should be 41 tally marks drawn.
8. 28

Day 163
1. 7th
2. 14
3. 7
4. 9
5. yes
6. a ruler
7. 22 children
8. 82 rocks

ANSWER KEY *(cont.)*

Day 164

1. 74
2. 16
3. 18
4. 75
5. 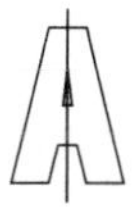
6. The camel should be circled.
7. Devon: 30 tally marks
   Marshall: 23 tally marks
   Travis: 27 tally marks
8. 15 birds

Day 165

1. Drawing should show 4 tens rods and 2 ones cubes.
2. 19
3. 5
4. 9
5. The circle should be colored.
6. Answers will vary.
7. Paints: 8
   Clay: 5
   Colored Pencils: 3
8. 10 eggs

Day 166

1. forty-three
2. 13
3. 9
4. 10
5. A hat should be drawn on the bear.
6. 3:30
7. 12 students
8. 8 pieces of candy

Day 167

1. 6, 5
2. 10
3. 9
4. 80
5. yes
6. 21
7. 3 more children
8. $2 + 7 = 9$
   $7 + 2 = 9$
   $9 - 2 = 7$
   $9 - 7 = 2$

Day 168

1. $>$
2. 14
3. 5
4. 7
5. There should be an oval drawn with a line through the center of it, either vertically or horizontally.
6. yes
7. 17 children
8. 67

Day 169

1. 53
2. 10
3. 6
4. 9
5. Drawing should be of a shape with less than 4 sides (a triangle, circle, or oval).
6. February
7. 3 more boys
8. 14 markers and colored pencils

Day 170

1. 2 rows of 3 bananas in each row should be drawn;
   6 bananas
2. 15
3. 7
4. 15
5. A circle should be drawn to the left of the triangle.
6. 2 or two
7. Answers will vary. Possible answer: 1 more child walks than comes by car.
8. a rock

Day 171

1. 88, 89, 91
2. 13
3. 5
4. 13
5. The rectangle should be colored.
6. February should be circled.
7. 6 children
8. 13 toys

Day 172

1. 63
2. 16
3. 9
4. 6
5. 8 angles
6. 15
7. There should be 10 tally marks.
8. 52

Day 173

1. The 4th tree should be circled.
2. 18
3. 8
4. 94
5. yes
6. 10:30
7. 4 more students
8. 11 hats

ANSWER KEY *(cont.)*

Day 174

1. 36
2. 12
3. 4
4. –
5. The letter V should have a line drawn vertically down the middle of it.
6. a clock
7. 7 yellow pencils
8. 16 stuffed animals

Day 175

1. 10
2. 14
3. 6
4. 9
5. The rectangle should be colored.
6. November
7. Answers will vary. Possible answer: a baseball or bat
8. 4 bicycles

Day 176

1. ninety-five
2. 15
3. 9
4. 6
5. A coin should be drawn next to the piggy bank.
6. The belt should be circled.
7. Answers will vary. Possible answer: What is your favorite food?
8. 72 movies

Day 177

1. 7, 4
2. 19
3. 13
4. 3
5. A square should be drawn with a line through the center of it, vertically, horizontally, or diagonally.
6. yes
7. birds and lizards
8. $7 + 6 = 13$
   $6 + 7 = 13$
   $13 - 6 = 7$
   $13 - 7 = 6$

Day 178

1. <
2. 26
3. 7
4. 50
5. yes
6. 9
7. 1 more award
8. 2 outfits

Day 179

1. 47, 48
2. 13
3. 3
4. 5
5. A shape with more than 5 sides should be drawn. Possible answers include: hexagon or octagon.
6. 6:30
7. 3 students
8. 5 blue and red cars

Day 180

1. 89 should be circled.
2. 17
3. 3
4. 14
5. A cloud should be drawn next to the airplane.
6. half past 12 or half past twelve;
   12:30
7. monkey bars
8. 5 runs

REFERENCES CITED

Kilpatrick, J., J. Swafford, and B. Findell, eds. 2001. *Adding it up: Helping children learn mathematics.* Washington, DC: National Academies Press.

Marzano, R. 2010. When practice makes perfect...sense. *Educational Leadership* 68 (3): 81–83.

McIntosh, M. E. 1997. Formative assessment in mathematics. *Clearing House* 71 (2): 92–96.

CONTENTS OF THE TEACHER RESOURCE CD

Diagnostic Item Analysis Resources

Diagnostic Assessment Directions	directions.pdf
Practice Page Item Analysis PDF	pageitem.pdf
Practice Page Item Analysis *Word* document	pageitem.doc
Practice Page Item Analysis *Excel* spreadsheet	pageitem.xls
Student Item Analysis PDF	studentitem.pdf
Student Item Analysis *Word* document	studentitem.doc
Student Item Analysis *Excel* spreadsheet	studentitem.xls

Reproducible PDFs of Practice Pages and References

All of the 180 practice pages are contained in a single PDF. In order to print [illegible] days, open the PDF and select the pages to print.

NCTM Correlations Chart	correlations.pdf
Practice Pages Day 1–Day 180	practicepages.pdf

